W9-BQX-043

LECTURES ON COUNSELING

JAY E. ADAMS

BAKER BOOK HOUSE
Grand Rapids, Michigan

Acknowledgment is made to Jay E. Adams
for permission to reprint the following titles:
THE STUDENT PASTOR-COUNSELOR TODAY, © 1977;
YOUR PLACE IN THE COUNSELING REVOLUTION, © 1975;
COUNSELING AND THE SOVEREIGNTY OF GOD, © 1976;
COPING WITH COUNSELING CRISES, © 1976;
THE USE OF SCRIPTURE IN COUNSELING, © 1976.

Reprinted 1978 by Baker Book House

ISBN: 0-8010-0122-6

First printing, January 1978
Second printing, November 1978

TABLE OF CONTENTS

THE STUDENT PASTOR - COUNSELOR TODAY

THE STUDENT PASTOR-COUNSELOR TODAY[1]

If I were a seminarian today and were shortly entering the pastorate, I would have in view the prospect of engaging in a significant counseling ministry. But if I entertained this purpose, I'd also like to know what I'd want from my theological training, what other resources were available and what I should do about them.

It was those sort of questions that I asked myself as I began to prepare for this lecture. I thought, if I could deal with them clearly and concretely then I might be of more help to you than if I simply chose some aspect of counseling that was of interest to me.

As I see it, there are three major facets of preparation for a counseling ministry that we should explore:

(1) I must consider what evangelical students entering the pastorate today are like; what their dispositions, characteristics and concerns are (i.e., their *stance* toward counseling);

(2) I must take a look at resources presently available to them; and

(3) I must say something about how such students may best use such resources to become effective pastoral counselors.

[1] This lecture was delivered at Concordia Theological Seminary, Ft. Wayne, Indiana on October 7, 1976.

1

CHAPTER I

Let's begin with today's students. I am not intimately acquainted with the typical Lutheran student, so it's possible that I could be speaking past you rather than coming to grips with your particular problems, interests and aspirations. I hope not. But I shall tell you what I do know from close association with one seminary and a rather good knowledge of a number of others. I'll have to leave it to you to judge whether I have scored or struck wide of the mark.

Now I want to make some observations about the seminary student as I see him:

First, the evangelical student of today has had it with traditionalism, i.e., with tradition for the sake of tradition. However, let me hasten to say that he is totally unlike the student who, as late as five or six years ago wanted to overthrow the establishment simply because it was the establishment. There is a new balance in today's student. He has reasons for what he opposes — some of which he gladly admits grow out of tradition (not traditional*ism*). Yet while he is freer to question and reject established practices and values than was his counterpart of the forties and fifties, he also can retain them more freely than the student of the 60's and early 70's so long as he believes they are true to the Word of God. Within the biblical framework, he can think independently, slavishly following neither the traditionalist nor the iconoclast. This sort of freedom to hear the Scriptures afresh makes him open to new ideas, but it also makes him critical of newness for newness' sake.

Thankfully, his immediate predecessor — yesterday's student who thought that freedom from traditionalism meant reacting to everything traditional simply because it was — has gone. Because he found it difficult to accept anything associated with the past, he

2

rejected much that was biblical, and, as a result, this determination to reject locked him into a destructive bondage to the very traditionalism from which he sought to free himself. This bondage — to say the least — was every bit as serious as that of the unthinking traditionalist that he abhorred.

One who only *reacts* — as did this predecessor of yours — is still tightly bound to what he wants to throw off. Because he *re*acted to traditionalism, he could not *act* on his own. The one who reacts acts only over against what exists; he doesn't move into the new, unexplored areas of creativity demanded by the recognition of unnecessary limitations and boundaries. For all his talk about the new, his stance is still backward, not forward. He does not look ahead or move forward because his sight and actions are yet controlled — negatively to be sure — but yet, controlled by the past. Thank God, I say, that we are through with this sort of student mentality; a mentality that will tear down something simply because it is there.

But no significant trend — and for awhile it was that — leaves those who live through its heyday and those who follow in its wake totally unaffected. In God's providence, there is always something worthwhile to gain from every movement, if one has a biblical perspective from which to view it. Today we are all able to capitalize on the concern for freedom that the rebels of the sixties sought but never attained, if we care to do so. In spite of the inevitable failure of such a destruction-oriented movement, it shook many things loose, opened a number of sealed compartments and provided a general sense of freedom that I, for one, appreciate. I refer not only to the more superficial matters like freedom to grow beards and wear leisure suits to church, but to more substantive questions.

I guess what I am saying is that the door was opened for us to attack the *evils* of traditionalism today in a way that was not possible when I began my ministry twenty-five years ago. So long as that attack continues to take the responsible course of questioning what hasn't been questioned adequately *according to biblical presuppositions and principles,* while accepting and cherishing what proves to be truly scriptural, no matter who believed it or how old it may be, I am for it.

But there is another side too. Today's student not only wants to reject error in thought and practice wherever it may be found; he is concerned to press beyond traditional thought and practices. He will correct what he must by offering new ways and means, but he also will explore new territories and push back the frontiers of ministry that for too long have been circumscribed by arbitrary and artificial barriers that no longer exist.

And . . . he wants to get on with his work; yet he is unwilling to settle for the mediocre approaches that characterized so many in the past. He is a high calibre exponent of the view that one stands on the shoulders of his fathers for one reason only — to reach higher than they could! Though he appreciates and appropriates the enormous amounts of truth inherited from the past, at the same time he is not content to eat fruit from the same branch as his teachers. He will reach above us; he is not satisfied with apples already well picked over.

As you have gathered, I like this student. He is exciting to teach. He is challenging; but he is also devout. He is balanced. God has screwed his head on right, but at the same time He has warmed his heart! I know his ambition is dangerous; but look at his potential! We simply can't hold him back because there is danger. He is needed in the church. We must warn him not to lose his balance. Then we must thrust him ahead. What God has provided, let not man reject.

There is one outstanding characteristic of this new student that especially thrills me as a professor of Practical Theology: he has a decidedly practical bent. That is one reason why he is so interested in pastoral counseling. While he is concerned about theory, he will not leave it there to stand on one leg. He demands that every presupposition and principle be carried to its conclusion — in *life*! In one sense this means that he is even *more* theoretical. His theory concerns theory about theory. It holds that God gave man all truth to change life. He believes intensely — whether he can fully articulate it or not — in the study of the Scriptures not merely to gather or communicate facts and data, but to discover the *telos* or purpose of each passage. He recognizes that he must provide more in his ministry than doctrine, accurately understood and faithfully taught. He wants to know and share the implications of every doctrine for family life, for business life, for social life . . . and so on. He staunchly believes in exegesis, but finds little satisfaction in discovering the grammatical-historical facts about a passage if that is what he is left with. As much as an evangelical biblical theology that finds the redeeming Christ as the heartbeat of every book of the Bible, including Proverbs, excites him, he does not want to join others who take biblical-theological excursions through the Bible merely to visit all of the Christocentric landmarks. He will not become a biblical sightseer. He wants to know (and to show) how the Christ of all the Scriptures can bless men in their daily activities. He is no tourist; his travel in the Bible is for business purposes.

Your fear that his practical inclinations may lead him to buy a bill of goods because in his zeal to help others he doesn't do the hard work of study to undergird his practical efforts may be well-grounded, but I doubt it. If I know him at all, I know that he is aware of and guards against this danger. He is not simplistic about all of this. His concern for a telic understanding of the Scriptures is insurance against it. Actually it leads him to ask more of the text than some of his fathers did. He will wrestle with a passage, in all of the old ways, but will not let go until it blesses him! He will make it disclose how the Holy Spirit intended to change him (and his congregation) through it. He will do the work of solid exegesis coupled with theological and historical reflection *so that* he can come to a correct *telos* of every passage.

Of course a shallow pietism is the nearest pothole into which he may fall. And if he successfully avoids it, his how-to emphasis that insists upon cheering the discouraged, and therefore lethargic, Christians by showing them that there are (after all) practical ways of achieving what the biblical writers told us even without first becoming an apostle Paul, could lead him into the even deeper pits of legalism. Yet if he holds to a scholarly concern for exegesis and theology, tempered by the fires of church history, as the *means* for obtaining his telic and how-to emphases, he will avoid both.

I like this new student because of these and other unmentioned factors that make up his profile. If I were to describe him in a word or two, I think I'd call him a scholarly pastor — a man who begins to approximate Paul's pastor/teacher of Ephesians 4:11. And it is because he is such a man that he recognizes the importance of discovering, developing and deploying the gifts of all the members of the body as verse 12 of that same chapter directs him to do. He is

5

not going to throw away his ministry doing things that God gifted others to do; rather, he will concentrate and focus his efforts on those tasks that are peculiarly pastoral and didactic. But I cannot pursue this tempting area any further.

Let me conclude my discussion of today's evangelical theological student — incomplete as it is — with this one word. In short, he has the makings of one of the most biblically well-balanced — i.e., to say Christlike — students in the history of theological education. I hope he makes it!

CHAPTER II

It is this sort of student who enters the ministry with a growing concern about pastoral counseling. I'm glad he is the sort of person he is. Any lesser man would fail. But what is there to help him? Our second task is to take a hard look at the resources available to him, that purport to enable him to become a counseling shepherd to needy and careworn sheep.

That the student I have described is interested in doing such work, pursuing the best training he can get, and utilizing all of the resources that he may, cannot be questioned. His orientation toward counseling necessarily accompanies the highly pastoral orientation that he brings to his scholarly endeavors. All over this land, and abroad, there is an awakening to the need for offering better help to Christians who are confronted with the catastrophic upheavals stemming from technological revolution, the ascendency of the New Morality and a galloping humanism — just to mention a few of the forces facing them today.[1] People — Christian people everywhere — are crying out for help as never before. Today's student wants to be prepared to give it.

But as he looks about, the resources available seem woefully inadequate. Experience in the vicarage frequently shows the sterility of past training (or lack of training) in counseling and provides few models for the student. Seminary curricula are heavily weighted toward other concerns, and counseling courses often are eclectically conditioned. Books are disappointing. The general situation is confusing. The resources seem slight, and what is on the market for

---

[1]This is apparent here, but in my lecture tour of Germany and Switzerland last April, where night after night 700-1000 persons turned out to hear about Christian counseling, it became evident that it is not only an American phenomenon.

the most part seems thin, outmoded (speaking to issues long-since dead) or just outright wrong. It will no longer do — for that matter it *never* did — for a pastor to tell a couple whose marriage is on the rocks, "Read this Scripture verse, pray and I'll pray for you too." There is nothing wrong with the verse or the prayer, but to leave people, who have already demonstrated their failure to relate God's Word to their marriage, merely with that — thrown out in such an abstract manner — is to court disaster. What makes you think that they will be able to use this passage in their present condition without explanation and concrete application? Why do you think they would be able to pray together at home when they can't seem to talk civilly to one another even in the counseling room? No, pastor-to-be, you must work and struggle with them, from the Scriptures and in prayer; not once but as often as necessary — perhaps over a six to eight week period. They need counsel of a caring, orderly, directive, systematic sort that grows out of a telically understood and ministered study of the Scriptures.

But since such concerns are recent — indeed, not yet existent among some older pastors and professors, there is little systematic scholarly biblical pastoral material on counseling available. True, there are popular books and booklets, pamphlets and tracts in abundance, but many of these are superficial and offer little more than the prayer and Bible verse approach. But even the best do not provide what the pastor needs — to show him how to show others. On the other hand, there are plenty of theoretical studies about counseling, but while providing at times some aid for the more creative men, these too miss the mark for the average pastor who has not been trained to think in terms of the concrete how-to . These books almost universally circumvent such problems, leaving him to pursue them strictly on his own. They may tell him the ins and outs of the divorce question, for instance — and this can be valuable — but they don't tell him how to use this otherwise excellent material to prevent a couple from getting a divorce. Know-what, is not know-how; and even know-how is not the same as show-how.

Of course there are other avenues that he can take. One leads away from the church to the office of psychiatrist or clinical psychologist. But the pastor who opts for this route recognizes sooner or later that he has made a wrong turn. Not only does he see

8

few persons helped, but far too often he discovers that the advice given — if any *is* given — is quite contrary to what he teaches on Sunday from the Bible. Moreover, if he allows himself to think about it, the man in the office down the avenue with the couch doesn't have more to offer than he. He doesn't have as much. What is needed to help people learn to love God and neighbor is the Bible. Psychology and medicine don't have the answers; he himself does in that Book about which he has learned everything else except how to use it to minister to men in need. It is not "psychology for living," but Scripture that we must have for living, after all. How can Freud, Rogers or Skinner — men who loathed the Bible and Christianity and developed systems that not only omitted God, but were opposed to His teachings — help wayward, suffering, sinning, parishioners to repent and to grow in grace? How can counselors who rely upon these systems help the members of your congregation to exhibit the fruit of the Spirit when they neither use the Spirit's Word nor rely upon Him — Who Christ said is the great Counselor — for help? Such musings disturb today's ministerial student and recent graduate. They are dissatisfied with the referral route — and for good reason.

But what of the books, tapes, lectures, courses and short term training sessions available for ministers today? These are — almost wholly provided by the same sorts of psychologists, psychiatrists and secularly-trained pastoral counselors. Why should the pastor think he can achieve what his friend down the street with a shingle couldn't by using the same approaches, gleaned in a half-baked manner? Moreover, the evangelical student who thoroughly immerses himself in the contents of this material is likely to come away disillusioned even more quickly than his friend who does referral. Sadly, he finds: no consensus or agreement about anything, and that — unlike other disciplines in which there is a growing pool of accepted information — the disagreements among counselors continue to grow greater every day as new systems, challenging others at every point, are added to the scene! To read of the dissension and despair among the practitioners in this field is warning enough for him to stay aloof. On top of that, he senses that there is an almost total lack of concern about value, even though that is the stuff that every counselor (without exception) is working with. Counselors, of every stripe, try to change lives. Yet how can they take it upon themselves to do so when so many show not even the slightest concern about the fact that they have no standard for determining what man's basic problems are, what man *should* be like, what is the goal and meaning of life, etc? They simply adopt their own values, the values of the counseling system or the counselee's values usually without careful thought about what they are doing. What pastor can be unconcerned about the values inculcated in his sheep by others?

No, there is no help there. The student that I described is willing to do two things: (1) He will scrap these approaches, eclectically incorporated in the past into existent patterns of pastoral ministry, because they do not square with the Bible and (2) He will gladly follow the lead of one who is biblically-oriented, even though this means plowing new ground in the field of pastoral counseling. But that's the problem on the horizon, there is hardly anyone for him to follow. Nearly everything offered is an eclectic potpourri that dishonors Jesus Christ by offering an unequal yoke of man's wisdom and the wisdom of God. In most instances, moreover, the Bible is bent to fit the psychological system into whose mold it is poured. Today's student rejects this; he will not play fast-and-loose with the Scriptures. So where will he turn, and what will he do to become the effective counselor that he yearns to be and that his people will need?

CHAPTER III

Since almost all of the resources available are either meagre, superficial or erroneous, what must he do? The answer is that he must do a lot of his own spade work. Since there is little for him to rely upon, he must break much new ground himself. That is the crux of what I have to say today. He will waste his time leaning on the bent reeds of the past . . . . He finds that they snap under the weight of serious pastoral concern. Instead, he must saturate himself with the Scriptures to discover there what God says about life on this planet as well as life in the age to come. He must break up the clods and dig out the stones himself, if he really wants to become a biblical counselor. He must tap the rich reservoirs of biblical truth lying offshore from mainland operations that are now petering out. This requires commitment and life investment. I call you to nothing less. I urge you to join me, the members of the Christian Counseling Educational Foundation Staff, and the growing numbers of pastors, professors and seminary students who are engaged in the task of opening up the tangled forest. This work is new, demanding and exciting. And its early returns show that it is a worthwhile investment of one's labors.

But can I do it? you ask. It is like you, today's student, to be humble about the matter. But that too is a necessary quality for the work because it requires nothing less than absolute submission to the authority of God's Word.

Yes, you can! With God's help you can! That is why I have taken so much time to describe today's theological student. God is doing things with him. No student in the history of American Christianity was more ready to take on this work. His pastoral concerns, his freedom from unbiblical traditionalism and his dedication to scholarly but practical, life-directed exegesis and theology form just

11

the proper combination for it. What a tragedy if he fails! So, in the name of the Lord Jesus Christ let me challenge you to join the ranks of those who are now beginning to undertake the task. Human guidelines are few, but what does that matter? That only serves all the more to drive us back to our Bibles. The risks are great, but the opportunities are greater. May God bless and use you in this task!

YOUR PLACE
IN THE
COUNSELING REVOLUTION

TABLE OF CONTENTS

FOREWORD

Because I was deeply concerned about the matters included in this book, I chose the subject for my Staley lectureship of January, 1975 which I delivered to the student body of Cedarville College, Cedarville, Ohio. And because the subject matter is pertinent to those who belong to a larger audience, I am sending these lectures forth to the Christian public in general, hoping that in some measure God will use this humble effort as one small contribution to bringing about the revolution in counseling that may in time spark a new revival of the Christian faith in this country.

The book has been released with two sorts of target audiences in mind. First, this includes the large number of Christian men considering a ministry of Christian counseling. Secondly, I have in mind the average church member who must determine to support efforts made in this direction, or the coming revolution in counseling will not materialize. I want to convince the former that they should consider the work of the pastoral ministry, and I wish to inform the latter about what is happening in the Church of Christ, and enlist not only their support but their participation as well.

If at first the word revolution sounds too sweeping and belligerent, let me urge you to reserve your judgment about this until you have finished reading. By then, I hope that you will see the necessity for nothing less. I like the definition of a revolt (or revolution, as we now call it) in Crabb's English synonyms. He writes:

> Revolt . . . signifies originally a warring or turning against the power to which one has been subject; but revolt is mostly taken either in an indifferent or a good sense for resisting a foreign dominion which has been imposed by force of arms.

That definition in every way is appropos of the situation that until

17

recently has prevailed. If "force of arms" may be considered figuratively referring to the warnings by which pastors and Christians have been intimidated, the picture is complete. A power, foreign to the Christian Church, has held her tightly in its grips for a long while. There have been many collaborators. But, at long last, tired of the failure, convinced that within the Church itself there are resources that have been virtually untapped, many are awakening to the need and to the opportunities and are beginning to throw off the yoke of oppression. The collaborators, understandably, are not happy. Hopefully, some of them can be won to the cause. But largely, the revolution—as indeed most revolutions are—has begun as a grass-roots struggle. To better alert and inform those at the grass-roots level who sense its importance, I send forth this book. I have revised very little, and have purposely attempted to retain the lecture style. If it seems somewhat abrupt at points, read the text aloud.[1]

[1]Tapes of the lectures are available from Westminster Theological Seminary, Chestnut Hill, Pa., 19118.

CHAPTER I
DON'T BE SHORT CHANGED[1]

Introduction: I thought at first of entitling this address "Anyone who goes to a psychiatrist ought to have his head examined," but thought better of it and settled for "Don't Be Short Changed."

Counselees, or those who urge them to receive counseling, are interested in change. In one way or another, the uppermost concern is to change their lives.

—Perhaps they have *had it* with wives/husbands/parents/children. . . . They want a change.

—Possibly they seek relief from depression or worry or fear or mysterious voices speaking out of nowhere.

—Or . . . they are anxious to learn how to get along with others/how to control tempers/how to communicate with persons they love/how to keep a job/how to rope and tie a runaway sex drive. Any one of these . . . or dozens of other problems . . . impel people everywhere to seek counsel of others, hoping they will provide the change that will bring peace and joy.

Counselors are people who try to help them effect that change. Many of these people who counsel are well meaning and enter the field from altruistic motives; others are themselves confused, seeking answers; some are in the work for the prestige, the power or the money, and some for the gratification of baser desires.

But in this attempt to effect change, profound and urgent questions arise, such as: Who sets the standard for change? The

---

[1]Lecture No. 1 was published in a slightly different form in Jay Adams, *Shepherding God's Flock,* Vol. II (Presbyterian and Reformed Publishing Co., Nutley, N. J.), but was delivered as part of the Staley lectureship.

19

counselee? The counselor? Someone else? Does the counselee know enough? May the counselor's values be accepted? And—who answers the question about who sets the standard? Who effects the change? Counselee? Counselor? Both? Another? What means will be used for bringing about the change? All those that work? Then is brainwashing acceptable? Surely, there must be *some* limitations in *some* directions—but that's just the problem: where shall the lines be drawn?—and who shall draw them? These and many other similar questions inevitably arise in the minds of all thoughtful counselors.

The trouble is—there isn't one in a thousand who can begin to answer them. Yet, without answers, where are we; what shall counselors do; and what of the counselee?

Counselors read, experiment, debate, write, yet they are no nearer to agreement on these questions than when they first began. Seated in his plush, expensive study, lined with learned tomes, the typical counselor, seemingly serene and secure, is nothing of the sort if he is a man of integrity and a diligent student of his profession. Daily he is harassed by the silent but strong protests over every action he takes and every word that he speaks coming from the authors who observe him from their perches on his shelves. "Too directive," cry some. "Why don't you reflect his feelings?" shout others. "Get rid of all that nonsense about value; focus on the behavior," demands a third. From all sides competing 'isms and 'erapies woo and warn.

In his better moments he tells himself: "Toss the whole business overboard. After all, who can know what is right? I don't even have time to learn all of the systems, with their presuppositions, principles and practices, let alone try them out! Why, there are classical Freudians, Dynamic Freudians, and Neo-Freudians, Adlerians and Jungians, Logotherapists, Integrity Therapists, Reality Therapists, Radical Therapists, Rational-emotive Therapists, Gestalt Therapists, Contract Therapists, Primal Screamers, Laingians, Transactional Analysts, Skinnerians, Behaviorists by the buckets, Rogerians, Group Therapists, Family Therapists, etc., etc., etc. Why in the world should I suppose that what I am doing is right?"

And . . . think of the poor counselee—in confusion meandering from one counselor to another—looking for someone who can help him. In the process he is diagnosed, misdiagnosed and rediagnosed. He may be told that he is sick, or that he has been poorly socialized by parents and peers, or that he has been wrongly conditioned, or that his difficulty is genetic, or that he has failed to live up to his full potential. He may be assured that the problem is illness, or bad training, or learned behavior, or emotional immaturity, or chemical, or interpersonal, or constitutional, or existential, or whatever in origin. Appropriately he will be treated or trained or encouraged or taught or medicated in widely varying ways. "Let it all hang out," says one. "You need to get it all together," says the next. "Tell me about your childhood, your sex life and your dreams," says another. "Take these pills four times a day and see me in six weeks," or "Renegotiate all of your personal contracts," or "Get rid of those inhibitions—find a man with whom you can have successful sexual relations," or "You must have a series of E.S.T. treatments (i.e., electroshock therapy—or, to put it more realistically, grand mal seizures, artificially induced)," or "We shall recondition your behavior," or "Hypnotism will help," or "Get a frontal lobotomy," or "Talk it out," or "Scream," . . . or . . . . Well, that's just about what one feels like doing when he hears even so small a portion of the whole as this.

In the process, persons have been advised to urinate upon their father's graves, punch pillows until the feathers fly, file for a divorce if they don't get along with a life partner, and just about anything else one could imagine. Before he is through, a counselee may run the gamut, being assured that all will be well if only he medicates, or copulates, or urinates, or meditates or ventilates!

What is he to *do*? In whom shall he *believe*? Where is he to *turn*?

And . . . in the face of all of this uncertainty, don't fail to notice what it is all about. Remember, all of these views, all of these persons, all of these methods are concerned about *changing people's lives*! If physicians were so divided and uncertain, would we entrust our bodies to them? If airlines and airline pilots differed so widely about flying principles and practices, who would fly? Yet, think, people by the millions turn to such counselors to *change their LIVES*! That means—to change their values; to change their attitudes, to change their beliefs, to change their behavior and to

21

change their relationships to significant persons! DARE we allow anyone to meddle in such matters when all is in flux?

Think about the trick a psychiatrist played upon his fellow practitioners—he sent twelve persons—sane as you or I—into twelve of the nation's leading mental institutions for the expressed purpose of discovering how accurate psychotherapeutic diagnosis is. What do you think happened? You guessed it; some of them were wrongly diagnosed as having serious mental illness. How many do you think? Would you believe half? Wrong. Would you believe three-fourths? Still wrong. Would you believe all twelve? Right! *All Twelve*! A one hundred per cent failure!! And, listen to this, of the twelve diagnoses, eleven were diagnoses of schizophrenia! Moreover, these "patients" made no attempt to deceive, but acted normally during the entire period of diagnostic evaluation! No wonder Karl Menninger, commenting on the farce, said: "Schizophrenia is just a nice Greek word."

Surely, by now we should be asking not only where can counselees find help, but also—how can they be protected in their gullibility and vulnerability from misguided (even though well-intentioned), from incompetent, from foolish and from unscrupulous persons? Who (or what) will preserve them from making changes of thought and action that can only disappoint and that may lead to ill consequences equally as bad or worse than those previously experienced?

And, surely, all of this confusion, contradiction and chaos not only must give us pause before approaching or sending someone to the self-styled experts or professionals, it should make us ask an even more basic question: What is behind the disorder or (as Zillborg called it) the "disarray?" Other fields, while having healthy disagreements, seem to make progress and seem to be able to tack down many areas of common agreement. Yet, in counseling, there is a consensus about nothing. Is there not something radically wrong in the discipline of counseling? *What could it be?*

As I gather it, coming here today necessitates an answer to that question. As you might suppose from what I have said, giving that answer is no small task. Indeed, after hearing something of the various opinions and ideologies to which I have alluded, you may

22

wonder why I came—how I could accept the invitation in good faith, and what brings me here anyway. Certainly I could not be arrogant enough to imagine that I had the final word, could I? Do I come to make another vain thrust and thus stir up more sediment to further foul the pool? Dare I even think that I could introduce the idea that would clarify the situation and point toward a pathway that emerges from the fog? No, if I came with another such word I should be not only a fool but a charlatan. I do not so come.

"Then, what brings you here?" you ask. Answer:

To point to the path leading to the clear light and sunshine; to explain what is behind the confusion and how it may be swept aside; to herald a new day of counseling that has already begun to dawn—and about which you may possibly hear much more in the not-too-distant future; to challenge you to join the ranks, and to hope that this meager effort may bear some fruit toward these ends!

"Wait a minute," you reply.

First, you said that you were not bringing in another opinion or ideology; yet now you seem to say just the opposite. You'd better explain—and make it plain; I've heard just about all I want to take of confusion and contradiction for one day!

OK; OK—I'll give it to you straight. I have not come to offer one more opinion, system or ideology. I would not dare; as a matter of fact, I wonder continually at the audacity of those who do. Instead, I have come with good news. There is hope in the midst of the chaos; but it is not found in *my way*.

Remember the question I asked earlier, but did not answer? It went something like this: since other disciplines (engineering, business, medicine and even non-clinical and non-counseling psychology) seem to be able to arrive at some measure of order and cohesion—enough at least to produce some concrete results—must not something be radically wrong with counseling? The answer to that question is "yes." Something *is* radically wrong with counseling, and *this is it:* almost to a man counselors have rejected the only true standard of human values, beliefs, attitudes and behavior. Yet those matters comprise the stuff of which counseling is made. They have *looked* everywhere else, *tried* everything else, but have totally *ignored* the one Book that can bring order out of chaos. Only a word from God Himself can properly tell us how to change. In the Bible alone can be found the true description of man, his plight and God's solution in Christ. Only the Scriptures can tell us what kind of persons we must become. Only God can command, direct, and give power to effect the proper changes that will enable men He redeems to renew the image corrupted by the fall. Two Skinnerians in a room with their latest sausage grinder, by which they claim to be able to grind any sort of sausage one wishes, cannot agree about what kind of sausage they want; i.e., what sort of man to produce. Each wants sausage that thinks like himself. God has not only *told* us what man must become, but has *shown* us in Christ! In short, counselors are in their present state of confusion, swayed by every new fad, precisely because they have rejected the one and only perfect and lasting textbook on counseling.

Textbook did you say? The Bible a *textbook* for counseling?" Yes, the Bible is God's basic text for living. It contains "all things pertaining to life and godliness" (II Peter 1:3). In it is all that a counselor or counselee needs to know in order to honor God by loving Him with all that he has, and by loving his neighbor as himself. As a matter of fact, on those two commandments—and in the scriptural explanations of how to fulfill them—hangs all of the work of counseling.

In counseling—per se—we do not find many persons presenting problems about the troubles they are having with *things*. ("You see Doc, there's this chair that I have been having difficulty with . . . . " or "I came here to discuss the state of the carburetor on my Toyota.") When those with organic difficulties have been eliminated by sending such persons to physicians, what is left is that large number of people who are in trouble in one way or another with other *persons*—with God and their neighbors.

"But," I can almost *hear* the objection, "you don't use the Bible as a textbook for engineering or architecture or medicine, do you?" Of course not. "Well, then, why do you use it as a textbook for counseling?" Because, while the Bible was never *intended* to be a textbook about business or engineering, God Himself, in the passages cited, as elsewhere, tells us that it *is* a textbook concerned precisely with the problems encountered in counseling. And from the confusion seen uniquely in that field, it should be evident that just such a text is what is desperately needed.

How extraordinary, indeed, it is for Christians, those who claim to believe in the inerrancy and authority of the Scriptures, and who have been saved through faith in Jesus Christ, whose death for their sins is recorded therein, to doubt the fact that the Bible is the textbook for living—and, of course, for effecting every change in living! How could it be otherwise? God alone can tell man what values to espouse; no one else originated the Ten Commandments! God alone can disclose the chief goal of man, explain the core of his problems and offer the fundamental solutions to them. Indeed, if counselors, apart from the Scriptures, could do so, the Bible—and, to be sure, Christ Himself—would have been given in vain! But counselors *cannot*. That is precisely why we are presently in this thick soup.

Well, then, what is the alternative? "There is hope, you say? Then tell me about it—I shall listen cautiously."

To begin with, God everywhere in the Scriptures commands change: "As obedient children, do not be conformed to former lusts . . . but like the Holy One who called you, be holy yourselves also in all your behavior" (I Peter 1:14,15); "You must walk no longer as the heathen walk" (Ephesians 4:17); "Grow by grace, even by the knowledge of our Lord Jesus Christ" (II Peter 3:18). I could go on and on, but you know already that this is true. What you may not have realized, however, is that every biblical exhortation, every insistence upon change, implies hope. God never demands of His children that which He has not provided for them. We are not only *saved* by grace, but our sanctification (i.e., our continued growth and change from sin toward righteousness) as Christians also is the result of God's grace. As Paul told the Galatians, we did not begin the Christian life by grace . . . only to complete it by our own efforts (Galatians 3:3). No, all is of grace. That means, therefore, that God Himself has provided the instructions and the power to live and grow according to them. The instructions—the goals, values, presuppositions, principles and practices—are found in the Scriptures; the power for Christians to live by them is provided by His Spirit. That is the good news about counseling that I bring today. And everywhere—throughout the country—and even elsewhere in this world, Christian ministers are awakening to the fact. The same Book that says that God has provided what is needed for counseling says also that it has been provided for the equipping of ministers for the work of changing lives: that the *"man of God"* (a term picked up from the Old Testament and used in the pastoral letters to refer to the pastor/teacher) may be adequate, thoroughly equipped. While every Christian should do counseling, it is to the minister that He has assigned the task as a life work.

No wonder there has been confusion! The wrong persons, using the wrong standards, have tried to do all sorts of wrong things without power.

But what of the Christian "professionals," most of whom espouse an eclectic view ("Something from Freud, something from Rogers, something from Skinner . . . and a little from the Bible")? Hal Brooks once said "If you don't know where you are going, any road will do." *That* is the problem with eclecticism . . . . It is good only for those who do not know where they are going. Skinner does not eclectically use Rogerian methodology; nor does Rogers use Skinnerian. Why not? Both see man's problem differently and therefore have different objectives in view. Each is committed to the different methodologies that will take them most surely to those destinations. Christians have an entirely different objective than all the rest—to change men so that they may become like Christ. Only God's road leads to that. It is time for Christians to stop riding on the world's bandwagons; they are headed in the wrong direction! The Bible, and the Bible alone, points the way. Therefore, as in salvation, so too in counseling—no other road will do.

But to be more specific, just what *does* the Bible provide? Let us look a *bit* more closely at II Timothy 3 to see.

In this fundamental passage concerning the Scriptures, it is important first to note that their twofold *"use"* or "purpose" is described *in terms of change:*

(1) Salvation: they are able to make one "wise unto salvation;" and

(2) for those who *are* saved, they provide four things:

(a) Teaching—they become the standard for faith and life; they show us all that God requires of us.

(b) Conviction—they show us how we have failed to measure up to those requirements in our lives. The word used is a legal term meaning more than to "rebuke" or "accuse" but speaks of pursuing the case to its end *successfully*. The Scriptures show us our sin; they flatten us in repentance.

(c) Correction—the word means (literally) "to stand up straight again." While it is true that the Bible knocks us down, cuts and bruises, rips up and tears down, it is equally true that this is done only to prepare us for its work of picking us up again and heading us in God's proper direction. The Scriptures also bind up and heal; they plant and build. By God's Spirit, who works in and through them, they not only help us put off sin, but also enable us to put on righteousness.

(d) Finally, they "train us in righteousness." It is not enough to quit the past ways, break old habits and stop sinning. If that is all that occurs, one will find himself soon reverting to past ways. He must not only do so, but learn *as a way of life to* walk in the new ways (Ephesians 4).

And what does all of this amount to? Change. We have just been describing the process of *change*. Change in depth. Change as profound as one could imagine. Eternal change. And it is all found in God's Book, the counselor's textbook on human change, the Bible.

I urge you—consider the facts and make the decision. Perhaps God is calling some of you to such a ministry of vital change. If so, answer in faith. With such powerful resources available why should you or your counselees be *short changed?*

CHAPTER II
THE PICTURE ON YOUR WALL

All right. So we have located the fundamental failure in modern counseling—God and His revealed Word have been omitted from the counseling picture. In discussions among counseling people, including Christians, the names of Mowrer, Glasser, Perls, Harris, Rogers, Skinner, Lazarus, and Erickson are more frequently heard and their views are better known than the names of Paul, Peter, David, Solomon and even Jesus Christ. God, and His viewpoint, for most are not a viable option. *That* is the problem. Now what? How can we rectify that situation?

"Isn't that simple enough to answer?" you may ask. "After all, if God is missing from the picture, what we need to do is to bring Him into it."

Well, that reply can be either right or wrong, depending entirely upon what you mean by "bringing God into the picture." The suggestion, of course, is not revolutionary or new. For years people have been writing books with titles like *Psychiatry and the Church, Freud and Christ,* etc. But when you begin to explore the ways and means that have been used to achieve this end, and even how some Christians have conceived of that end itself, you soon begin to recognize that there are problems connected with "bringing God into the counseling picture." The matter is more complex than at first it might seem. And, in my opinion, that is precisely why so many Christians have unwittingly fallen into the sin of accommodationism, which consists of accommodating Christianity to some other view. I find it necessary to define this sin because, it seems, so few say anything about it. Moreover, there is more than one way in which Christian counselors have attempted to include God in their counseling, and as a result, more than one way that accommodationism can take place. And, finally, I think that further

28

study of the problem will convince you that these attempts to bring God into the picture mainly have been unsuccessful.

But, before we turn to the discussion itself let me go one step further and state categorically that this issue is not merely an academic matter. It is not something that we can leave to the counselors to squabble over as an intradepartmental feud. Instead, it is nothing less than a question fraught with large practical consequences for both the counselor and those whom he counsels. The wrong answer to the question involves grave dangers to both, and grave dangers to the Christian Church. Counselor and counselee—alike—stand in personal jeopardy.

"*That* is *strong* language. Are you sure that you are not overstating the hazard? Why do you make such an extreme statement? Wouldn't it be better merely to say that the matter is of *some* moment to all of us because it has practical consequences?"

No, I am *not* overstating the case. Indeed, I will go so far as to say that if God is not brought into the picture properly—i.e., if He is not included in counseling in a manner that accords with what He Himself has required in the Scriptures, it is worse to introduce Him than to leave Him out altogether.

"*Wait* a minute. How can you *say* that? How could leaving God out of the counseling room be less dangerous than including Him—wrongly perhaps—but including Him? Aren't you the one who is always complaining about people leaving God out of counseling? I don't think that I *understand* you. Have I caught you in an inconsistency, or can you clarify what you are saying? I should think that even a little consideration for the place of God in counseling is to be preferred to none."

Well, your question is fair enough, and it surely represents the thinking of many persons today—one of whom may have influenced you by their writings. But, I must stand by what I have said. And, by the way, let me make it clear to begin with, that I do *not* wish to reproach anyone for his good intentions; that clearly is not the issue. There is nothing personal involved in my disagreement with the persons who have attempted to bring God into the counseling context. So there is no inconsistency in what I am saying. The real issue is whether, indeed, the wrong way of bringing God into the picture (to which I have alluded) does anything of the sort. That is to say, the issue is whether He will allow Himself to be brought into the picture that way. And . . . there is *one* personal matter, I confess, that I cannot avoid: *God is a Person*—who does make this sort of thing more than an academic issue with reference to Himself—He takes it personally!

In this brief consideration of the matter, I want you to understand that I can do no more than scratch the surface of the problem; its implications are numerous. I certainly would not claim even to know how many there are. But as I peel off a few bits here and there, I think that you shall see plainly enough from those samples, the depths of the subject that we have chosen to discuss. I shall focus on only one or two of these implications then, and through them try to give you at least some inkling of what I am talking about.

First, one way to bring God into the counseling picture *wrongly* is to introduce Him as an *additive*. This adjunctive use of God and His Name dishonors Him as God, denies His sovereignty, and deceives and discourages counselees.

"Wow! That's quite a charge. Can you substantiate it?"

Without a doubt. Ask yourself this question: When God is *added* to an already existing picture, to *what* (precisely) is He added? Well, the very fact that He is needed as an addition tells you, doesn't it?

"What do you mean?"

Just this. If there was a need to bring God into a picture in which He had no place before, the fact is that the picture to which He is added is an *ungodly* one. But I think that you can see that the very idea of associating God with such a picture by attaching God's name to a godless system is repugnant. To attempt to put Him into a system that was designed with no thought of Him, and in the final analysis is (therefore) bent upon leaving Him out is to dishonor Him. God refuses to be thus associated. He will not be identified with the golden calf. He rejects every idolatrous system created by men. Indeed, He declares: "I will not give my glory to another" (Isaiah 42:8). Do you think then that He will allow you to add His Name and that He will give His blessing to any system that was

30

conceived in a proud autonomous spirit—a system, that by its structure finds no need for the living God?

"Well . . . "

There are no wells about it. God will not allow us to add Him on to a system that by its basic presuppositions, by its principles, and by its practices, excludes Him. The result would lead to God's participation in that unequal yoke that He Himself condemns. Christ simply does not associate with Belial!

Therefore, to baptize counseling systems like Freudian Psychoanalysis, Skinnerian Behaviorism, the Rogerian Human Potential Movement or the Berne/Harris/Steiner views of Transactional analysis into the Christian fold unconverted, by adding on God's Holy Name and sprinkling in a few assorted scriptural proof texts, ultimately amounts to taking His Name in vain. It means to represent God as in favor of ungodliness. To say the very least, the attempt to bring God into a picture in which there is no place for Him and into which He will not come can only be futile.

"Well, I can see your point, but are you talking about what people actually do or are you fighting a straw man that wears clothes that *you* bought for him, then stuffed yourself?"

I can assure you that this is no straw man that I have been describing. As I have shown in my books, he is alive and all too healthy; and his practice is widespread. But before I give you a concrete example of what I am talking about, let me at least mention one other implication of the God-as-additive approach.

While the most serious error has been mentioned—i.e., misrepresenting God by saying that He is in favor of godless systems—there is another aspect of that fact: counselees thereby are seriously deceived. By labeling a system Christian, when in fact it has no place for God, the counselor leads his counselees to believe that they are receiving *Christian* counseling (that is to say, counseling that from the ground up is from God; straight from His Word). Affixing a smattering of Christian activities or symbols to that system may give it a Christian appearance, particularly to an uncritical, hurting Christian who is confused and perhaps overly anxious to obtain help. In fact, although the additive counselor himself may be a Christian, and may think and speak of his counseling as Christian, in truth it is not. What is hard for counselees to understand is that the mere fact that a counselor is a Christian is no assurance that the counsel that he gives is Christian. Yet, the addition of a Christian counselor and Christian trappings to an ungodly system does not make it more godly. It simply makes it more dangerous. Thereby the true content of the system is disguised. And, as a result, the trusting counselee stands in greater danger because he lets down his guard. If the system were plainly labeled for what it is, he might have been able to protect himself.

"Then that is what you meant when you said that bringing God into the picture wrongly is worse than leaving Him out altogether!"

Exactly. There is no vital change in the picture itself when God words and God symbols are added to it. The picture has been *retitled.* The new title only *misrepresents* the facts; it does not *change* them. The fact that a painting depicts Whistler's mother cannot be altered by renaming her portrait "Whistler's Mother-in-law."

This deception, in which godless systems are depicted as godly ones, has many grave effects upon counselees. Let me mention just two.

On the one hand, this retitling of the picture leads to a false assurance in counselees (and perhaps also in self-deceived counselors). They think that the blessing of God is upon what they are doing when it is likely that it is not. (Of course, it is possible for God to work sovereignly even in such a context if He so wills. But then He will work against the system, in spite of it, and not because of it.) The deception leads counselees to trust in an unscriptural system as if it were biblical, thus according to it an authority and giving to it a kind of submission, that it does not deserve. The presence of a counselor, whose personal Christianity cannot be doubted, the use of prayer and the sprinkling of a sufficient number of Bible verses often is all that it takes to make the deception complete. But these Christian additives, no matter how good they are in and of themselves, will not sanctify systems that (at their core) are godless, and therefore, anti-christian. To put it another way, even when employed by Christians, together with Christian additives, the effect of any anti-christian system always must be harmful rather than helpful. And because God may choose to bless in spite of the sinful circumstances, that does not justify those circumstances for either the Christian counselor or counselee. Nor may either *expect* such help from God in that situation.

And, not only is there a false assurance, but on the other hand, when the system at length fails to produce godly living (and that is something that no ungodly system *can* produce; the fruit of the Spirit grows and is harvested nowhere but in His field), the failure contributes to doubt and despair about God ("God's counsel didn't work," says the counselee).

OK, I've tried to tell you what it is like to attempt to *add* God to counseling and I appreciate the fact that you have been waiting patiently for my answer to your earlier question. You've been wondering whether anyone really does such a thing or whether I'm beating a stuffed mule. Well, you realize, of course, that people don't *speak* about *adding* God to ungodly systems as I have, but they *do* it. The most recent example of this that I can cite appeared in a widely circulated Christian magazine. In an article on counseling, surveying what Christians are doing today, Vernon Grounds quotes Quentin Hyder as saying,

> The actual psychotherapy I had given him was not significantly different from that which he would have gotten from a non-christian psychiatrist. However, there were three factors which were different. First, he felt more easily able to express his problems in biblical terms and knew that I understood what he was trying to say. Second, being reassured that I was myself a committed believer, he was much more readily able to accept my explanations and respond to my suggestions. Third, I was able to read a few relevant passages of Scripture to him and we often concluded our sessions with prayer together.[1]

Significantly, Grounds comments: "It is this stance and spirit that most Christian counselors appear to identify with today."[2] Notice

[1] *Eternity* Magazine, January 1975, p. 19.
[2] *Ibid.*

several things about Hyder's description of his counseling. First, he considers neither the Scriptures nor prayer to be part of the psychotherapy as such. Secondly, notice what Hyder added to the pagan system of psychiatry that he uses: biblical terms, a few passages of Scripture and occasional use of prayer. But thirdly, and probably of most importance, notice how the counselee let down his guard. Hyder says that because he was assured that the counselor was a Christian, he more readily accepted the non-christian explanations and suggestions that were offered. The great danger of such a misrepresentation of the facts is that the willing counselee gullibly will accept as Christian what is not because of its Christian packaging.

Just let me mention another example. John Drakeford, Director of the Marriage and Counseling Center at Southwestern Baptist Theological Seminary in Fort Worth, Texas, has identified himself so closely with O. Hobart Mowrer that, in fact, the main dish on his menu is little more than Mowrer warmed over. Recently, Mowrer wrote this concerning Drakeford: " . . . when he returned to his seminary he reorganized his whole program along Integrity Group lines." Integrity Groups is the name that Mowrer uses for his humanistic group counseling system. He mentions also a booklet that "Drakeford compiled . . . called 'The Little Red Booklet,' which" (says Mowrer) "is an encapsulated version of Integrity Groups."[3] This booklet is a perfect example of the additive syndrome. After setting forth unadulterated Mowrerian dogma from start to finish, pagan and humanistic as it is, on the last page Drakeford *added* eight scriptural passages! Mowrer does not believe in the existence of God (he told me personally that the Bible could be improved by eliminating the vertical element in it) and his system is from start to finish ungodly; yet Drakeford baptized it unaltered into the faith.

So, you see, I am not tilting at windmills. The problem of using God as an additive to sweeten all sorts of bitter psychiatric potions is a very real one.

Closely related to the additive view (and sometimes linked with it) is what I call the Eureka view. This way of trying to introduce God into the counseling picture differs slightly, but significantly, from

[3]Unpublished mimeographed ms., 1974.

the first. This difference makes it all the more subtle and, therefore, all the more dangerous. The advocates of the Eureka view differ from those who follow the first because instead of attempting to bring God in from the outside in order to tack Him on as an adjunct to a godless system, they purport to discover that He was in the picture all the time. The zeal and growing ability of some of these advocates of the view to find all sorts of parallels and similarities as well as outright identifications of Christian truth with pagan theory, at times is truly remarkable. As they comb the writings of the framers of the unbelieving systems they may be heard to cry continually, Eureka! as they supposedly discover one after another. Some maintain that there is a positive identification while others, or even the originator of the system, think otherwise. Accordingly, Freud's Id has been identified with the biblical view of original sin, Rogerian listening with the Christian concept of listening, Glasser's idea of responsibility with biblical responsibility and even Skinnerian reward and aversive control with the scriptural reward/punishment dynamic.

In actuality, there is no discovery of anything that was there in the picture; instead, the desire is the father of the fact—God is first projected into the picture, then found. This is accomplished by reinterpreting the contents of the picture to conform to Christian vocabulary. Tragically, at the end one is left with the same picture, but the Bible has been bent to fit it.

"I'm not about to ask you whether you can cite any examples of this trend because I suppose that you can. But tell me this—how can they get away with it? Can't people see that this is going on?"

Well, I'll give you some examples later anyway, but first let me answer the immediate question that you have raised. Remember from the previous discussion how gullible and disarmed a Christian can be when he is anxious to get relief from a pressing problem and he finds a Christian "professional" who claims to be using Christian counseling. Add to that the psychotherapeutic jargon and the ethos that the medical model lends to the *psychiatrist,* and you have the basic ingredients for easy acceptance. The poor counselee may think, "I don't see it," but then he remembers that Dr. so-and-so says that it is so, and he acquiesces. "After all," he reasons, "the good Dr.

said that the problem was too deep for me anyway." Moreover, many things that unbelievers suggest do resemble Christian methodology. But careful investigation of similarities always reveals fundamental differences.

The problem of the Eureka mentality is a serious one; the practice of crying Eureka is nearly universal. In an almost ludicrous statement, Marion Nelson wrote: "I have never found any command or exhortation in the Bible which, properly translated, interpreted and applied, contradicts any psychological principle." I say that this is almost ludicrous, because at first it brings a chuckle as one thinks of Nelson trying to retranslate and reinterpret hundreds of biblical passages in order to square them with thousands of conflicting psychological principles made by the advocates of scores of conflicting systems. But upon further reflection the smile must give way, for it is because of the acceptance of this palpable nonsense that many lives will be ruined. The only way for Nelson to support his thesis, so far as I can see, is for him to judge which principles are the true psychological principles. He could only do this, of course by using a standard, and if that standard is the Bible, then the statement is nonsense since the Bible would eliminate all principles which conflicted with it.

Gary Collins is perhaps typical of the tendency to cry Eureka. In his book,[4] *Effective Counseling,* he not only equates Fromm's view of love with I Corinthians 13, but even finds Freud in favor of religion.[5] Without saying more, let me finally mention the astounding statement of L. I. Granberg, who had the temerity to write: "The Christian who considers thoughtfully the findings of the psychotherapist sees many of the processes associated with the Christian's rebirth and sanctification operating in another context and described in a different vocabulary."[6] How blind men can be, to identify what psychiatrists do with that which the Bible teaches may be done by the Holy Spirit *alone.* Paul plainly states, in I Corinthians 2, that the natural man neither understands the Spirit's work, nor what has happened to men who have been transformed by His work.

[4]Marion Nelson, *Why Christians Crack Up* (Moody Press, Chicago: 1960), p. 16.
[5]Gary Collins, *Effective Counseling* (Creation House, Carol Stream: 1972), p. 59.
[6]L. I. Granberg, "Counseling," *Baker's Dictionary of Practical Theology* (Baker Book House, Grand Rapids: 1967), p. 194.

Usually the pious label that is gummed on the Eureka process is "common grace." But common grace is another thing. It does not mean that pagan dogma can be taught as Christian truth by translating it into Christian terms. The goodness of God is manifested in common grace as He makes the sun to shine upon both believers and unbelievers alike. He restrains evil in unbelieving men so that they do not totally destroy one another, and He allows them to excel in many of the arts and crafts of society. But, as Calvin so well put it, "many monstrous falsehoods intermingle with those minute particles of truth scattered up and down their writings . . . . To the great truths, what God is in Himself, and what He is in relation to us, human reason makes not the least approach."[7] And, as we saw in the previous lecture, it is with those truths that counseling deals.

In short, every Christian must become wary of the sort of confused thinking that leads both counselors and counselees alike to conclude that any slight alteration of the prevelant pictures of counseling will do. No such tinkering with ungodly systems will ever make them Christian. We can settle for nothing of the sort. Nor can we merely hang another picture in their midst. No indeed; all of the pictures must be removed from the wall. In their place a new one must be hung. It is a picture into which God and His Word are neither intruded as an extraneous appendage, nor is it one in which He is projected and then discovered. Rather, God is in the *background* of the picture at every point, *He* is its theme and its subject, and certainly not of the least importance is the fact that He Himself is the artist who painted it. When we hang that picture on the wall of every Christian counseling room, the world will begin to cry EUREKA—at last we've found it!

[7] John Calvin, *Institutes* III, IV, 4.

CHAPTER III
TURNING THE TIDE BY COUNSELING

"We see the problem as you have presented it. You've helped us to understand how some Christians have wrongly tried to solve it. But now, don't you think it's time to say something about what can be done to turn this sad situation around? After all, we are looking toward our futures in the Lord's vineyard. And many of us do not yet know how our gifts ought to be used there. Perhaps you can say something that will be of help."

An extremely reasonable request. And, I am so entirely caught up with it that I plan to spend the time in both today's and tomorrow's lecture talking about it. What I hope to show you today is that counseling is tied far more closely to your future than you may realize.

To begin with, I want you to understand that the opportunities for serving Christ were never greater than they are today. You will take your place in the church and in society at a remarkable time. The decline of the liberal churches, the political and moral confusion on every hand, and the self-confessed failure of psychiatry and psychology to really help men with their problems have combined to make people everywhere examine again the basic issues of life. People everywhere are beginning to recognize the need for what you have. To meet that need, God has been blessing His faithful churches with numbers, finances, resources and increasing influence. The time is ripe for a sweeping proclamation of the saving gospel of Jesus Christ, with its impact for good in every area of our culture. All is ready. All, but *one* thing . . . .

There is one major obstacle: Christians. Christians by the thousands, just like their non-christian neighbors, are suffering from unresolved personal problems. They are turning in droves to counselors of all sorts. Pastors are overburdened by husbands or wives threatening to dissolve their marriages, by parent/teen struggles, and by interpersonal conflicts among various members of their flocks. There is immense power abroad in the church today, but much, if not *most* of it is being drained off by these energy-wasting difficulties. If even a small proportion of the energy of God's people that is now consumed in anxiety, worry, guilt, tension, anger and resentment were able to be released into productive activity for the kingdom of God, the world would soon know that Jesus Christ is at work today. Sadly, instead, the world still searches for the answer to its problems, seeing little or no difference in the lives of professed Christians.

Yet, potential for untold change now exists; God has enmassed in the church an enormous amount of resources that are virtually untapped. Were the holes in the barrel, through which so much power is being lost, repaired, the effect for good could be overwhelming. In a vital sense, then, a necessary preliminary to any real impact upon those around us who do not know Christ, is for us to become the sort of Christians whose lives, in the midst of confusion and chaos nevertheless, shine. But shining lives today are rare. The church is shot through with the same attitudes toward life that may be found in any other place. There is little distinctive living. Christians look too much like the world. God has told us that usually it is not our distinctive teaching or belief that first makes an impression, but rather, as Peter explained to Christian wives, they would have to win their unsaved husbands without a lot of talk by *demonstrating* their faith in daily living (I Peter 3:1,2ff.). What Peter told wives, holds true elsewhere: when others *see* Christianity in action, they will be ready to *hear* about it in words.

That's where counseling comes in. Not only is there the need for the kind of counseling that always was and always will be essential to the welfare of the church and to the evangelization of those unsaved persons who come to Christians for help, but if I am not entirely mistaken, in this period of national breakdown there is a special need for Christian—truly Christian—counseling. If the church can be repaired, the holes plugged, and the power preserved and harnessed, the effect upon the surrounding society might even occasion another Great Awakening. Surely, the need is apparent. The opportunity appears to be present too. But will we seize it? That is the question that I come here to put to you. All of the evangelism programs that may be conceived, no matter how true and how biblical, will not bring about the desired results if on two fronts weakened lives stand in the way. First, as I have indicated already, Christians must be strengthened in the witness of their lives, demonstrating in their personal decisions, in their practical actions and in their expressed attitudes and comments that Jesus Christ enables them to weather the economic, political and social storms that are raging uncontrolled. Indeed, others need to see in us that peculiar combination of realistic joy and peace that comes from righteous living empowered by the Holy Spirit (cf. Rom. 14:17). Secondly, Christians whose lives are weakened by unending strife and turmoil make poor recruits for evangelism. They are too much embroiled in their own problems to be of much help to others. So, in one sense, it does not seem to be going too far to say that today proper counseling is a prerequisite for evangelism.

But be that as it may, how shall we reach the goals that we have described? What sort of strategy must be followed in order to plug so many holes soon? Where will the counselors come from and how shall they be trained? How shall we alert the church to the solution, and convince Christians that there is hope even in the midst of the present disorder? Those are large questions that require more detailed answers than I could offer here. Yet, they are not abstract issues; they are deeply practical, and you will be involved in their answer, because you belong to the generation that will constitute the emerging leadership that can either carry the day or lose the battle. The outcome largely will depend upon how well you enter into, energize, more sharply define and bring to its fullest flower, the counseling movement that some from our generation have conceived and have gotten under way. We have begun and I hope begun well (that will be for your generation finally to determine). But, at any rate, the real task we must bequeath to you. We stand near the close of a transition period, most of us will die in the wilderness. It is up to you to lead the church into the promised land.

So, if you are going to take up the challenge, you will need to know something of the history of what has happened so far, as well as what is expected of you in the future. You need perspective. It is hard to know where to begin, but perhaps it would be best to go back to the situation that existed when some of us entered the ministry about twenty-five years ago. Liberals were riding high; they had nearly all of the ecclesiastical clout that did not belong to the Roman Catholic Church. Conservative churches were in the minority: weak in finances and nil in national influence. Great blows successively had been struck at the church. Evolution had all but successfully destroyed belief in creation and in the fall of man. Adam had come to be considered but a mythical character. That meant that the whole question of man's sin in Adam and the consequences of the fall were up for grabs. To move from questions about the origins of man and his fall into sin to doubts about the second Adam and His death for guilty sinners was but a short journey. None, however, except the most extreme wanted to eliminate Christ from the picture; after all, His life and many of His words could be used (or misused) to support some of the idealist values and programs of the new humanism. So, through the advent of a so-called higher criticism of the Bible that purported to be *scientific,* Jesus was stripped of His deity and made instead to be the first and best Christian. His role became that of an example and a teacher who taught self-sacrifice and good deeds. By following in His steps we could bring about a new and better world in which to live. The portions of the Scriptures that so obviously taught the miraculous and the redemptive, and that contradicted the views of the liberals, were no problem to them since the Scriptures were no longer considered to be *God's* revelation to man, but *man's* best endeavor (to date) to reveal God. They were conditioned by their times (as indeed, was Jesus Himself), and they were caricatured as filled with local and dated elements. Belief in the Supernatural (to which now "Science" had given the gate) posed no problem, since it could be discarded as a form of magic. After the layers of such accretions had been scraped away, and after the mythology had been reinterpreted in scientific terms, presumably one could find the true historical Jesus and his teaching lurking behind. It was simple enough for each one to remove what was not wanted at any point by this highly subjective process.

Well, the attacks were relentless and the gains were substantial. Everywhere, denominations, institutions of learning and organizations that had been developed by Bible-believing Christians and dedicated to the service of the Lord Jesus Christ fell into the hands of unbelievers. Funds, resources, programs and institutions which had been given to further the teaching of the gospel now were used to destroy faith. Those few who did not capitulate, those men and women who under trial, loss and even persecution held true to the Word of God, were thrown on the defensive. Energies that previously could be used for the positive work of evangelism and edification were now spent in fighting battles, most of which took place within the borders of the church itself. Many of these battles were lost. For the badly outnumbered, battle-worn troops, that meant retrenching. With supplies, personnel, resources and strategic positions all in the enemies hands, they found themselves faced with the mammoth task of rebuilding again what had crumbled, but this time not in virgin territory; it had to be done in the midst of the Samaritans who did all that they could to hinder. Vast amounts of energy were consumed in these battles and in the rebuilding of the church in America. The critics jeered, the opposition sneered, and even capitulating Christians (of which the woods was full) heaped discouragement upon the faithful few who from their several denominational and ecclesiastical backgrounds tried once more to build on a sure foundation. The infighting had been exhausting; the opposition had been bold and ruthless; but the current situation shows plainly enough that in spite of all, God has blessed those who persevered.

But there were losses even in the ultimate gains. With energy consumed in waging war within and without, with resources and manpower poured into rebuilding, there was little energy and little time left over to spend cultivating one's personal and family faith. Few books, few efforts were forthcoming in these areas. Consequently, the Church, the family and the individual suffered greatly. Some Christians, indeed, forsook the battles and the rebuilding and went off to the caves. There they developed subjective mystical and deeper life concepts based upon individual communion with God and personal experience. But far from helping the situation, this factor brought more division and confusion. Then too, there were those who saw in the defeats and the growing apostasy, the end at hand and, in the spirit of eleventh hour thinking, gave up all hope of restoring the faith. Their energies also were diverted and dissipated as they turned to the study of prophecy with *such* a vengeance that little else mattered.

In all this, concerns about Christian living were largely missing. In the confusion, church discipline evaporated. Personal ministry of Christian to Christian was mostly unknown. Young people were raised with little or no instruction about marriage or the home. They were taught the doctrine that they needed, to withstand the foe— and that was good—but rarely were they taught either the implications of biblical truths for daily living or how to study the Bible in such a way that one can discover those implications. My generation therefore has grown up knowing little or nothing about these matters. Consequently, our homes and our lives have suffered. We have made some terrible mistakes. Nor have we taught our children what they needed to know—that is why some of you find yourselves in some of the dilemmas that you face right now. Currently, evidence of that need is apparent in the size of the crowds that seek help from those who give such basic instruction.

Some of us who have begun our Christian lives and have entered into our ministries during this period of tumultuous upheaval, have found ourselves veering from one of these emphases to another. But, as a consequence, at last we have come to see the great need for balance. We fought, and were ourselves at times consumed with fighting. We built, and often became so weary in the work that at times we became weary *of* the work. We argued prophetic viewpoints until we were able to divide and subdivide not only the times and the seasons, but ourselves. We lived at church and found no time to live before the world and in our homes. Now we have come full circle. We want to hand you a better and more balanced approach; one, that while neglecting none of these emphases, nevertheless knows how to put each in its proper place according to biblical priorities. That is one reason why I have tried to paste together this historical/personal collage for you. It would be wrong for me to entreat you to put an emphasis upon counseling which is unquestionably *needed* at present, if by doing so I were to cause you to neglect the other factors that are essential to maintaining the faith collectively and individually. That is also one reason why I have tried to point out what I think is a valid connection between counseling and evangelism. In other words, I am trying to get you to see that a strong emphasis upon counseling is the strategy for today. But at the same time, I want to warn you that if we are to enter into the opportunities that lie just ahead, we must not reject the emphases of the past, imbalanced as they may have been at times, and we must not become so caught up in counseling and biblical truth about Christian living that we forget other vital matters. While the practical must not be sacrificed for the doctrinal, neither is it right to move in the opposite direction. We must not lose the true gains that have been won so dearly by creating a *different*, but nonetheless, *another* unhealthy imbalance.

There is need for continued doctrinal warfare with the forces of the evil one. The building of the church must have our continued efforts. Zeal for evangelism and missions must not flag. Prophetic study is important. But, while doing these things we must also restore the home and the quality of relationships that we sustain to one another and to God. Otherwise, all of these other efforts will be in vain. Yet, we may not allow this concern to water down our theology like those who have been teaching what is called the new Relational Theology. Those who have taken more than a *taste* of Keith Miller's *New Wine,* have become *intoxicated* with it and have found their ability to walk in the straight paths of biblical orthodoxy, seriously impaired. Theology does not come from experience; it always must issue from the Scriptures. Experience must be judged by the Bible. What we need, then, is not a new theology, but a concern for personal living that grows out of a solid theology and that at every point is conditioned by it.

So, Christian young people, I call you to get involved in the need of the hour. Get involved by beginning to square off your own life with God and with your neighbor. Examine each area of your life to discover how anger and resentment, fear and worry, envy and personal ambition, laziness and lack of discipline, guilt and depression have been hindering the development of your gifts for ministry and service to one another and to the world that so desperately needs to hear of a Savior. Take an inventory of your relationships, beginning with your relationship to God. Are you in proper fellowship with Him and with your parents and peers? You cannot begin to counsel others until you have begun to learn how to receive God's counsel for *your* life.

When you have sufficiently attended to these matters, and when you have learned how to maintain loving relationships with God and your neighbor, get involved in helping others. There are so many who need your help. Some of you will be called to counseling as a life calling in the ministry. Others will not. Nevertheless, you must recognize that God has called every Christian to a ministry of counseling someone at sometime. In a number of passages every Christian is called to become competent to counsel someone.[1] But, in closing, let me just read one other passage to you that says it so clearly:

> Brothers, if a man is caught in any trespass, you who are spiritual should restore him in a spirit of gentleness, looking to yourself, lest you too be tempted. Bear one another's burdens, and so fulfill the law of Christ (Galatians 6:1-2).

That is what we need—and by the grace of God that is what we shall have if you respond in obedient faith!

---

[1]Cf. esp. Romans 15:14; Colossians 3:16; these verses strongly attest to the fact.

CHAPTER IV

YOUR PART
IN THE COUNSELING REVOLUTION

Today we come to the concluding lecture in this series. It is last, but in many ways it is the most important of all. I could not present what I have to say until first I took time to set the stage for it. That, either adequately or poorly, I have done. Let me summarize what I have said. The current despair and disorder both within and without the church create the need. Combined with that, the growing resources accumulated by the faithful churches of Christ newly emerging as the victors in the century-long struggle with liberalism, provide the opportunity. The roadblock to seizing the opportunity, and thus meeting the need, is the weakness of Christians themselves, and the resultant weakness of a church that, otherwise, might be powerful. An outstanding and strategic answer to this problem, that will plug the holes and conserve energy, that will repair the disunity and bring about the release of the strength of love working in concerted effort, is biblical counseling. But godly counseling will not be forthcoming if we incorporate the world's failures into the church, baptizing them as Christian when, in fact, they are not; rather, it is only to be attained by digging deeply into the mine of scriptural truth to discover those presuppositions, principles and practices that God so graciously has provided, and that we so ungratefully have neglected. God's power in the church is going to be released widely, with great impact both within and without, only when Christians everywhere begin to straighten out their lives and their homes before Him and before one another. Then in the spirit of gentleness they may begin to minister both formally and informally to one another. That, as I say, is the background that I have tried to sketch out. Now against that background, let me explore the last statement in some depth. We shall bring it into the foreground. It is

46

this: God has obligated Christians to minister to one another both formally and informally as each other's counselors.

Counseling, as you already know from the quotation with which I ended the last lecture, as well as from other sources, is not unknown in the Bible, nor was it unknown to the Churches of the New Testament. Galatians 6:1,2 is explicit: each individual, as God gave him occasion, was to restore his brother whenever the need for such restoration was necessary. He could not remain disengaged. Whenever, in the providence of God, he discovered a brother caught in any sin from which that brother was unable to extricate himself, he was obligated to move in and help. That, in contrast, is rarely done today. And, it is clear from the large number of passages that have to do with mutual ministry in the New Testament, that this practice was universally taught by the apostles and was followed widely. Many of the scriptural passages that require this sort of activity contain the key words "one another," and many of the "one another" verses refer to exhortation, encouragement, restoration, admonition, rebuke and the giving of other sorts of counsel.[1] What is of greatest importance to note is that all of them are concerned not with the ministry of someone who is called to counseling as a life calling, but with the ministry of individual, every-day-man-in-the-pew Christians to one another.

While it is impossible to provide the training or know-how for counseling that you as a Christian may need in a lecture series like this, it is proper to urge you to consider your responsibility to find such help. Much of what you lack can be obtained by personal study of the subject as it is taught in the Word of God. God will bless you with increasing wisdom and finesse if you prayerfully and earnestly search the Scriptures and faithfully attempt to put into practice what you find there. But remember you must show in it all the spirit of gentleness. The biblical encouragement to engage in counseling of one another is given with that clear qualification. Increasingly, other helps to understanding and applying the Scriptures are becoming available. Books, short courses, counseling materials and courses on

---

[1]Cf. Galatians 6:2 to begin with.

cassettes have been prepared for such purposes. Moreover, and of the greatest importance, many pastors who themselves have been studying their obligations anew and who also have become concerned about mobilizing their congregations for mutual ministry, are preaching about these matters and conducting courses to supply what is needed. It may well be that with some slight encouragement on your part your pastor would be willing to organize a course of study in your church.[2] Many pastors as a first step already are working with their elders and deacons to prepare them to join in the work of counseling.

But mutual ministry means more than merely helping others; it also means willingness to ask for and to receive help from others when needed. There is no one of us who at some time or another does not need the counsel of his brother. We must not become too proud or too embarrased (which is only another way of saying the same thing) to seek help when we recognize that we are at the end of our own resources. What God has provided through brotherly counsel we dare not turn down. It is not always easy to accept help from another. But whenever a brother approaches us to resolve some problem between him and ourselves, or to restore us when he thinks that we are caught in a trespass, we must learn to humble ourselves and receive him with thanksgiving. It helps to remember that in so doing, he is being obedient to God. His effort honors God because he honors God's Word by following it (cf. Matthew 18:15ff.). We must be thankful for that, no matter how difficult anything else in the encounter may seem. And remember too, probably you should have taken the initiative yourself before it had to come to this (cf. Matthew 5:23,24). There is none of us who from time to time would not be all the better off for having had just such an encounter.

Now let us consider the second way that you can further the counseling movement in the days ahead. I can report that there is a significant amount of concern to become involved in biblical counseling abroad in the land today. During the last two years I have been receiving upwards of a hundred or so letters each year

---

[2]One way to begin might be to purchase a copy of *Shepherding God's Flock,* Vol. II, as a gift for your pastor. The book discusses the concept of lay counseling. See inside back cover.

from young men (not to speak of young women who write) who are majoring in psychology and who have decided to enter the field of Christian counseling. A fair number even come for personal interviews. Most of them want me to make some recommendation about the proper graduate training to get in order to prepare themselves for a ministry of Christian counseling. I make one reply: "If God has called you to the work of full time counseling then go to a good theological seminary. *That* is the proper place to obtain the training that you need. And when you are through, get ordained and serve Christ in a pastorate, because *that* is the proper place in which to do Christian counseling as a life calling.

"Incredible! What do you have in mind when you steer them into the seminary and then into the formal ministry of the Word? Are you interested in luring more students to Westminster?"

No, that is not my goal. As a matter of fact, I consider it just as much my job as a seminary professor to keep the wrong men out of the pastorate as it is to persuade the right ones to enter it. We already have too many men in pastoral ministry who do not belong there. We don't need any more of the sort. What I have in mind is just this: a *number* of those who write are precisely the sort of men who *ought* to consider the gospel ministry seriously. They have exactly the right qualities and the proper concerns, but they have never considered the ministry. Reasons vary, of course, but for many, I discovered, it is the model of the pastor, and the model of the pastorate they have known that has turned them off. A part of this grows out of the matter of balance of which I spoke in the previous lecture, and the weaknesses of both the members of the congregation and many pastors in the areas of Christian living and personal confrontation. But when I sketch for them something of the biblical picture of a pastor and something of his work as it could be carried on, some begin to reexamine their goals. A number of these men now are preparing to serve Christ in the pastorate.

Now, in order to give you some indication—and of necessity what I say must be greatly abbreviated—of what the pastoral ministry of the future will be like, when carried on by men well-trained in biblical counseling, who intend to do the proper work of the pastor (rather than all sorts of things to which God did not call them), I

49

shall offer a slice of an imaginary, but typical sort of conversation with one of these men.

"The pastorate? Why do you suggest that? All of that visitation, organizational work, and preaching is not for me. I want to work with people and to help them to get out of their problems."

I am certain that you do, but that's exactly why I suggested that you consider the pastorate. You see, there is no better place in which to do what you want to do than in the pastorate. And it is just the very combination of factors that you think would keep you from truly helping people out of their difficulties (organization, preaching and visitation) that God designed to accomplish that purpose. Any other sort of counseling endeavor that you undertook would be severely truncated, in comparison to the work of the pastoral ministry, by the omission of these factors.

"Frankly I don't see it. You are going to have to spell it out a lot more clearly than that before I could buy it."

Gladly. Let's begin by taking up one of your previous comments. You want to help people get out of trouble, is that right?

"Exactly. I can think of few things more rewarding."

Fine, but let me help you consider one that might be. Here you are five or six years from now, deeply involved in the work of counseling. You have just said goodbye to the third person this week who came in with the same problem. Who knows how many times before and after you will see others with that problem. Under your breath you say to yourself as she leaves, "If only I could get on the housetop and warn people before they got themselves into this mess; here is the third case this week!" But, alas, you can't. The counseling that you do is remedial, not preventive. It is repair work, after the fact. But, God designed a place where there is a rooftop from which to issue the warning—the Christian pulpit. There you can warn, rebuke, encourage and guide men, women, and children around those pot holes into which so many have stumbled. Preaching, among other things, is preventive counseling. Organizational work gives you an opportunity to plan for proper teaching in the church school, youth group, etc. You can't do preventive work without access to people early enough to help them avoid the dangers. And nothing can reach them like an organized program. Moreover, before things grow so bad that it is hard to do anything about them, as a pastor you have the opportunity and the right to initiate counseling. Nipping problems in the bud, before they ever get so large that the person might think about consulting a counselor, is a significant part of true pastoral concern (which, incidentally, is what the word visitation means in the Bible). That word does not mean making all sorts of useless house calls, as some have misunderstood it to mean. It means shepherdly concern that leads to whatever help is needed. When the Bible speaks of "visiting widows and orphans," for instance, obviously it does not mean to make house calls on them; it means to look after them, to care for their needs. So, if you are really concerned about helping people get out of difficulty, you certainly should be equally as concerned, if not even more concerned about keeping them out of those difficulties in the first place. And the person who can do this best is someone who has had to help pick up the pieces in remedial counseling. Only the pastorate provides a balanced opportunity to do both preventive *and* remedial counseling.

"O.K., I can buy that, but what about all of the other organizational activities that a pastor has to become involved in?"

Well, the problem is that some pastors have become involved in many things that they have no business doing, and have failed to do the things that they ought to do. I am interested in seeing you consider the ministry because I suspect that you would not be like many of the pastors who have failed in this way. You see, you are not rejecting the pastorate that is described in the New Testament; what you dislike or fear is a model that was originated in modern times. For example, organization in the New Testament was structured in order to do two things: to allow the pastor to become a pastor and teacher (and nothing·else) and to allow the entire congregation to exercise their gifts in mutual ministry to one another and to the world around, and to assist the pastor in his work. It is all found in concise form in Ephesians 4:11, 12, but it is worked out in detail in many other places. Let me quote those two verses for you:

God gave some . . . to be pastors and teachers, for the equipping of the saints for their work of ministry.

That is the New Testament picture. A pastor is a shepherd; the prime task of a shepherd is to know and to care for his sheep. You get the picture when you read the twenty-third Psalm this way: "The Lord is my pastor; I shall not lack." It is the shepherd's task to provide the concerned care for sheep that God requires. A large part of that will involve personal counseling (cf. Acts 20:31). Christ, the chief Shepherd, set the pattern for all of His undershepherds, by laying down His life for His sheep.

"I never thought of it that way."

You haven't heard the half of it. The pastor can counsel with authority—the authority of the living God Himself, as he counsels in His Name. He has the power of church discipline. Moreover, he can provide *total* care for the counselee; not merely care that extends to one hour one day a week. He can follow up his counseling as no other counselor is able to. And think of the resources that are available to Him. He has an entire congregation to draw upon. To assist him in counseling, he has their prayers, their strengthening reassimilation of a forgiven offender, and their many specialized abilities, to name but a few. Take the latter. Why should the pastor spend his time as a counselor helping a counselee to get his finances in shape when he has a half-dozen men in the congregation who are experts in such matters? At that point in his counseling, he simply makes an appointment with one of them for the counselee and thus provides expert help while reserving his own counseling time for what could not be supplied by others. Moreover, by involving him, he has helped another member to use his gifts in ministry and thus has brought blessing to someone else. If a place is needed for a young person to stay while he is trying to kick a drug habit, he has six homes in his congregation ready and able to provide the needed care. He has trained the members of those homes himself. If . . . .

"Wait a minute, I don't know many churches like *that!*"

I agree, you probably don't. That is one reason why you have not considered the pastorate. But there are *some,* and increasingly we see more; there will be *many* more when young people like yourself catch the vision for the pastorate that is set forth in the Scriptures rather than shying away because they see in most of today's congregations and in many of their pastors something quite foreign to this. I do not say that it will be easy to make all of the changes that are necessary to bring this about. Pastors now working at it have discovered that it can be hard. But it is possible. And by God's grace it can happen all over. The idea must be taught and Christians everywhere must become convicted about the need. The change will require nothing short of a revolution. Even if you are not called to counseling as a life ministry, you can help by supporting such efforts, as indeed a growing number of laymen are today. I did not say that it would be easy. But a man with the heart of concern for people that *you* show is just the sort of man that God loves to use to bring about such things.

And, let me mention one final fact. The place to study for a counseling ministry is in a good theological seminary, because *that* is the only place where an adequate education for counseling as a lifecalling can be obtained. I am not referring primarily to the counseling courses offered in such institutions. Rather, I am thinking of the Greek, and of the Hebrew, and of the theology, and of the exegesis courses and so forth; those studies that enable one to become intimately and accurately acquainted with the Bible. That is what a counselor needs above all. If he is to withstand the pressures of the age, if he is to rely on the living God and not upon the wisdom of men, if he is to help counselees to love God and to love their neighbors as they should, he must have "the Word of Christ dwelling in him richly" (Colossians 3:16). That is the basic need for counselors today.

Well, you have heard me out. I don't know whether you have been influenced by what I have tried to say or not. But one thing I know; you already are involved in counseling more than you may recognize and that involvement will increase. Remember, what you do to support biblical counseling may make a great deal of difference not only to you, and some day to your children, but also to the future course of the church of Jesus Christ in the land. May God convict you all of the great need, and of the great opportunity that lies at hand, and move you to do whatever you should.

COUNSELING
AND THE
SOVEREIGNTY OF GOD

COUNSELING AND THE SOVEREIGNTY OF GOD[1]

A fourteen-year-old girl is abducted by a married man, the father of three children, who carries her off to an unknown destination. During the horror of the uncertain days that follow, what can sustain her parents? What is the supreme fact to which the Christian counselor can appeal that will bring hope and some measure of relief?

A family of seven, barely scraping along on the meagre salary of a blue-collar worker in this inflationary era, is suddenly plunged into disaster by the closing down of the plant at which he works and his inability to obtain other work. They face the problem of survival amidst the uncertainties of a volatile world economy poorly managed by greedy and godless men. How can the family survive this blow when a gallon of gasoline strikes a low of 54¢ and it is a bargain to buy three loaves of bread for a dollar? On what basis do they try to go on? Is there any use? Is there any meaning to it all? Any hope? To help them understand and cope with this dilemma, what does their pastor tell them? To what bottom-line truth should he point?

There is but one—the sovereignty of God.

Knowing that God knows, that God cares, that God hears their prayers, and that God can and will act in His time and way to work even in this for good to His own . . . *that,* and nothing less than that conviction, can carry them through. And what that hope may be reduced to is: a confident assurance that God is sovereign.

---

[1]This lecture was delivered at Westminster Theological Seminary, October 10, 1975 on the occasion of my inauguration as Professor of Practical Theology. In addition to the main subject, the address also concerns theology and counseling and the relationship of Christian Counseling to Psychiatry and Psychology. This lecture is included in the author's "What about Nouthetic Counseling" (1976).

It has always been so.

When the problem of evil burned like an inextinguishable fire in his bones, and in the frustration of his situation he cried for a personal hearing before God in order to vindicate himself and discover why he had become the object of such pain and sorrow, Job received one answer, and one alone. From out of the whirlwind came the final unequivocal word to be spoken concerning human suffering:

> I do in all the world according to my own good pleasure. I scattered the stars in the sky as I saw fit, and I created the beasts of the field and stream according to *my* desires. Job, where were you when all this took place? And who are you to question what I do with my own? I am sovereign.

In discussing the outcome of the remarkable course of history that through slavery and temptation and imprisonment at length raised him to the second highest political position in the world, Joseph assured his brothers:

You did not send me here but God did (Genesis 45:8). And in a further affirmation, that was destined to become the Romans 8:28 of the old testament, he declared:

> You planned evil against me, but God planned it for good (Genesis 50:20).

His firm conviction of this truth, doubtless growing stronger throughout the span of those hard days, was what made it all endurable.

When Moses protested that he could not undertake the task to which God was calling because of his slowness of speech, God did not acquiesce, argue or plead. He simply asserted His sovereignty in powerful words by means of a stinging statement: "Who made man's mouth?" (Exodus 4:11).

Under the most extreme sort of pressure to engage in idolatrous worship, Shadrach, Meshach and Abednego (according to the words of their unflinching testimony) rested solely upon the sovereignty of God:

"Our God," they said, "is able to deliver us" (Daniel 3:17). And true to their word, in what may have been a preincarnate Christophany, that God in sovereign loving care walked through the fire with them.

In addition to these, others, who endured taunts and blows, fetters and prison, who were stoned to death, tortured, sawed in two, run through with the sword— *others,* I say, in faith rested upon the promises of a sovereign God whose Word they believed to be true, and whose promise they considered to be unfailing. Threat of death itself was not enough to shake their confidence in a *sovereign* God.

Yes, it has always been that way; the sovereignty of God is the ultimate truth that meets human need. That is why the pastoral counselor, above all men, must believe this truth and search out its implications for each and every counseling situation.

And . . . that is why today, in the midst of the many modern crises that individuals and families undergo, the pastoral counselor who most assuredly affirms the sovereignty of God will bring the most significant help of all. Freudian fatalism, Rogerian humanism and Skinnerian evolutionary theory all fall woefully short of this help. Nothing less than this great truth can satisfy the longing heart or calm the troubled soul.

That is the way that it always has been, and that is the way that it always will be.

A counselor's theology, and his use of it in counseling, then, is neither a matter of indifference nor a question of insignificance. Rather, it is an issue of the most profound importance. Truth and godliness, the reality of God and the welfare of His people are inseparable. The godly man, who copes with life, is always the one who has appropriated God's truth for his life.

Take, for instance, the question on the lips of nearly every counselee—Why? Why did *this* have to happen? Why did it have to happen to *me?* Why did it have to happen *now?* Why? Why? Why?

Evolutionary explanations do not satisfy; they only aggravate. If man is no more than an animal, what hope is there? And of what significance is any attempt to change? The only value is the preservation of the herd.

Deistic determinism is no better. According to those who espouse such views, suffering merely follows as the inevitable consequence of the onward motion of impersonal law, in which the plight of the individual does not touch the heart of God since He has safely distanced Himself from His creation.

Existential embarrassment over the equivocation of a call to an authentic acknowledgment of the *absurd* can do no more than increase the pain.

Arminian answers that intimate that the problem may be a cause of frustration to God as well as to the counselee only serve to point the discouraged, defeated disciple to a pathway that leads ultimately to atheism.

The only explanation that can fully set to rest this insistent human inquiry into the ultimate reason for the existence of misery and death is that the all-powerful God who created and sustains this universe for His own good ends sovereignly has decreed it.

By this reply, simultaneously are swept aside all notions of man in the clutches of a blind, impersonal force, every concept of a weak and unworthy deity who is to be pitied along with the rest of us because He can control His runaway world no longer, and any lingering suspicion that the destiny of a human being is nothing more than a move in a cosmic chess game in which he is as ruthlessly dispensed with as if he were a pawn—heedless of the welfare of any other piece than the King. He *is* sovereign; all *does* exist for the King. But this kingly God of creation plays the game according to His own rules. He is altogether sovereign and, therefore, the Originator of the game as well—rules and all. And as He faultlessly makes each move across the board, His strategy for winning the game involves the blessing of His loyal subjects as well as His own glory. And each subject, whose every hair is numbered, moves as He moves in a responsible manner that He has sovereignly ordained.

So, you can see that a firm dependence upon the sovereignty of God is a dynamic concept in counseling—one that makes a difference, *the* difference—and, therefore, one that must undergird every effort at counseling. If, indeed, God is sovereign, ultimately all turns out well. All problems have solutions; every blighting effect of evil will be erased and all wrongs righted. The counselor who knows

God as sovereign has found fertile ground in which to plant his pastoral ministry. He will soon send down a taproot through which he will draw the living waters of life for many thirsty souls. Rooted and grounded in this foundational doctrine, his standpoint allows him freedom to view and to evaluate both the grand sweep of things and the plight of a poor sinner agonizing in the throes of personal grief. The sovereignty of God is the ground of hope and order in all that he does in counseling. It is the basis for all assurance that God's scriptural promises hold true. It is the cornerstone of Christian counseling.

But, before going any further, let me warn against two distinct, but dangerous, tendencies of those who, while superficially holding the truth of the sovereignty of God, draw faulty implications from that great teaching. The biblical doctrine lends no support whatever either to those who, with near profanity, so glibly cry, "Praise the Lord, anyway" in all sorts of inappropriate situations, nor does it provide comfort for mechanistic fatalists who wish to discount the idea of personal responsibility before God.

Taking the first matter seriously, there are at least two things to be said. On the one hand, counselors must affirm clearly that sin exists, and—along with it—that "misery" of which the catechisms so meaningfully speak. There can be no Christian Science-like denial of the stark tragedy of human existence since Adam. There can be no facile self-deception aimed at alleviating misery by attempting to conceal its true nature beneath a heap of pious expletives, symbolized in the phrase "Praise the Lord, anyway." This vain effort, in the end, only lets one down hard. The counselor must give full recognition to sin and its terrifying effects if he wishes to be a faithful minister of the Lord Christ. After all, the Man of *Sorrows,* who was acquainted with *grief,* also believed in the sovereignty of God. Yet, He wept.

On the other hand, with equal vigor, every counselor worthy of the name of Christ must impress upon his counselees the truth that the existence of a sovereign God is truly a cause for great joy and hope in the midst of tragedy and sorrow. For if God is sovereign, life is not absurd; it has design, meaning and purpose.

Unlike existentialists, who vainly try to find meaning in man himself, the Christian pastoral counselor will show that this misdirected humanistic viewpoint is what constitutes the unbearable *angst* of which they so powerfully speak. Instead, the counselor directs the counselee's attention from creatures who, in Adam, have done little better than to get themselves involved in a kind of global Watergate affair before God. It is to the sovereign Creator and Sustainer of the universe, rather than to fallen creatures, that he bids the counselees to look for the final explanation that he seeks.

Apart from such a God, who knows the end from the beginning (because He ordained it), human beings cannot explain their existence because they have no eschatology; death ends all. But, in Him, there is a *denouement*. There will be an ultimate disclosure of the unrevealed particulars of His divine purpose. Those things that now so often seem to be but meaningless functions in the course of human activity will all come alive with significance. Each piece of the puzzle at last will be put in place—the dark purples of despair, the fiery reds of anger and affliction, the sickly yellows—and we shall be permitted to view the whole as it now exists in the plan of God alone. The comforting conviction that there is a beautiful, meaningful picture on the cover of life's puzzle box, to which each piece of distress and pain bears a faithful resemblance, belongs solely to those who affirm the sovereignty of God. Without such a conviction, there is no hope.

Likewise, one can escape the fear of a disorderly world, relentlessly rolling on like an avalanche that is out of control, only by an adherence to the doctrine of the sovereignty of God. Because of the certainty of order and control that the doctrine requires, even crazy and bizarre behavior in human beings is not inexplicable to the Christian counselor. Behind its baffling facade lies an etiology that can be traced immediately to personal rebellion against God and His laws, or (as a physiological consequence of Adam's sin) may extend all of the way back to Eden. Either way he knows the deviant human thought and action is not the result of mere chance. It is explicable in terms of a violated covenant and the judgment of a personal God.

Thus hope wells up in the heart of every man to whom God reveals Himself savingly, for there is One who came to pay the penalty for the broken law and to keep covenant with the Father. Because of His perfect fulfillment of all that God demands, men may be saved here and hereafter from the penalty and from the grip of sin. Ultimately, the evil consequences of sin will be removed altogether from the lives and from the environment of the redeemed. Indeed, so great will be the effects of salvation that those who were created lower than the angels will in Christ be raised far above by His grace. They will share with Him in His glory. So, you see, there is meaning in it all, after all. Where sin abounded, grace more fully abounds. Even the absurd and the bizarre take on meaning as the foil against which the glory of God's grace may best be displayed.

And, lastly, there is hope also in the fact of God's sovereignty because His is a personal rule over His subjects. The atonement, by which the redeemed were reconciled to God, was no impersonal or abstract transaction, as if Christ died for "mankind." He is a *personal* Savior, who loved particular individuals and shed His blood for them.

Cicero, in *De Natura Deorum* (2:66), wrote: "Magna dei curant, parva neglegunt." ("The gods are concerned with important things; trifles they ignore.") No such God is the sovereign God of our salvation. A sick child was of no consequence to Venus or Aphrodite. Larger questions—like some of the ongoing rivalries and disputes with the other gods and goddesses of the Greek and Roman pantheons—occupied their time and attention. Such gods brought no comfort or hope to men, because they were not sovereign. Much of creation slipped by beyond their purview.

But there is hope in the presence of the true Sovereign because He is in control of everything. Not a sparrow falls without Him. He is the God of trifles. Jesus taught us by His works and words what this sovereign God is like. The way that He put it was:

"He who has seen me has seen the Father."

And, it is in that very Gospel of John in which these words are recorded that we are so pointedly shown Jesus' deep concern for individuals—Nicodemus, the woman at the well, the blind man, Lazarus, Mary and Martha .... It is in the same Gospel that we hear Him speak of His shepherdly concern; a concern that extends to the hundredth sheep and that calls each by name. The sovereign

Shepherd of Israel is great enough to care about trifles—like us. He labors under none of the limitations of the classical gods. Nor does He stand at a deistic distance in disinterest. This sovereign God is the Father of a redeemed family over which He exercises total care and concern. There is plenty of hope for every Christian counselor in that.

Moving now along a continuum full of factors that might command our attention, I suggest that we pause for a moment to urge every pastoral counselor to remember the sobering fact that the existence of a God who is sovereign neither removes nor lessens, but (rather) *establishes* human responsibility to that God. If He who is sovereign over all men and over all their actions has determined that they shall be responsible to Him . . . then that settles it. That is how it is when a sovereign Creator speaks. It does not matter whether it is difficult to reconcile responsibility with sovereignty or not, because that is precisely what God decreed: Men shall be responsible to Him! And if He sovereignly determined to create man as a being fashioned in His image and governed by His moral law . . . so be it! That is the prerogative of a sovereign God.

Shall the pot say to the potter, "Why have you made me thus?" When you stop to think about it, to whom could one be more responsible than to the One who created him and sustains his every breath? To put it another way—because God is sovereign, He is the *only* one who is not responsible to another. Did not the Lamb of God Himself, who according to the sovereign plan of God was "slain from the foundation of the world," nevertheless declare:

"It is proper for us to fulfill all righteousness"?

That statement presupposes responsibility.

It should be eminently clear, then, that God's sovereignty neither encourages the utterance of pietistic platitudes like "Praise the Lord, anyway" as the solution to the problem of human suffering, nor does it leave us unaccountable. Indeed, it is this very truth that *demands* of us nothing less than a realistic, eyes-wide-open response to the existential situations of life, for God will hold us answerable both as counselors and counselees.

All counseling that measures up to the biblical standard must fully acknowledge both the tragedy of sin and the fact of human responsibility; it must reckon with God's ultimate purpose to glorify Himself in His Son and in a people redeemed by His grace. While all things will turn out well, they do so, not apart from, but precisely because of the responsible action of the Son of God who came and actually died for those who from all eternity had been ordained to eternal life.

It should be obvious that I have not attempted to open up the many practical implications of the doctrine of God's sovereignty in any concrete way. The doctrine is so foundational that the number of such implications is large. I wish rather to invite others of you to join with me in extracting the ore from this virtually untouched mine.

The sovereignty of God has been taught and preached, largely in an abstract way—but little has been done to explore the applications of this doctrine for life, and (therefore) for counseling. Moreover, Christian counseling has failed to measure up to its name principally because its early theorists were unskilled in exegesis and theology. Largely, they came to counseling through a background of psychology. Yet as important as psychology (rightly conceived and practiced) may be, it can never be foundational to counseling, but only ancillary.

Counseling—as we shall see—has to do with the counselee's relationship to persons. God and all the others who people his horizon are its concern. Only incidentally does the counselor concern himself with other matters. Clearly love for God and one's neighbor is a prime interest of the minister of the Word.

That is why here at Westminster Theological Seminary over the past ten years the attempt has been made to teach pastoral counseling from the starting point of God's sovereignty. In everything that has been done and every word that has been written, it has been our goal to take that doctrine seriously, following its implications obediently, no matter where they might lead. Often the road has proven both difficult and unpopular; yet travel along it always has been satisfying. Temptations to veer to the right or to the left have been numerous. It has not always been easy to resist them. God alone knows how well we have succeeded in doing so.

"But," you inquire, "can you tell me more about the ways in which the doctrine of God's sovereignty has affected the theory and practice of the teaching of counseling at Westminster?" The basic answer to your question is this: Both theory and practice have been affected in *every* way.

But to become more concrete, let me mention what I consider to be the most significant influence the doctrine has exerted, an influence that has had marked effect upon both theory and practice. Early in the development of a counseling stance from which to teach, the question of encyclopedia arose. To what task does the pastoral counselor address himself? In counseling, does he handle a very narrow band of "spiritual" or "ecclesiastical" problems, or is his field of legitimate activity substantially larger? Is his counseling activity bordered (and thereby limited) by others from clearly distinct disciplines, namely psychologists and psychiatrists (whose titles, curiously enough, might be translated—not too freely—as "soul specialists" and "soul healers")?

Over the years the question always has been kept in view. Gradually, the Scriptures have driven us to an answer; an answer that one hardly would have chosen by himself. The conviction has grown that it is God's answer. And when God speaks by His inerrant Word, what He says is *sovereign.*

Because of the teaching of the Scriptures, one is forced to conclude that much of clinical and counseling psychology, as well as most of psychiatry, has been carried on without license from God and in autonomous rebellion against Him. This was inevitable because the Word of the sovereign God of creation has been ignored.

In that Word are "all things pertaining to life and godliness." By it the man of God "may be fully equipped for every good work." And it is that Word—and only that Word—that can tell a poor sinner how to love God with all of the heart, and mind, and soul, and how to love a neighbor with the same depth of concern that he exhibits toward himself. On these two commandments hang all the law and prophets. They are the very summation of God's message to the world and to His redeemed people. And, as a consequence, it is the calling of the shepherds of God's flock *(par excellence)* to guide the sheep into the pathways of loving righteousness for His Name's sake. Putting it that way—that God's Name is at stake—shows the importance of this task.

"All of that sounds quite biblical and . . . it all sounds very innocuous," you may say. "But," you continue, "I don't see where that puts psychologists and psychiatrists in conflict with God. You'd better explain that one more fully." OK. Let me screw the two things together for you so that you can see the interconnection that leads to the conflict.

In assigning the pastor the task of helping sheep to learn how to love God and neighbor, God has spoken sovereignly. If this is the pastor's task, clearly delineated in the Bible, then he must pursue it. This puts him in the counseling business. But, immediately, upon surveillance of the field, he discovers all sorts of other persons already out there trying to do similar things, and saying that to them, not to him, belongs the task of counseling. There are competitors in the vicinity. Indeed, even a cursory investigation indicates that they are not merely in the vicinity but in the sheepfold itself. And, as a result, the true shepherd soon discovers that they are leading the sheep astray.

"But," you ask, "is there no basic difference between the work done by psychologists and psychiatrists and that done by a pastor?" There is no way to distinguish between the work of the pastor as it is sovereignly ordered in the Scriptures, and that which is attempted by others who lay claim to the field. Persons who come to counselors for help are persons who are having difficulty with persons. They don't come complaining, "You see, I've got this here problem with my carburetor." That is why love for God (the Person) and for one's neighbor are such vital factors in counseling. Nothing could be more central to a pastor's concern. Yet, it is with this concern about persons that psychologists and psychiatrists also busy themselves. They want to change persons and the relationships between persons.

I contend, therefore, that it is not the pastor who is responsible for the overlap; it is the psychologist on the one side, who has moved his fence over on to the pastor's territory, and the psychiatrist on the other, who also has encroached upon his property. Unfortunately, until recently, pastors have been all too willing to allow others to cut their grass. At long last, largely under the impetus of the Westminster emphasis, there has been a noticeable change in attitude by conservative pastors everywhere.

"Now, wait a minute. Are you saying that psychology and psychiatry are illegitimate disciplines? Do you think that they have no place at all?"

No, you misunderstand me. It is exactly not that. Remember, I said clearly that they live next door to the pastor. My problem with them is that they refuse to stay on their own property. I have been trying to get the pastor to mow his lawn to the very borders of his plot.

Psychology should be a legitimate and very useful neighbor to the pastor. Psychologists may make many helpful studies of man (e.g., on the effects of sleep loss). But psychologists—with neither warrant nor standard from God by which to do so—should get out of the business of trying to change persons. Psychology may be descriptive, but transgresses its boundaries whenever it becomes prescriptive. It can tell us many things about what man does, but not about what he should do.

Similarly, the neighbor who lives on the other side of the pastor's lot could be a most welcome one with whom the pastor could live in real harmony were he satisfied to play croquet in his own yard. Psychiatrists, for the most part, are a tragic lot. I say this not only because among the professions psychiatrists have the highest suicide rate, but more fundamentally because they are persons highly trained in skills that they hardly use, and instead spend most of their time doing what they were never adequately trained to do. In the United States psychiatrists are physicians, who (for the most part) use their medical training to do little else than prescribe pills. Freud, himself, acknowledged that a background in medicine is not required for the practice of psychiatry. That is why in other parts of the world psychiatrists are not necessarily medical persons. And that is why clinical and counseling psychologists do the same things as psychiatrists without specialized training as physicians.

The pastor recognizes the effects of Adam's sin upon the body; he, therefore, has no problem working side-by-side with a physician who treats the counselee's body as he counsels him about its proper use. From the days of Paul and Luke, pastors have found kinship with medical personnel. Why, then, does the psychiatrist present a problem? Certainly it is not because of his medical background. The problem is that he will not stay in his own backyard. He keeps setting up his lawn chairs and moving his picnic table onto the pastor's property.

If he were to use his medical training to find medical solutions to the truly organic difficulties that affect attitudes and behavior, the pastor would be excited about his work. But the difficulty arises as the psychiatrist—under the guise of medicine—attempts to change values and beliefs. That is not medicine. The pastor is disturbed at having residents from the adjoining lots digging up his back yard to plant corn and tomatoes. He does not object to—but rather encourages—all such activity in the yards next door.

So, in effect, the issue boils down to this: the Bible is the textbook for living before God and neighbor, and the pastor has been ordained to teach and guide God's flock by it. When others take over the work, and substitute other textbooks, conflict is inevitable. The most recent change has occurred because the pastor has taken a fresh look at his title deed, and resurveyed the land. In the process he has discovered an incredible amount of usurpation by others. He dare not abandon the tract to which God in the Scriptures has given him a clear title. The idea is not to destroy psychology or psychiatry; pastors simply want psychologists and psychiatrists to cultivate their own property.

In all of this, the sovereignty of God has played the conspicuous role. So often, however, when thinking of His sovereignty, we restrict our concerns to the matter of the relation of regeneration to faith. But it is not only in regeneration that God is sovereign; He is sovereign in sanctification as well. If, in order to accomplish His purposes in the believer, He has given His Word to be ministered by His church in the power of His Spirit, that is how these purposes must be accomplished; there can be no other way. And pastors, as key persons in all of this, must see to it that this is the way that things

71

are done—whether it pleases others or not. The ministry of the Word to believers in counseling can be dispensed with no more readily than the ministry of the Word in preaching.

In conclusion, therefore, I wish to emphasize the fact that what has been going on in the practical theology department at Westminster in the area of counseling has issued from a tight theological commitment. The position that has been developed and articulated is the direct result of Reformed thinking. Those who hold to other theological commitments, it might be noted, have viewed the problems in the field quite differently. Because of their failure to acknowledge the sovereignty of God at other points, they cannot hold the line against the defection of autonomous thought and action in counseling either. So, if there is anything that has been done here over the last decade that is worthy of mention, it is but the natural outcome of the faithful efforts of those who labored before. For it was they who, against unthinkable odds, held tenaciously to, and in clarity and with power delineated, the scriptural truth of the sovereignty of God in all things. The principles that they taught us we now are making every effort to apply to the task of Christian counseling.

We call upon you—whoever you are, and in whatever way you can—to join with us in this work. It has just begun. During the next ten years far more can be accomplished if you do. The needs are great, the opportunities are numerous; the human resources are few. We would stagger at the enormity of the undertaking but for one fact. It is a fact that brings hope and confidence; a fact that is the source of all humility and gratitude.

It is the fact that God is *Sovereign.*

COPING WITH COUNSELING CRISES

(First Aid for Christian Counselors)

TABLE OF CONTENTS

CONTENTS OF CASES

List of Crisis Cases

INTRODUCTION

I delivered these lectures at Talbot Theological Seminary in October, 1975 as the Lyman Stewart Lecturer for that year. In January of 1976 they also were delivered at Capital Bible Seminary, and in February at a Christian Education Seminar of the Presbyterian Church of America. Although a few emendations have been made for publication, the book is substantially the same as the lectures. However, I have added ten sample cases that may be used by students, either individually, in classes or as a part of other groups, to provide practice in applying the biblical principles of crisis counseling presented in the lectures. I hope that this addition will be of significance. Questions and directions for role play accompany each case.

My goal is to help prepare the Christian counselor to aid his people in facing the many sorts of crisis situations that they inevitably encounter in a world of sin. My prayer is that God will use this book to that end.

Jay Adams
Professor of Practical Theology
Westminster Theological Seminary
1976

CHAPTER I
FIRST AID FOR COUNSELORS

Much of the New Testament is crisis oriented. A number of the epistles, especially, were written to meet crises in the lives of individuals and churches. These crises involved all sorts of problems—heresy, apostasy, congregational division, lawsuits, disorder, death, persecution, immorality . . . . You name it, and in one form or another, you will probably find it in these letters. Christian counselors, therefore, are privileged to have the biblical resources to which to turn. Without a doubt, there is a rich lode of theoretical and practical ore available in the Bible to the crisis counselor.

Each minister of the Word, during the course of his ministry, must help others to face the many crises that unavoidably arise in a sinful world. Among other things, we must come to understand the pastoral ministry as a calling that involves helping persons in crisis. It is evident that in thoroughly equipping him for every good work,[1] God supplied an abundance of materials from which the "man of God" may abstract and marshal an impressive array of pertinent principles that is adequate to forge the practical programs and procedures that are needed to help persons in crisis. As a matter of fact, this fertile, inerrant source of help is intended to qualify him in a unique way for this work.

"Why, then, have you chosen to speak on this subject? If there is so much in the Scriptures about crisis counseling, surely by now all that could be said has been. The mine must be nearly exhausted. There must be a plethora of books on the subject and . . . . "

Excuse me. May I break in for just a moment? I agree that this is

---

[1] II Timothy 3: 15-17. For further exposition of the bearing of this passage upon counseling, see *The Christian Counselor's Manual,* pp. 8, 23, 93, 158, 187, 212, 233.

precisely what one could expect (and *should* expect), but surprisingly, the facts show otherwise. To the best of my knowledge, no one has even begun to do the job; the Scriptures are still uncharted territory for the crisis counselor. Virtually nothing has been done to locate the principal deposits or to set up mining operations. The *first* word has not yet been spoken.

In this series of lectures, therefore, I should like to invite you to accompany me on trips up unexplored rivers and into virgin forests. It is inevitable, I suppose, that we shall miss much on our journey, and I should be remiss if I did not warn you of this probability. It is even altogether possible that I shall fail to show you the grandeur of some of the mightier rivers while investigating their tributaries. There are mountains to traverse, and at times the going will be hard. I cannot even tell you how far the territory extends. After all, it is a *continent* that we shall explore! Most of the way we must use the machete; there are no trails.

But, in spite of the hazards, I am convinced that the trip will prove worthwhile if only I can accomplish two objectives. First, with your help, I should like to establish a beachhead. Then, I hope to enlist some of you to become fellow explorers—and even colonists—in this vast, undeveloped wilderness. There is much to be done in this land by those who catch the vision. The opportunities are limitless.

I should say that despite these warnings, I have some solid confidence in what we are about to do. I shall try not to be a blind guide leading the blind. I have made a sufficient number of forays into the land already to assure you that we shall not get lost. But I confess that this is the first time that I have been the leader of a full-scale expedition; heretofore, I have always gone alone.

But why has there been so little exploration?

I am not altogether sure. I can only suggest one or two reasons. For one thing, until recently, we have viewed the Scriptures largely from other perspectives. I do not wish to infer that these perspectives were unnecessary or unimportant; I only wish to note that our field of vision has been limited.

Another consideration should be noted: it has been only during the last few years that a growing concern about crisis counseling has emerged. That concern, to our shame, has stemmed almost exclusively from non-Christian quarters. Now, a number of Christian counselors, like Johnnie-come-latelies, have begun to show an interest too. But, that interest has produced little-or-nothing fresh, little-or-nothing distinctively Christian. Eclectically, Christian counselors again have opted for adaptations of the existing approaches that seem to be well on their way toward becoming established among non-Christian counselors. They have not bothered to do the hard work of asking, "What do the Scriptures have to say?"

In the area of counseling, as in all others, the eclectic spirit is rife. As a consequence, the highly unsatisfactory views of Lindemann and Caplan (top of the totem pole gurus in the secular crisis counseling movement) are being accepted and assimilated into the church in a totally naive fashion. This is both astounding and alarming since, in their view, human beings rigidly are caricatured as responding monolithically to grief and other crises, irrespective of the vast differences that underlie the crises and that characterize the individuals who face them. More often than not, the "grief work" (or "crisis work") theory is uncritically adopted without the slightest thought about the theological or anthropological presuppositions underlying this position. This is most disturbing, since the Lindemann grief work theory makes no room for essential distinctions between Christians and non-Christians, allows for no differences of attitudes or behavior in individuals, and views the sense of guilt, fear, anger, sorrow and other expressions of emotion as but simple states that may be handled satisfactorily by helping the counselee to progress normally through a succession of predetermined stages. Moreover, in this popular analysis, there is no place for repentance, grace, forgiveness or sanctification. The work of Christ is ignored, and what the Scriptures declare to be the fruit of the *Spirit,* crisis interventionists claim to be available apart from the work of the Spirit. How Christian counselors could propose to help people in crisis without these biblical essentials is beyond me. Lindemann's humanistic views *must* be unacceptable to the thoughtful Christian counselor.

The trip that I have planned for us is not an excursion tour that a minister might consider optional; on the contrary, it is of the greatest importance. To begin with, according to the Bible, the pastor is to be an example to the flock in all things (Titus 2:7). That means that every pastor himself must know how to meet a crisis. If he cannot, eventually he will lose credibility as a counselor. And even when *that* eventuality may be postponed, his best efforts to help others will be torpedoed by the resultant weaknesses in his own thinking and personality.

Moreover, as leader and protector of the flock, it is crucial for the pastor to know how to care for the sheep in a crisis. Otherwise, in their hour of need, he will become part of the problem rather than a part of God's solution.

It is possible, of course, for one to be able to make others aware of proper information and correct procedures and yet fail to be able to effect these in his own life. Since all counselors are sinners, to some extent this inconsistency between knowledge and practice will be present in every counseling context. No sinner—not even a redeemed one—is able to apply fully the truths of the Scriptures to his own life. Therefore, to some extent, there always will be something of a loss.

On the other hand, there are those who, because of their past training both in precept and by example, are able to meet personal crises in a manner pleasing to Christ, but, when they try to help others to face the very same sort of crises, fail. Why? They may fail because they are not able to analyze, abstract and articulate the biblical principles behind the actions by which they overcame the threats and dangers of the crises. Or, they may fail because they do not know how to raise hope in the counselee, or . . . for any other number of reasons relating to the acquisition and communication of truth. *Know how* is not the same thing as *show how*. To some extent, of course, all counselors also fail in this way. Sinners must seek perfection now, but they will attain it only in the life to come. What is true of all of the qualifications for elders in the epistles to Timothy and Titus is true also of those that pertain to counseling: they must be applied approximately, not absolutely. As Blackwood so aptly put it in the title of his last book, *The Growing Minister,* a pastor must mature continually in both knowledge and life. Yet if he knows neither how to live in this world of crises nor how to advise others to do so, he does not possess the qualifications to be a minister of the

Word. Until he can demonstrate some genuine competence in these things, he ought not to be ordained to a work for which he is ill suited. Otherwise, both he and the members of his flock will suffer the consequences. That means that you, now while you are still in Talbot Seminary, must begin to develop your ability to handle personal crises, and you must begin to learn how to help others to do so if you wish to minister to a portion of God's flock upon graduation. You need not search out crises; they will come soon enough on their own. If your professors here are anything like my colleagues at Westminster, I am sure, by their assignments and examinations, they will provide more than enough opportunities for you to face crises during your stay in this institution.

"But," you ask, "does a minister really deal with that many crisis situations? I mean, is it really worth all the effort? After all, I have a lot of Greek and Hebrew to study . . . . "

You wonder about this, possibly, because you may have known ministers who have had to counsel relatively few persons who are in crises. They may even tell you that it is *not* worth the time and effort since the opportunities to do crisis counseling are so limited. In response, let me simply suggest a few things:

First, people do not think or operate that way in other areas of life. Although there are relatively few instances in which those who are adequately trained in first aid find it necessary to perform a tracheostomy, it is, nevertheless, vital for them to know the procedure, or someone, someday whose life they might otherwise have saved may die of suffocation. Let us suppose, for the sake of the argument, that a given minister receives only a half-dozen or so phone calls from persons threatening suicide during his entire ministry. Is it not still important for him to know what to do when such a call comes? Or, can he simply write off those six persons as "a limited number of cases?" May he rationalize by saying "After all, I shall preach to hundreds, perhaps even thousands, so I must concentrate all of my attention on preaching?" Any such attitude falls far short of the spirit of the Good Shepherd who not only feeds the ninety-nine sheep at hand but also seeks the hundredth that is lost.

But then, if a minister tells you that he has relatively few crisis counseling cases, in most instances (if he has been in the pastorate for any significant length of time), you can begin to question whether that man has an effective ministry to his people. There is no dearth of crises and no lack of persons—even Christian persons— who are failing to meet them God's way. Why, then, do those sheep to whom he ministers not seek him out more often? In contrast, *truly* ministering pastors tell of the overwhelming number of such cases that they see.[2]

Particular circumstances, in certain situations, may (of course) limit the number of crisis cases that a minister may encounter for reasons not attributable to him. But, in general, it may be said with assurance that the effective pastor is at least as deeply involved in crisis counseling as anyone else in any other profession, and much more fully than most.

Simply for the sake of the many who experience crises in their marriage and families, and in order to minister well to the sick and dying, the pastor should find a study of biblical principles and practices pertinent to crisis counseling essential. You can be certain that every hour you spend increasing your knowledge and developing the skills involved in crisis counseling will at length prove profitable.

Since it should not be necessary to extend the present argument further, I shall make two additional responses briskly, then move on. Some pastors are so unacquainted with the particular features and peculiarities of the crisis situation that they don't recognize a crisis when they see one. These same men often are the ones who are so insensitive to the needs of their people that they fail to discern the symptoms of persons going through a crisis. Secondly, there are some pastors, I am afraid, who do not want to recognize a crisis. Like the priest and Levite, they close their eyes and walk by. They try not to become involved either out of laziness or fear. Crisis counseling is hard work, and it runs risks. It takes both effort and time, and requires courage and wisdom.

---

[2]In response to a student questionnaire by students at Westminster in 1973, 13 out of 35 ministers said that 50% of their counseling was crisis counseling. The rest estimated that crisis counseling constituted anywhere from 5% - 90% of their counseling.

That fact leads to a discussion of the counselor himself. In the lectures that follow we shall have occasion to consider the crisis situation and the person in crisis. We must not forget the counselor. We have just said that he must be a man of wisdom and courage. To that let me add the need for commitment and concern.

By concern, I mean something more than sympathy. Concern is not *only* weeping with those who weep—as essential as that may be—but also the willingness to help another to do something about his problems. Sympathy, too often, means "sympathetic *agreement.*" But that sort of expression of solidarity with the sufferer goes too far, since seeing a crisis only as the counselee does, in fact, precludes the possibility of helping him. If the counselee is perplexed it may make him feel better temporarily if you share his perplexity, but sharing it will not help him out of it. If he has lost hope, acknowledging the hopelessness of his situation may be comforting for a time, but it will not restore hope. The counselor must be able to enter into the counselee's problem, but he must be able to get beyond it as well. If he is merely caught up in it, he too will be disabled by it. Because he has the Scriptures, he need not stop with the problem. He may move quickly along the biblical path that leads out of it.

Scriptural concern, therefore, is not the expression of sympathetic agreement; rather, it is the expression of sympathetic *disagreement*. It is only by *countering* perplexity, and hopelessness, and depression, and temper, and fear with biblical alternatives that the counselor maintains his integrity as such. The Christian counselor is not a neighbor who holds pity parties on the phone each afternoon; he is a man with a biblical alternative.

But the counselor must have wisdom in order to manifest the right kind of concern. It takes wisdom, for instance, to maintain a balance between sympathy and disagreement. He must know how deeply to allow himself to enter into the counselee's situation while, at the same time, assuming a stance over against the counselee's present helpless position. To see the problem only as the counselee does is not merely a matter of abandoning one's place as a counselor; of far greater import is the fact that when he does so, the counselor misrepresents God. As a Christian counselor, he is required to know and articulate God's solution. Therefore, when he fails to do this, the counselee is led to believe that God does not have an answer to his problem. There is always *something* that can be done, even if it is to take the first step toward the biblical solution. Frequently, it will involve a change in the attitude and responses of the counselee. But whatever it may be, the Christian counselor must hold the conviction that in some way biblical help *will make a difference*. No one ever needs to go away from Christian counseling the same. If he has been confronted with the Word of God, he can be different in some way, that day.

It is in learning the facts of the crisis situation, in evaluating them biblically, and in discovering the biblical responses required by them that the Christian counselor must develop knowledge and skill. It is in confronting the counselee with these as an alternative to his present stance that he will need wisdom and courage.

Sympathetic agreement takes no courage and calls for little wisdom; sympathetic disagreement demands both. It is not easy to tell a depressed woman that she must get off the couch and get to work, that she must stop feeling sorry for herself, and that she must confess and forsake any other sin in her life. To tell an irate husband whose wife has given notice that she plans to leave him, that his resentment is sin and needs to be abandoned may not be popular, but it may be the only way for him to handle the tragedy in a manner that is pleasing to God. And, incidentally, if he does, that change in him will probably do more to persuade her to reconsider than anything else he could do. Certainly, allowing him to storm about the study, or permitting him to excoriate his wife in bitter language solves no problems. Sympathetic *disagreement* calls for settling him down and confronting him with his own sin first. That type of concern requires the courage to confront.

Now, on balance, I must hasten to say that sympathetic disagreement is quite a different approach from that which was taken by the counselors who confronted Job. Doubtless, their breed did not die quickly; today, we meet their representatives frequently. Like Job's friends, they fancy themselves as being quite biblical. Yet it is they who bring biblical confrontation into disrepute. People are constantly confusing *their* approach with the biblical one. It is important, therefore to take time to distinguish between the two.

When Job's friends came to offer counsel, they surely disagreed—of that there can be no question. There was confrontation—of *that* the record leaves no doubt. Since they are called "friends," there is even a likelihood that there was a measure of concern. But what Job's friends lacked was sympathy, not the sentimental sort that could never ride side-by-side with disagreement and confrontation, but the sort of sympathetic concern that includes these and combines them with a full analysis of the situation and a loving belief in the word of the counselee. Presumably they had the capacity for neither; thus they failed to provide the help that Job needed. The Christian crisis counselor must excel precisely in the three things they failed to do:

1. First, they came with preconceived notions about the cause of Job's problem. As a result, they failed to gather the data that might have led to a true analysis of the situation.

2. Secondly, they refused to listen to Job when he protested that their assumptions and (therefore) their conclusions were wrong. They failed to follow the biblical maxim that leads to successful counseling: "love believes all things." In love, the biblical counselor doubts the word of the counselee *only when the facts demand that he do so.*

3. Like many modern counselors, Job's friends began with their own assumptions and doubted that Job was telling the truth. Because of these two fundamental errors, they also fell into a third: Job's counselors failed to uncover Job's real problem and, therefore, could not help him with it. By focusing their attention upon supposed prior failures in Job's life that they considered to be the cause of Job's crisis, they missed entirely the meaning and depth of his true struggle. This is tragic since, as the record shows, Job *needed* the help that they might have provided. Instead of providing help, they succeeded only in aggravating the situation. Job was not responsible for the crisis, as they supposed, but God held him responsible for how he would handle it.[3] The heavenly discussion

---

[3]Counselors must remember that this is often so. The daughter of a drunkard who beats her and fails to provide for her may not be responsible for this situation, but she is responsible for handling it God's way.

between God and Satan focused, you will remember, upon *this* issue: "What will Job do when trouble comes?" But the problem as these would-be-counselors saw it was, "What has Job done to bring this crisis upon himself?" They confronted him—but at the wrong point. The real question was "How will Job face a crisis?"

So, from one perspective, a good crisis counselor is one who has enough courageous concern to take a different and more biblical view of the crisis than the counselee, yet he will always reach his conclusions in the matter by examination of carefully collected data. Unlike Job's friends, he will work hard to discover all of the dimensions of the problem. Then, and only then, out of concern, he will take a biblical stance toward it, no matter how sharply this may require him to disagree with the counselee's conclusions.

Now, let me attempt to define a crisis. One dictionary says that it is a stage in a sequence of events at which the trend of all future events is determined. Although that definition seems a bit overly dramatic for some crises, nevertheless from one viewpoint it certainly seems to describe Job's situation reasonably well. The glaring fault in this definition, from the Christian perspective, is its uniformitarianism or determinism—i.e., its failure to take God into account. The same dictionary further defines a crisis as a "turning point" and "a point at which a decisive change occurs." I am not in the habit of quoting the dictionary to prove points, since it rarely does that. However, in these definitions you will notice that there is more than one way to speak about a crisis. It is that fact that I want to make clear. A crisis is described either as a point in time at which something decisive occurs (or is about to occur), or as a condition, state or critical stage of instability leading to a decisive change. Since otherwise there might be confusion, I want you to understand that in these lectures I shall use the word to refer to both the state and the turning point. Putting the two together, we may say that a crisis is any situation into which God has led the counselee that either now or later demands decisive action that will have significant consequences. A crisis requires change.

And, while we are at it, let me say too that it is important to go beyond the dictionary and make a further distinction: a crisis may be either real or imagined. The emotional impact upon the counselee will be just as real and just as powerful even if the crisis is only imagined. If he is told convincingly that he has cancer, whether the fact is true or false, his emotional response will be exactly the same. When discussing crisis counseling, therefore, we may speak not only of the person in the crisis, but also of *the crisis in the person*. That means that counseling may be just as essential in an imaginary crisis as in a real one. Indeed, the problem may be even greater, and the counselor may need to make an *exhaustive* analysis of the situation in order to be able to discover and convince the counselee of the imaginary nature of the supposed crisis.

A crisis, then, is any circumstance to which a person senses a need to respond, in which he believes that his response may have life-shaking effects.

Fundamentally, there are three elements to be considered in every crisis:

1. The crisis situation (real or imagined),

2. The individual who is in crisis, and

3. The response that he must make to the crisis issues.

The counselor must be concerned with each of these elements. In each crisis he will find it helpful to simplify his task by breaking it down into these elements. Immediately, when he does so, he may discover that he needs to *focus* his attention upon one or more elements. If, for instance, the attitude of the individual toward God is proper, and if he possesses adequate resources otherwise, the counselor's task may be reduced to analyzing the crisis situation and helping him to determine how to respond to it. If, on the other hand, the counselee understands the crisis well enough, knows what God wants him to do and how to do it, but refuses to do so, the counselor must focus upon the person, rather than upon the situation or the decision. So, you can see how helpful it can be to divide a crisis into these three elements.

Each of these elements must be considered fully in relationship to the obligations and the promises of God. The Christian counselor seeks to bring scriptural aid to the counselee in one or more of these three areas. Full aid, i.e., aid in all three areas, involves helping the counselee:

1. To make a biblical *analysis* of the crisis situation,

2. To take a personal *inventory* of his state, attitudes, behavior and resources, and

3. To follow biblical *directions* in responding to the issues in the crisis situation.

Thus, the framework for crisis counseling consists of three critical factors corresponding to the three elements in the crisis. Those factors are:

Analysis, Inventory and Direction

For a counselor to analyze a situation, take the inventory of the state and resources of a counselee, and be able to give biblical direction about the proper response to a crisis, he must acquire the knowledge and skills necessary to do so. During each of the next three lectures I shall consider one of these three factors with a view to helping you become acquainted with some of that knowledge. Skills, and the wisdom with which to exercise them, must come from the prayerful application and use of this knowledge.

"But," you may ask, "how did you arrive at the three elements of which you speak?" That is a fair question to which I have time to address myself only briefly. Let me say right away that this framework has emerged from the study of a number of crisis situations in the Scriptures. In each of these situations these three elements frequently appear as matters of concern. I do not claim that they all are present in every situation, nor am I sure that we would all agree about labeling all of the situations considered, "crises." Moreover, that there may be other elements that should be isolated and included in this framework, is altogether possible. And, finally, that others might prefer to breakdown the total crisis context quite differently—and perhaps more accurately—is not unlikely. Therefore, let me say as plainly as possible that while I think that this framework is biblical and (therefore) useful, I do not say that it is as fully biblical or as fully useful as another might be. But at present it is the only one that I have.

To support my contention that there is biblical support for this framework let us consider a passage or two in which a crisis is met in a thoroughly biblical fashion.

The Book of III John was written by the apostle to Gaius as a stopgap measure to help him to handle a crisis in a manner pleasing to Christ. The congregation to which Gaius belonged was in jeopardy as the result of the pride and ambition of Diotrophes, who (in all likelihood) was the pastor of the church. Diotrophes had refused to show hospitality to travelling missionaries whom John had sent forth to preach the gospel on the basis of his apostolic authority. Because he did not wish to share the limelight with them, Diotrophes not only rejected the missionaries himself, but forbade his members to show them hospitality upon pain of excommunication. Gaius had warmly received the missionaries, and presumably had been thrown out of the church. As he sat outside on the curb scratching his head, he wondered "Did I do the right thing or not?"

When he learned of these affairs, John wrote to Diotrophes about his sinful actions, but instead of repentance and compliance, he received a slanderous rebuff. It was not a personal matter with John; the problem was that in rejecting his apostolic authority Diotrophes was rejecting the authority of Jesus Christ. Now, in this letter to Gaius John says that he plans to come and handle the matter personally as soon as he can. But, meanwhile on a single sheet of papyrus John penned this letter and shot it off to Gaius in order to help him face the crisis in his life and in the church.

We shall have occasion to return to this crisis situation later on, but for the moment, notice how fully all three elements appear. John completely analyzes the situation, carefully assesses Gaius' attitudes, actions and resources in relationship to it, and clearly directs him in the responses that are proper to make. All three elements—the crisis situation, the individual in crisis, and the proper response to the crisis—figure prominently in the letter.

Because he was an apostle, writing Scripture, John did not need to base his counsel directly upon Scripture passages. Perhaps, for this reason it would be appropriate to consider next the letter of Jude. Jude also writes by divine inspiration, but makes no personal claims to apostolic authority. He more nearly approaches our context then. In the crisis of which he wrote, we see the same three elements once again. Dropping his reed in the middle of a sentence, Jude crumbled up the sheet of papyrus upon which he had been writing, took up another and addressed himself to the startling news that had just reached him. His words . . . "it became urgently necessary to write at once and appeal to you to join the struggle in defense of the faith that God entrusted to his people once and for all" (v.3), plainly reveal the crisis nature of the situation about which he wrote.

There is neither time nor space to discuss the letter in depth but upon study and reflection I think you will see those same three elements and those same three counselor responses protruding. Jude carefully analyzes what is happening, in terms of Peter's second letter. In the strictest sense of the word, he makes a *biblical analysis* of the situation. Then, using Peter's writings and data from other biblical sources, he discusses the state of the congregation, pointing out the personal and congregational resources that God has provided for such contingencies, and finally, he urges decisive concrete action upon his readers.

If I were to give a subtitle to these lectures, it would be something like "First Aid for Christian Counselors." In a medical crisis, one can not do everything immediately; often all he can do is give *first* aid. Yet that is important. We have all been made newly aware of the vital nature of that initial aid by the TV program, "Emergency." Of course, more sophisticated help—in greater depth—is given later in the hospital.

Similarly, important things can be accomplished in crisis counseling; but not everything. It is only during the period of more regularized counseling that many other things can be done. This should be kept in mind, so that not too much will be expected from crisis counseling. So long as the emergency element prevails, counseling must be limited to crisis approaches. So, one of the goals of crisis counseling always will be to eliminate the elements of urgency and emergency in order to allow for the fuller, and the more sophisticated approaches of pastoral counseling.

In summing up, let me push the First Aid analogy a bit. If a crisis consists of a crisis situation—a person in crisis—and decisive responses that must be made to resolve it, and if good crisis counseling addresses itself to these three elements: by making an *analysis* of the situation, taking an *inventory* of the attitudes, actions and resources of the person in crisis in order to give *direction* to the counselee about the biblical responses required, then in the simple mnemonic, A-I-D (Analysis, Inventory, Direction) you have it. Just think of crisis counseling as a sort of First *Aid* and in days to come that little three letter word may come to your aid as you endeavor to aid another!

CHAPTER II
ANALYSIS

It is impossible to escape all crises in a world of sin. In the providence of God, for His sovereign purposes, crises come. Some we bring upon ourselves; others (as in the case of Job) come through no fault of our own. Some crises are simple and straightforward: "Shall I divorce my husband for incompatibility?" Others are far more complex: "My whole life has suddenly caved in—my hopes, my values, my goals—everything, and I don't know where to turn or what to do." Some crises are imagined; some real. Some are contrived (in order to avoid responsibility or to manipulate others); many are not.

Distinctions like these are arrived at by means of *analysis,* and constitute one aspect of the work of analysis. Apart from such work, it is difficult for the counselor even to *begin* to help a person in crisis, since he must determine the nature of the crisis situation in biblical terms before he can develop a scriptural strategy with which to meet it. If the crisis is contrived or imaginary, to treat it merely as if it were legitimate or real would be the height of folly. In my last lecture, I suggested that John and Jude had first fully analyzed the crises about which they wrote. The fundamental place of analysis, therefore, should be obvious. Everything else in crisis counseling depends upon it.

When Paul faced the council in Jerusalem, it was through analysis of the speaking situation that he arrived at the decision to explain his mission in the terms that he chose—terms true enough, but *also,* terms that he knew would divide his accusers into two camps.[1] Strategy was based upon analysis. In the messages of the risen Christ

[1]Acts 23:6.

to the seven churches (some of which were in a crisis or were about to face one) the same procedure is evident: first, there is a summary of the results of Christ's analysis, introduced in each case by the phrase "I know " ("I know where you dwell . . . ;" "I know your tribulation;" "I know your deeds."); then counsel is given that grows out of and is appropriate to that analysis. *This,* is the sort of thing that I am talking about; until with Jesus the counselor can say "I know . . . ," he is not ready to offer help. To call for an analysis of each crisis, therefore, simply means to ask seriously, and to answer thoroughly out of careful study of the particular situation, "What sort of crisis is it that my counselee is facing?"

There is more to analysis than that, as we shall see soon, but before looking into other aspects of the question, let me make a remark or two about a connected issue of some importance.

Because it is not possible to avoid all crises, we must learn to deal with them. But few persons have ever been taught how to do so. Ask yourself, has anyone ever taught *you*? Well, that is one reason why there is such a need for crisis counseling today.

C. S. Lewis opened his book, *A Grief Observed,* with these plaintive words: "No one ever told me . . . . " Doubtless, if someone had more adequately prepared him for the crisis of grief about which he wrote, he would have been able to handle it in a better manner than he did. Pastors must learn to help the members of their congregations *preventively* by preparing them for crises. It is foolish—not to say tragic—to wait until a person has come unglued in a crisis to begin giving instruction. The pastor, if he is a faithful shepherd of the sheep, will not be content to lock the door after the sheep has wandered out. Christian ministers always should be concerned to hang the traffic light at the corner *before* someone is killed in a bloody accident.

Yet, at present, there is neither enough remedial work being done by Christians, nor anywhere near enough preventive effort. We are woefully deficient in both. Since I cannot discuss preventive measures as such in these lectures, I wish to underscore the need for them by these few brief comments, and urge each of you to give further thought on your own to the matter. The members of your congregations in years to come will thank God for your ministry if you make the effort to teach them how to handle a crisis before it comes. Young married couples should be helped to discuss grief *before* losing their parents. Teenagers, who often live from one crisis till the next, must learn *as pre-teens* how to avoid bringing on crises that are unnecessary and how to handle the many jolting boy/girl experiences that they cannot avoid.

But it is not only because I want to urge you to think through preventive crisis instruction on your own that I mention the subject. It should also be obvious as we go on, that many of the same principles that pertain to counseling someone who is already in a crisis, apply equally as well to preparing for a crisis and meeting it on one's own, before God, by His help, and without the assistance of a human counselor.

At times it might be useful not only to teach the biblical principles for handling crises, but also to dramatize these through acting out some typical crisis situations. Well . . . that is all that I can say now about preventive measures. But remember, as we proceed, in this lecture (as well as in those that follow) to keep this matter on the front of the shelf where you can get your hands on it easily from time to time.

Now, let us return to the question of analysis, the A in AID. First, let me be clear about how the word is being used. Whenever I speak of the analysis of a crisis, I use the word to refer to the process of breaking apart the situation into its constituent elements. By putting it that way I imply that:

1. Every crisis has parts, aspects or elements that, for purposes of understanding and solution, can be separated in *some* sense.

2. It is an error to impose an artificial structure upon the crisis situation so that each and every crisis is dissected in the same way. Like a diamond, each crisis must be studied individually to determine the peculiar points at which it ought to be cut. This decision comes from within; it is not imposed from without. The nature of each crisis itself, like the nature of the diamond, always must dictate where the chisel is to be placed.

In order to handle crises successfully, the counselor must divide the whole into its parts—or at least some of its parts. It may be important to divide and even subdivide more fully in some areas than in others. For instance, Jude in writing to one faction of the church, divides them from at least two others. In addition to his readers, there are the heretics who have invaded the church, and those who have been influenced by them. While the heretics are lumped together, in his analysis the persons who were being caught up in the heresy are not. Instead, Jude subdivides this group into three classes, each having a distinct relationship to the heretics and to their false teachings. By distinguishing between them, he is able to recommend specific and individualized help that is appropriate to each class: "have mercy on some who are doubting; save others,—snatching them out of the fire; and on some have mercy with fear, hating even the garment polluted by the flesh" (22,23).

Crises, then, usually come as wholes, not in parts, and virtually scream for analysis (or, as we are now thinking of it, *division*). Frequently, it is this very wholeness that constitutes the crisis element in the situation: "The woods are too vast, too dark, too tangled. What shall I do?" Such complaints are the constant cry of persons who need help in facing crisis situations. In such cases, taking the crisis apart, setting up a biblical plan for dealing with each element in some order according to a schedule, and beginning to focus upon the first element right away, may be exactly what the counselee needs to solve his problem.

But, how can I determine when this need for division is one of the factors that is fundamental?

You will probably need to make an analysis of the situation in almost every instance anyway simply to sort things out, to know where to begin your counseling. So, the question is not as important as at first it might seem. If in the process of sorting out, the counselee comes alive, begins to participate in the process himself and starts to see light, keep working at it together and you may discover that principally what he needed was the handle on the problem that you have now given to him. Surely that is much of what the New Testament is all about, when (as in James) Christians undergoing temptation are shown that God cannot be blamed for their temptation, but that they must look at their own evil desires, or when (as in II Peter) the scoffer's charge of slowness in keeping a promise is distinguished from the longsuffering of God by which He patiently waits till the last one of His elect comes to faith.

But, to answer your question more specifically, you can almost be certain that your counselee needs to divide and distinguish the things that differ, or that he needs to take on a part rather than the whole:

1. *When he continually speaks about the enormity of the crisis.* Whenever he expresses his problem in language like "This is too much," or "This is more than I can take," or "How will I ever get all of this done?" you may begin to suspect that you have a situation that needs division into its parts. He is overwhelmed by the whole. If he says, "I've bitten off more than I can chew," why not agree and help him to slice up the whole into chewable bite size portions?

2. *When he is confused over the complexity of the crisis.* Language denoting a tangled, can-of-worms situation about which the counselee expresses confusion also gives a clue: "I just get all confused when I try to think about it" or "I just don't know where to begin."

3. *When he is worried about having to do more than is realistic on a given day.* This is expressed in language taking the form of "But, what will I do if . . . ?" The what-if formula connected to strong emotion is almost always indicative of worry. In such cases, the counselor must help the counselee to learn how to take apart his problems each day and allocate those that belong to the present a place on today's schedule; the rest must be rescheduled for consideration in the future. Christ once said, when speaking of worry:

Do not worry about tomorrow . . . . Each day has enough trouble of its own (Matthew 6:34).

The biblical word for worry—interestingly enough—means to "separate, divide or take apart." The counselor, therefore, must help the counselee to take apart the situation, before the situation takes him apart.

4. *When a counselee complains of unfairness.* In such cases he fails to distinguish human responsibility from divine sovereignty. Language like "Why did *this* have to happen?" or "Everything always happens to *me*" or "Joe isn't even a Christian, and yet *he* doesn't suffer like this" is indicative of the sort of difficulty that James, Peter and the Psalmist, who keeps warning us not to fret over the fortunes of the unbeliever, were confronting. The irresponsibilities of scoffers and their way of thinking must be distinguished from God's providence. One's own evil desires must be sorted out from God's testings, and the temporal prosperity of the wicked must *not* be contrasted with the temporal suffering of the believer, but the temporal condition of each must be compared with the eternal state of each.

In all of these instances, in one way or another, various elements in the situation need to be sorted out. And it is this kind of basic analysis of the whole—in which constituent elements are isolated for comparison and contrast, or for proper scheduling, or for easier understanding and handling—that must come first. Often, as I have said, such analysis *itself* will do much to resolve a crisis.

Let's take a typical crisis situation in which it is this approach that makes the difference.

> I'm ruined. I'm at the end of my rope. All of the chickens have come home to roost. I am a financial disaster! I'll lose my house . . . . Pastor, what can I do?

Where does t⊙ counselor begin? He asks, "Gary, how much do you owe?" In response, Gary says, "I don't know; I just don't know. But it is more than I can handle—I know that!"

Immediately, a good counselor would be suspicious. How could Gary be so concerned about financial ruin when he cannot even substantiate it? Something is wrong. The first task this counselor needs to accomplish is to *get the facts.* He must separate emotion from reality, generalizations from specifics. Consequently, he will try to discover how much is owed to whom for what, what Gary's financial resources actually are, and which creditors (if any) are breathing down his neck. He will also try to discover what precipitated the crisis. When an analysis of the situation is in, the facts can be sorted out and a program can be designed to meet the problem. The likelihood is, as in Gary's case, that once doing so, the answer will be readily apparent. In many instances, ruin is the last word by which the situation now can be described. The "ruinous" or "crisis" element was introduced by *Gary* who allowed his obligations to pile up without keeping records, etc. Reintroducing the element of organization as an obligation of faith, it may be achieved first by sorting out the facts and dividing the urgent from the less urgent, and then by planning accordingly. This often makes the difference. But notice, analysis had to come first.

Now, let us turn to a different matter. We have said that a crisis is a situation in which action leading to serious consequences is required. That is one way to look at it. But you will recall that I criticized the dictionary definition because it left God out. The Christian counselor must not do that. Indeed, that is precisely what makes his counsel unique; he will analyze the situation from a biblical (that is, from a theistic) point of view.

God is sovereign. No matter how bad the crisis may appear to be, it is never beyond His ability to resolve. And furthermore, neither is it beyond God's purview or His concern. Every hair on the counselee's head is numbered. He works all things together for *good* to those who love Him; who are called according to His purposes. Even this crisis, then, is a part of God's sovereign purpose. The time will come when the Christian will see *how* it was all for his benefit— but that time is usually on the *lee* side of the crisis. That is why it is so easy to leave God out of the picture, and that is why the counselor must make every effort to reintroduce Him. By bringing God into the picture, I do not refer to reading a Scripture verse or two, with prayer. That is necessary. But too often, the way in which the Scriptures and prayer are brought into the picture is quite superficial. They do not intrude so dynamically that the entire crisis situation must be re-evaluated; rather, they merely are tacked on. But God cannot be tacked on. He will not allow Himself to be a party to an essentially humanistic analysis of the circumstances. Rather, He must be seen to be the most basic, the most vital, the most dramatic and the most hopeful element in the situation.

One of the principal reasons why Christian counselees freeze before a crisis is because they view it in essentially the same way that

58823

an unbeliever might—apart from God and His purpose. The counselor's task is to relate God *fully* to the crisis. It is crucial for him to restructure the entire picture as one in which God is at work achieving His purposes for the blessing of His own, for the furtherance of the gospel and for the honor of His Son. To do this so profoundly *changes* the crisis, that it takes on an entirely new dimension. It becomes a crisis *in which God is involved.*

That is what Paul did for his Philippian readers when, in answer to their perplexed inquiries about why the greatest missionary of all had been shelved by imprisonment in Rome, he wrote:

My circumstances have turned out for the greater progress of the gospel (Philippians 1:12).

In the verses that follow, he showed them how imprisonment had occasioned an opportunity to evangelize many men among the Praetorian guard, how many other brethren were now coming forth to proclaim Christ with a new boldness, and how he was about to be afforded the opportunity to present the gospel to Caesar himself. If Paul, like his readers, had failed to see the sovereign purpose of God at work in his imprisonment, he could have looked on the imprisonment only as a terrible tragedy. He might have doubted either the wisdom of God or His power to control all things. And, doubtless, in such a frame of mind, he would have lost his witness to the guards, failed to stimulate other Christians to proclaim Christ, and wavered in his witness before the emperor of the world. Because he so firmly believed that God *was* involved in the crisis, he was able to look for and work toward the outcomes; that when he wrote the letter, he was able to share this with the church at Philippi.

I shall say more about God's place in a crisis in another lecture, but before I leave it, I wish to make two vital points about the effect of such a radical Christian theistic analysis of a crisis situation—the first is this:

To acknowledge God as sovereign over the crisis *limits* it.

Don't miss this point. God is in control. The crisis is not a broken thermometer—with bits of mercury irretrievably going everywhere. God made the mercury and He knows where every little bead is. If He wills, He can gather them all together into one lump again.

101

Therefore, the counselee's thoughts and language can be and must be changed; the situation is neither "hopeless" nor "impossible." It is neither "too much" for him nor "out of control." The One who said "I will be with you till the end of the age" is here; Christ is in the crisis. Therefore, it is *limited* —limited to His purposes, to serve His ends, controlled at every point by His power. The crisis is in God's hands; it will not continue a fraction of a second longer than He wills, nor will it extend a millimeter beyond the limits of His design.

Secondly, if God is in the crisis: There is *meaning* to it all.

The vicissitudes of life are not merely tragic moments of absurd episodes in the saga of human existence. There is purpose, meaning, *joy* in the midst of pain and sorrow. If there is meaning, the believer can rest on that; he can search it out insofar as it is possible in this life; and he even can participate in bringing it about. In short, if God is involved in the crisis, he can be too. Life is not just a crazy, dirty, sordid, meaningless mess from which one ultimately shrinks; no! There is something worthwhile, something exciting, something adventurous, something *holy* in it—God is in life, doing inscrutable, magnificent things that *some* day we shall understand fully. So with a sense of basic joy and anticipation we can slave, and serve, and sweat, and soil our hands—because there is a point to it all: God is in the crisis!

So analysis not only means *slicing up* the crisis into its fundamental elements to see what it is made of, and isolating and identifying these more manageable pieces for study and control, it is a matter of *sizing up* the crisis as well. Analysis involves seeing the situation for what it actually is—an incident in the plan of God, bounded on all sides by His purposes and love.

We have seen that since God is in the crisis, all language and thought that speaks of the crisis as if it were beyond limits ("it's too much," "impossible," and so on) is wrong. It is wrong not merely because it is inaccurate; it is wrong because (like the dictionary definition) it is *pagan* to speak that way. But when we size up a crisis *biblically* we discover that it is of *limited* extent; it is limited by God's will. As Job discovered it can achieve only His purposes—and nothing more.

Further, consider this important fact: every crisis is limited by the faithfulness of God to his children. We read:

102

There is no trial that has overtaken you but what is common to man, and God is faithful, who will not allow you to be tested beyond that which you are able to bear, but (with the test) also will provide the way out of it, that you may be able to bear it (I Cor. 10:13).

God promises three encouraging things:

1. No trial is unique. Others have gone through it successfully before you. There is hope and responsibility in that.

2. Every trial is uniquely fitted to each Christian. None *exceeds* his ability to bear— *if* he handles it God's way. Again, there is hope and responsibility in *that*.

3. God will deliver His children from the trial. It will not continue on and on; there will be a way out—by rescue from it, change within it or solutions to it. The promise of this verse means that God's presence in the crisis assures us that it is limited to what each believer can endure and handle successfully. And note, God backs up this promise by His faithfulness; that means it no more can fail, than His faithfulness can fail. There is hope and responsibility in that.

Lastly, the presence of God in a crisis means that there is adequate strength and wisdom available to meet the crisis. When Paul wrote "I can do all things through Christ who strengthens me" (Philippians 4:13), he was not penning pious platitudes. He wrote those words in a crisis; he was speaking about his experience of Christ's faithfulness in other crises, to people who had seen a demonstration of the fact in still another crisis. When this letter from prison was read in the Philippian church, there was present a jailer who must have remembered the manifestation of Christ's strength in Paul during a previous imprisonment. No, these are not the words of an untried seminarian, still wet behind the ears; this is the apostle Paul speaking. In the midst of every crisis, Christ had proven Himself faithful in supplying the strength to do everything that He requires.

This is a biblical analysis of a crisis; one that—in whatever ways he can—the counselor must convey to the counselee: the crisis is limited by the presence of God. He limits its power, its scope, its purpose. The crisis has meaning; it is part of the plan of God.

Therefore, not only can it be faced and met successfully by His strength, but the counselee can participate in it as part of God's inscrutable goodness toward him.

Probably, it is most important for the counselor to understand and believe this himself. Whether or not he is able to articulate every aspect of the biblical perspective, the counselor *will* convey his attitudes. If he understands and accepts this biblical viewpoint, the two critical ingredients of hope and responsibility will come through. And that is exactly what the counselee needs in the analysis of the problems that he must solve.

Enough for the theological and presuppositional stance toward a crisis. Let's turn, in the time that remains, to a *practical* approach to analysis.

Practical Steps

In analyzing any crisis situation, the counselor must work with facts. He cannot work with abstractions and theories, or with guesses and suppositions; he must become concrete: just what is it that the counselee faces? Is the crisis what he *thinks* it is, or something else? Is it as serious as he suspects or even more so? How can these, and a dozen other questions like them, be answered? Only the facts, gathered, reinterpreted, assessed, sorted out and programmed for action, in a manner that is in full accord with the Scriptures, can answer these questions. There is no other way to reach satisfying solutions than through the hard work of dealing with facts. Analysis means, in the *final* analysis, doing whatever is biblically legitimate to get a *grasp* on the facts.

I have mentioned five activities that will help the counselor (and through him, the counselee) to get a biblical grasp of the facts. They are: gathering facts, reinterpreting facts, assessing facts, sorting out facts and programming facts. Let's take a quick look at each activity to understand it, in a way that will enable us to get down to the facts and apply this approach to any crisis situation.

First, it is essential to gather the facts about the situation. Contrary to counseling theories that stress the person and the expression of his feelings, and ignore the situation in which he is involved, biblical counseling is always concerned about both. Indeed, it is impossible to express meaningful concern about the person without becoming involved in his predicament. The facts of his problem are important. Since I have discussed this matter in detail elsewhere,[2] I shall do no more than remind you of this crucial difference today. Again, in my book, *The Christian Counselor's Manual,* I devoted more than one chapter to the discussion of data gathering. Since so much has been said already about this question, I shall make but one or two additional observations.

To begin with, data gathering in a *crisis* may be more difficult than at other times, particularly if the person in crisis is in a state of high emotional excitement, or if the data must be gathered quickly. Very seldom will it be possible to collect information by means of a Personal Data Inventory or some equivalent data-gathering instrument. Often, the amount of data that it is possible to obtain will be far less than at other times. Since early returns on any dramatic event tend to be confused and inaccurate, much of what is gathered ought to be held tentatively. Sometimes, if he is in shock, or if he is overwhelmed, the person in crisis cannot be relied upon to give adequate, accurate information in logical sequence, and the counselor may find it necessary to interview other involved persons in more depth. So, it is clear that in order to get a satisfactory grasp of the facts in a crisis, more often than he might like, the counselor must accommodate his normal process of data gathering in flexible and creative ways. But, note, the key word here is *adapt;* I did not say *abandon.* The same principles of data gathering still pertain.

"Concretely," you ask, "what are some ways of adapting?" Let me be specific. For one thing, the more highly emotional the person in crisis may be, the more structured the counselor's approach must be. If, for instance, the counselee is pouring forth all sorts of information in disconnected bursts, he cannot be depended upon to structure the process himself. That means that the counselor must be definite and sure about what he wants to know.

Closely related to the definiteness of the counselor, who must assume the proper sort of take-charge attitude in a crisis where there

[2] *Competent To Counsel.*

105

is no structure evident, is the matter of selectivity. Not everything one would like to know can be obtained readily. The materials sought must be determined by the counselor, therefore, through a much more narrowly-oriented approach that settles for less information in lesser detail. That means that in approaching the counselee in the crisis situation, the counselor must know what he wants and go right after it without any preliminaries or any further ado. While most of the information on the Personal Data Inventory will not be appropriate, he (for instance) will probably want to ask what we have called the three basics: What happened? What have you done about it so far? and What do you want me to do?" Yet even here, he may find it necessary to settle for answers that are spotty and partial—answers that would never do in a more relaxed or slower moving counseling context.

But since it is important for the counselor to be clear about what to ask, so that he can structure the data gathering process in the most efficient way, let me further suggest that his questioning focus upon three areas:

1. *The persons involved in the crisis*. Who are they? In what ways are they involved? Are there others besides those who are immediately apparent to the counselee? The focus on persons is critical. Few counseling crises have only to do with things. The most emotionally-laden aspect of the crisis is the personal element. Even financial reverses become crises *only* because of the personal implications of the loss. And, while we are discussing this area, let me remind you again to be sure that the counselee has a clear view of *the* Person and His altogether critical role in the crisis.

2. *The relationship of the counselee to each person who is involved, and what his reponsibility is to each.* Does he owe money? Must he seek someone's forgiveness? Has someone slandered his name?

3. *The issues that have emerged already, or that are likely to emerge very soon.* What are they? Of what sort? etc.

So, three all-important areas of data gathering, then, are: the *persons* who, directly or indirectly, are involved in the crisis, the *relationship and responsibilities* that the counselee bears to each, and the *issues* that need to be resolved. And, into each of these areas the three basic questions can be introduced: What happened to you and to any other persons who might have been involved? What have you done about the actions of any of these persons? What do you want me to do about them? Or, take the second area: What happened to your relationship to each of these persons? And what are your responsibilities to them? What have you done so far to deal with the problems in each relationship? And what have you done so far to meet your responsibilities to each individual? Again, in the third area: What are the issues that have arisen? What have you done about them? and What do you want me to do about them? These three questions, in these three areas, quickly will uncover most relevant data initially needed for helping the counselee to meet the crises.

And, may I point out in passing, that care in gathering data, plus homework based upon the data that are gathered, separately (or in conjunction) will expose which crises are real and which are imaginary; which are contrived and which are genuine. Stress upon feelings alone will never disclose such information; counseling that is abstract also will fail; it is only when we become concrete, ask for facts and take them seriously that the truth will come out. You cannot deal in facts for very long without discovering what you need to know about these matters. You can go on deceived for months, or even for years, if you fail to work with facts. This first activity, then, is foundational to all else. Do it well, if you wish the rest to proceed smoothly.

Secondly, having gathered whatever facts he can, the counselor will be concerned to reinterpret them for the counselee in biblical terms. I say *re*interpret, not interpret. If the counselee had not put some interpretation upon the facts already, he would not yet knowingly be in crisis. And if he had not placed an erroneous interpretation upon the facts, the chances are that he would not be in need of counsel. We never take in data without placing some interpretation upon it; it cannot be learned apart from tagging it and responding to it. Language, in particular, becomes the vehicle for interpretation. So the counselor will be intensely interested not only in the basic thrust and import of the counselee's answers to his questions, he will be concerned also with particular words and phrases that most pointedly reveal the counselee's understanding and present stance toward the crisis. He will be most intensely interested in such telling words or phrases when they are repeated frequently. If the counselee continually says "I'm ruined!," or "It's too late!," or "What's the use of going on?," or makes any number of other such statements, the counselor knows that it will be necessary for him to reinterpret the situation in the light of the true, biblical import of the facts that he has gathered. As I have shown previously, when counselees speak of hopelessness and helplessness, it may be of importance to challenge this attitude by an exposition of I Corinthians 10:13, which then can be applied more specifically to the facts at hand. "Impossible," for instance, becomes "hard, but not too hard for God;" "out of control," becomes "difficult to control, but not out of God's control."

I wish to urge an important caution at this point. When reinterpreting, never so reinterpret a situation that in effect you *minimize* the severity of the problem. Take every problem most seriously, but insist that the counselee take God and His promises *just* as seriously.

The reinterpretation of facts can be all important. For instance, if a man who is a homosexual, looks on homosexuality as a sickness, the counselor will want to reinterpret the facts in biblical terms as *sin*. That can be crucial. If homosexuality is hereditary, or if it is a sickness, there is no hope for change. If it is sin, there is all the hope that there is in Jesus Christ. Labels, like "sickness" and "sin" are the results and signs of interpretations. But they are more than that; they also are *signposts* that point to solutions, or at least to the direction that one must turn to attempt to find a solution. "Heredity," for example, points not to Christ (He died, not to change our hereditary makeup, but for our sins.), but up a dead end street (Who can get new parents and start all over again with a new set of genes and chromosomes?). "Sickness" points to the physician; "sin" points to Christ.

Thirdly, in getting a grasp on the facts through analysis, the counselor will want to help the counselee to assess the facts. Here he is concerned in narrowing the working field. Consequently, he will try to divide matters into separate categories, as for instance, questions of immediate concern ("How do we get Mary to unpack her bags and remain?," or "Is it really true that she is pregnant, or does she only *think* so?," or "You have got to put down the gun, John, so that we can talk about whether your life *is* worth living?"), and questions less pressing ("You can decide about selling the business and moving to another state at a later point," or "Let's schedule the discussion of what to do about your financial condition in general after we decide what to do about the one creditor who has been phoning you for a week").

Another way of assessing priorities is to ask "What are the *simple* issues and what are the more *complex* ones?" Often, as we saw in the last lecture, it is not so much a question of *what* a person does at the outset of a crisis as it is a matter of doing *something*. Simpler issues, usually, therefore, are to be preferred over more complex ones at such a time. John simply told Gaius, for the time being, to continue showing hospitality to the missionaries and to concentrate on doing it well. The more complex matters of Gaius' relationship to Diotrophes and to the church were left for later on. Closely related to distinguishing between simple and complex matters is the assessment of issues as having greater or lesser consequences. Again, it is wiser to begin with the latter.

Fourthly, in gathering, reinterpreting and assessing the facts, certain data will fall out as uncertain, tentative, possibly more matters of emotion than fact, conjecture and speculation, or even bizarre. This material must be sorted and sifted out from the working data. It should be rejected, deferred and shelved, or similarly disposed of whenever possible. If the data are basic or of central concern and cannot be separated from your approved accumulation, then they must be handled on the spot. But this is rare. Even when a dramatic matter like having hallucinations may *seem* to be a significant part of the problem, and when it deeply troubles the counselee, it is often possible to defer a full investigation and discussion of the question by observing that in many instances that are not drug related, hallucinations occur as a secondary complicating problem as the result of significant sleep loss. If it is at all likely that this is the situation, the matter of hallucinations should not occupy too much time and thus divert attention from the issues over which the sleep was lost. Simply put the counselee to bed!

Sorting out usable facts from questionable or unusable materials is an essential step to take before taking the fifth one. But, when you have sorted and sifted the wheat from the chaff, you have yet one vital matter to which to attend—the programming of the factual data that remain in the sieve for discussion, decision and action. According to the interpretations and assessments made, this data must be scheduled in an order of priority for handling. Scheduling and priority setting are two activities that are absolutely essential for helping persons in crisis. Often, the counselee's judgment and sense of perspective is clouded or out of focus. He may tend to make decisions on the basis of feeling rather than out of conviction stemming from a prayerful consideration of the Scriptures. Unlike Moses, who traded the temporal riches of Egypt for the long term blessings of Christ, the person in crisis tends to confuse the short term with the long term. Often, simply scheduling matters of concern makes a significant difference. Getting it in order of priority, on paper, helps the counselee to see more clearly what is at stake. It gets him on track and keeps him there.

So, to conclude for today, remember, because the Christian counselor works with facts, he is concerned to analyze every crisis situation as fully as he can so that he may get a *grasp* on the facts about it. Getting such a *grasp* may involve five things:

G - Gathering facts

R - Reinterpreting facts

A - Assessing facts

S - Sorting or sifting out facts

P - Programming facts.

CHAPTER III

INVENTORY

"Do you always use mnemonic devices like AID and GRASP?" you may wonder. If you are not quite that kindly disposed, your question may take a slightly different form: "Really, don't you think that it's rather corny for you to pull something like this in a seminary context?"

Let me hasten to say that I understand such a response. Indeed, I thought long and hard about doing this before I came. I knew that I might run the risk of turning some of you off. But, in spite of the dangers you can see that I opted for it anyway. "Why?" you ask. I'll tell you.

First, let me say that I don't do this often. Even a quick survey of my writings will prove that. So, why now? Because of our present subject matter. We are talking about *crisis* counseling. In a crisis everyone—even the counselor—needs firm structure. A crisis is a time when emotion runs high, and it is a time when the things that ordinarily you can depend upon to stay tacked down, come loose. It is easy not only for the counselee to be swept along by the emotion and the pressures of the moment—the same danger also exists for the counselor. It is all too easy for him to become confused about what his role may be, what he must do, what is to remain central and what is peripheral.

Therefore, any legitimate means that will help the counselor to remember what to do and how to do it in a crisis can be useful—even if it is corny. In fact, for mnemonic purposes, sometimes—the cornier the better!

The lifesaving people—to teach the types of water-rescue techniques available, and the order in which to use them—a few

111

years back developed a little mnemonic. To many it might seem corny, but it proved its usefulness in saving lives. Here it is:

TOW/THROW/ROW/GO

But notice, it was intended to help out in an emergency—in a crisis. *That* is when a firm structure for thought and action proves most useful. And just—by the way—before you gum that label "cornball" on me *too* quickly, let me remind you of a rather similar use of the mnemonic device, found in the *acrostic* Psalms! "OK, OK," you say. "If a mnemonic a day will keep confusion away, I'll try to stomach it. What's today's not-so-clever little piece? So far we've had A-I-D (Analysis, Inventory and Direction) and G-R-A-S-P (getting a grasp of the facts by Gathering facts, Reinterpreting facts, Assessing facts, Sorting out facts and Programming facts). Now, what about the I in Aid; how do we take an inventory of the person in crisis? Why don't you tell us right off today rather than keep us guessing?"

As a matter of fact, I think I shall. But, for variety's sake, I've changed my style. Taking the principle of "the cornier the better" seriously, today I have a poem for you. As I read it, see if you can spot the five key factors in taking a personal inventory, of which this poem reminds you. Here is my little ditty. It is entitled,

"Inventory"

The counselee's *state*
  may be sorry or great
Depending on what he has *done.*

If his *motives* are true
  when he seeks help from you
Your battle's already half won.

112

What his *resources* are

    will determine by far

If he'll lose or gain victory.

And through crisis he'll *grow*

    if plainly you show

Opportunity through this [here] In-ven-tory.

All right; now that we've gotten past that, let's get down to business. In taking a personal inventory of the counselee, the first—and most obvious—place to begin is with the counselee's *state*. Remember,

    The counselee's state

        may be sorry or great.

Which is it? That is the first thing to determine. And it can be the all-important factor.

What I am referring to when I speak of taking an inventory of the counselee's state is asking questions like these:

1. *Is he in full possession of his faculties?* A drunk on the telephone threatening suicide is not. A counselee doped up by drugs (either self-administered or prescribed by a psychiatrist or physician) is not. A parent who is in shock after hearing of the sudden and unexpected death of his daughter less than fifteen minutes before is not. A counselee hallucinating as the result of significant sleep loss is not. These, and any number of other causes like them may lead to the judgment that no information, or only partial information may be obtained at present from the counselee himself. It may be necessary to gather data from other involved persons instead.

If the counselee is only confused or emotionally supercharged, heavy structure brought to bear on the situation by the counselor can make a great difference. If the counselor's own state is calm, cool and confident, if he exhibits a rock-ribbed faith in the promises of God, and if he communicates hope and order in the midst of chaos by the proper sort of take-charge manner, his modeling will exert a powerful influence upon the counselee. Remember the effect of Paul's manner during the storm at sea (Acts 27). In such instances, as a result, after a short time, the counselee himself may be in a position to cooperate fully with the counselor.

If, however, some of the more serious disorientations mentioned above seem to be present, another sort of action is called for. To keep him from injuring himself or others, the counselee may need to be placed under the supervision of someone until the effects of the disorienting factor wear off. He may need to be put to bed. Medical assistance at times may be required. In such cases, the counselor must postpone his offer of direct help in meeting the crisis in favor of ministering to the secondary needs of the person in crisis.

2. *Is he a Christian or non-Christian?* The counselee's state will be affected across the board by the fact, and the counselor's approach also will be affected at every point by the answer to this question. Paul wrote "we grieve (but) not as others who have no hope" (I Thessalonians 4:13).

I cannot discuss the matter of evangelism in crisis here at any length. Let it suffice to say that after helping minimally at first in whatever ways that he can in order to eliminate distress, confusion, etc., the Christian counselor soon should seize the opportunity to disclose the true nature of the crisis—i.e., that the counselee is trying to understand and solve the problems of a sinful world without Jesus Christ. The approach will vary from person to person as it must in all effective evangelism—Jesus never evangelized the same way twice. The abrupt approach to Nicodemus contrasts dramatically with the slower and more gradual one used in speaking to the woman at the well recorded in the next chapter. Both differ strikingly from the account of the evangelization of the blind man in Chapter 9 of John's gospel. *There,* we learn that Christ did not even mention the way of salvation on the first encounter, but merely sent him to the pool of Siloam for healing. When interrogated about his remarkable recovery he could say no more than "This one thing I know: whereas once I was blind, now I can see!" It was only during a second encounter that Jesus spoke to him about the healing of the blindness within. In each case, the *approach* differed; in each, however, the purpose and the message were the same. As soon as it was appropriate the Lord introduced them to Himself as Savior. The same basic approach to evangelism must be followed today. God, in His wise providence, sometimes brings about a crisis in order to cause the counselee to reconsider his ways. The counselor must be sensitive to the opportunity that ground well ploughed affords, and must sow the gospel seed. After all, every person who seeks counsel admits that he needs help. Evangelism is a matter of showing why.

3. *Is his attitude proper or improper?* If the counselee is bitter and resentful, or angry and sarcastic, or fearful and worried, it may be impossible to help him to discuss and to handle the issues involved in the crisis until the counselor has helped him to change his attitude. If he is guilty of having brought the crisis upon himself, that too may call for the counselor's immediate attention. Since I have said so much about how to handle these matters in other places, I shall spare you any repetition here. It is enough to point out that until he is right before God and his neighbors, all else that he may attempt will, judged by God's standards, fail.

Now, back to the poem:

The counselee's state

may be sorry or great

Depending on what he has *done*.

By this next line I am not speaking about what he may or may not have done to bring about the crisis. Rather, I am concerned about what he has done thus far *in response* to it. This, all-too-often neglected consideration can be critical.

Job's counselors put the emphasis upon responsibility for bringing about the crisis (as I noted in my first lecture) and thereby failed to help him since in reality he was struggling with the problem of how to understand it and what to do about it. Job's situation clearly parallels the one that I now have in mind.

If the fisherman tries to untie a knot in his line and, instead, succeeds only in putting six more knots in the monofilament, he has complicated the original problem by his faulty attempts to solve it. That is the sort of thing that I had in view when I wrote "Depending on what he has *done.*"

Let us take, for example, a typical crisis. Mary has packed her bags; she plans to leave Tom the next day. He is afraid and desperate. Obviously, he does not know how to communicate with her or the marriage probably never would have reached this bitter point. But he loves her; he doesn't want her to leave. He pleads with her not to go; he begs her to give him another chance. Yet, as he promises her that he will "do anything" that she asks if only she will reconsider, by his tears and begging he succeeds in further knotting the line. One of the things that disgusts Mary is his weak unmanly ways. Here he is—acting like a snivelling animal—cringing at her feet. Failing in this sort of appeal, he is angered and begins to tell her so. His pride is injured; he has humiliated himself before her and has been rejected. He loses his head and tells her off; the venom he pours forth opens old wounds. He stoops even to name calling. More knots. When you see them for counseling, the original issues over which Mary decided to leave may be very remote in comparison to the sting of the recent tongue lashing that she most vividly recalls. To focus only (or even first) on those distant issues and to neglect the more recent injuries therefore would be a colossal mistake.

Possibly in another case the two problems are confused. Difficulty over problems at work involving interpersonal rivalries together with unconfessed guilt over an extra-marital sex affair may lead to a number of sleepless nights for Roger. When he comes he says that it is because he has been hallucinating. He and his wife Jean initially talk about two or three weeks of depression preceeding the onset of hallucinations, but only vaguely intimate that something at work was troubling Roger. Yet, what could problems at work have to do with something as strange as these hallucinations? They tell you nothing about sleep loss. Only when, by probing, you discover this missing piece to the puzzle can you begin to make the other pieces fit. What they consider the most serious problem, the hallucinations, turns out to be secondary; the hallucinations are the result of sleep loss due to the sense of guilt.

In Roger's case, what he has done, namely losing sleep over his sin rather than confessing it in repentance, has tied *him* in knots.

Take one more example. Perhaps the counselee has seen another counselor first. If that counselor has filled his mind with blame-shifting excuses by saying that his greatest problem is his wife, and has been advised in getting a divorce, both notions must be dislodged before one can go further.

In any case, it is vital to investigate what the counselee has done. If he has become discouraged by failing in his attempts to solve his problems, that will be important to know—he will need to be given hope. If he has become wary of counselors because of unfortunate previous experiences, *that could be critical*. If he has done nothing, that could be the *most* crucial fact of all. So, never fail to take an inventory of the counselee's response to the crisis.

The poem reads:

> The counselee's *state*
>
> may be sorry or great
>
> Depending on what he has *done*.

But then it continues in these words:

> If his *motives* are true
>
> when he seeks help from you
>
> Your battle's already half won.

And it is!

Let's take a case. Bill has separated from Janet. She wants him back. When she comes for help the concluding words of her story are: "I'll do anything to get him back." A wary counselor will want to pick up those words and discuss them with her:

"Janet, I'm glad that you want Bill back, but your motives concern me. When you say 'I'll do *anything* to get him back; you are not speaking as a Christian should. I think that we must consider your agenda first."

It would be important for him to stress the fact that a Christian should want to do anything— *that God says*. That addition is not just a pious platitude; it is an extremely practical principle that on the one hand, limits her options and, on the other, sends her to the Scriptures to find out *what* God says to do. She discovers that she cannot lie to get him back; she must receive him only on the right basis, etc. Moreover, because of her strong motivation, the counselor will want to caution her:

> "Janet, if you put 'getting Bill back' first, you may get him but not on the right basis. In this crisis put pleasing Christ first— even before Bill—and whether you get him back or not, you will succeed in your major goal, and you will be blessed."

Motives are tricky. It is always wrong to make judgments about another's motives. The counselor, unlike God, can look only on the outward appearance. But, as in the case above, he can discuss the counselee's motivational comments with him. He should listen carefully for such comments. Apart from motivation-revealing comments, he must confine his counsel to the counselee's outward behavior.

Of course, the counselor can *ask* about motives: "What were you trying to accomplish when you called the police?" or "What made you think that life was not worth living?" Yet, since man's heart is deceitful, the counselor cannot always be sure of the answers that he receives. How can he be certain that he, along with others involved, is not being "used" or "manipulated" to achieve some purpose high on the list of the counselee's hidden agenda?

Well, the answer to that is simple: he can't! That is, he cannot be sure that he is getting a truthful account, right away. Should he be suspicious, doubt every word, take nothing for granted? If that is to be his attitude toward a counselee, would it not be better simply to start guessing from the outset rather than waste time in data gathering? Of course, that is where the logic of such an approach leads; and there are counselors who, because they hold that counselees either do not know or will not tell the truth, do just that. With a few supposed clues, from language, dreams and bodily action, in accordance with a prepackaged system they *guess* about his problems.

The Christian can do no such thing. He is bound to take the counselee seriously. In I Corinthians 13, Paul clearly says that love runs a risk. That risk includes the risk of being deceived, being used, and being manipulated. He writes "love . . . believes all things, hopes all things" (v. 7).

Does that mean that the Christian counselor must become a naive pushover? No, not at all. It does mean, however, that in love he will always give the benefit of any doubt. It means that he will not only teach the husbands and wives that he counsels to do so; it means that he will demonstrate the same attitude in his counseling of those same husbands and wives. But won't he be deceived? Yes and no. At times he will. But at times any counselor will, regardless of his theoretical base. Unlike the guessers, however, he will never be *self*-deceived.

But when a counselor takes a counselee seriously about his statements, two things happen:

1. Often, the counselee who might plan to deceive or misstate the truth, changes his approach. Belief out of love often breeds truth. Counselees have told me so.

2. But, secondly, suppose this doesn't happen; what then? The facts alone must drive the counselor to doubt. He questions the word of the counselee only when he can do nothing else. Well, won't he go on, and on, and on being deceived then? No. Since he is working with facts and commitment, the Christian counselor will *(more* rapidly than others) discover the truth. When he takes a counselee at his word, he follows up on that word, asking for more and more facts to get the whole story. It is difficult for most persons to deceive in detail. And, then, the counselor gives homework *based* upon the data that he has received. When the counselee balks, he will want to know why; when the homework cannot be done, he will investigate that. In a variety of ways, then, sooner than one may think, deception is usually discovered.

119

But to return to the original concern, remember, the counselee—even a Christian counselee—often will tend to become self-centered and humanistic in a crisis. His Christian value system may be set aside for whatever seems expedient. It is the Christian counselor's privilege and duty to stand-by and point to the fact that Christ *is* in this crisis and that in *all* things—even in this crisis— *He* must have the preeminence.

Let's continue to consider our little five part ditty. So far we have suggested taking an inventory of the counselee's *state,* his *responses* to the crisis, and his *motives.* Next, we turn to the matter of *resources.* Upon what resources will he depend to meet the crisis? Does he know what they are and how to utilize them? As I read from the poem once more, listen particularly to the part about resources; it stresses a key consideration:

The counselee's *state*

    may be sorry or great

Depending on what he has *done.*

If his *motives* are true

    when he seeks help from you

Your battle's already half won.

What his *resources* are

    will determine by far

If he'll lose or gain victory.

Many persons fail to meet crises adequately because they do not avail themselves of all of the resources that have been provided by God. This, also, is one of the major reasons why they lack hope. They see only what they can see of the crisis with their noses pressed hard against the wall; they fail to benefit from the viewpoint of another perspective outside of themselves.

The poem suggests that there are a number of God-given resources from which the counselee may draw help and hope to meet the crisis. Three of these are:

1. Personal resources

2. Family resources

3. Church resources

Under the heading of personal resources—i.e., those resources to which he can turn *on his own without involving other persons around him,* I would like to mention just two: the Word and the Spirit. In a crisis, a believer is driven first to God. Prayerfully, he asks God for wisdom, and then seeks it in His Word. He is strengthened—or as James put it—blessed by the Spirit in the obedient doing of whatever the Word requires (James 1:25). A wise counselor will always point a counselee to the Scriptures. Here, in doing so, he will force him to begin his search for solutions—and not merely solutions—*God's* solutions. A person in a crisis, like Peter, is sinking because his eyes and his thoughts are centered on the storm. He needs to be directed instead to the Christ of the Scriptures in whom is the solution to every problem. So, in taking an inventory, the counselor will be very much concerned about whether or not the counselee is facing the problem, *Bible* in hand.

What of prayer? Whenever I read the answers to the three basic questions, What is your problem? What have you done about it? What do you want me to do about it?, I find that in a majority of cases, question number two is answered the same way by Christians: "I've prayed about it." Some, perhaps, answer that way to sound pious; the larger number have really prayed. But their problem persists (otherwise they would not need to seek my counsel). Why? Because rarely is prayer *alone* the solution to a problem. It is never—by itself— the solution when God, in His Word, has required action as well. One may not ask for his daily bread and then sit back and wait for it when the Bible says that if a man will not work, he should not eat. More often than not, prayer constitutes the background for the solution that comes through dependent obedience. We should pray for wisdom and depend upon the Spirit to provide that wisdom as we search for it in His Word. We should pray for strength and depend upon the Spirit to provide that strength as we obediently step out by faith to do whatever that Word says.

Of course, not all knowledge and wisdom must be sought out anew in a crisis. Christians often have learned truth and developed skills in the past—by their study and practice of the Word—that can be newly activated to meet the present situation. Other sins have been confessed in the past; and God and those involved have forgiven them. Why shouldn't the admitted adulterer now seek forgiveness again? Why does he think that this sin of adultery is beyond the pale of forgiveness from God, or his wife or his church? What he needs to learn from the Scriptures at this time is not how to seek forgiveness—that he knows—but rather the fact that he now can have it. The counselor, accordingly, will read a passage like I Corinthians 6:9-11 that speaks so plainly of the forgiveness and cleansing of an adulterer by God. He will turn to II Corinthians 2:7-8 where Paul urges that a repentant excommunicate—one who was accused of incestuous adultery—be forgiven, comforted and received with a reaffirmation of love. What the Christian in crisis needs to learn in such cases, is not about repentance and confession of sin, but about forgiveness for *this* sin.

There are times when all that is needed to tip the scale toward the solution of a crisis is information. This was true of the Thessalonian church. Some of their members had died. Their loved ones were grieving, but added to their grief was an erroneous notion that they had picked up in some way—Paul didn't seem to know exactly how—that no Christian would die before Christ's second coming. When believing loved ones died, they were shattered, and were losing hope.

Hearing of the crisis nature of this double grief, Paul winged off a letter to set them straight: "I do not want you to be ignorant, brothers, about those who are asleep . . . ." Then, he tells them the truth. And at the end of that information he writes: "Comfort one another with these words." The answer to the crisis was information—accurate, truthful, detailed, dependable—as so often it is.

In Paul's case, he had given them the facts beforehand. Throughout his Thessalonian letters he makes a point of this; he says, for instance about another matter: "When we were with you, we kept telling you that you were going to suffer affliction" (I Thess. 3:4; cf. also II Thess. 3:10 and I Thess. 4:11). So Paul did not wait until the crisis had come; he anticipated as many crises as possible and in advance taught how to meet them. This crisis had come because they had forgotten his teaching, thereby leaving themselves open to distortions of the truth. When you take an airplane trip, you are told *beforehand* by the stewardess what to do if you should have a need to use the oxygen mask. A card in the pocket of the seat describes emergency procedures, and the stewardess is required by law to point out the location of all exits. All too frequently, counselors find that Christians have not been prepared *beforehand* by their pastors for the crises into which they will come. A significant portion of the Bible is preparatory. For instance, much of Daniel and all of Revelation can be understood as information given beforehand, in order to help those who must live through the events that are predicted, doing so in a manner pleasing to God. These are not books designed to arouse speculation and dissension; they are handbooks for living through times of crises.

But the counselee must be shown that these very personal resources that a man has—the Scriptures and the Spirit—also point him beyond himself. They stress the need of turning to others. The writer of Ecclesiastes rightly observes that two are better than one in a crisis and that a three stranded cord is not easily broken (cf. Ecclesiastes 4:9-12). This truth needs to be emphasized.

A person in crisis who has turned to a counselor, has sensed already something of this need. And if the counselor is a Christian, and if his counsel is Christian, the counselee has made a good move. Yet it is not only to pastors—or other supposed professionals in counseling—that one should turn. Galatians 6:1, Colossians 3:16 and Romans 15:14 are but three of the many passages that indicate that every Christian has a ministry of counseling. Parents should counsel children, member should stimulate member (to love and to good works). The whole body of Christ must be made available to each member in his crisis.

To begin with, the counselor should urge members of the family to take seriously their scriptural obligations and responsibilities in the home. A husband must be guided to assume the role of loving leader in time of crisis as well as other times. Submissive helper, is what his spouse must become. Children must be shown that they are in trouble because they have failed to rely upon the resources that God has provided for them in their parents. Parents must be taught how to care for and discipline their children without exasperating them and provoking them to anger, so that they find parental resources readily accessible. The family is a critical unit in God's order of things, containing such powerful resources that any counselor who does not recognize and draw upon them is a failure and a fool.

But, perhaps even more to our shame, we have almost entirely failed to use the corporate and individual resources that God has provided in the church and in its leadership. A boy wanting to kick the drug habit should have dozens of doors thrown open wide to receive him during the difficult period of withdrawal. A family in financial trouble should receive help from the deacons rather than turning to state welfare. There is no problem that can arise in which other members of the body can be of no help if they truly weep with those who weep and rejoice with those who rejoice.

A most powerful passage, that applies quite directly to Christians meeting each other's needs, is found in Paul's words to Titus when he says:

Let our people also learn to engage in good deeds to meet pressing needs, that they may not be unfruitful (Titus 3:14).[1]

The Church has not learned this; principally because it has not been *taught to* do so, or *how* to do so. If a crisis is not a "pressing need" what is it? That is, from one side, as encapsulated a definition of a crisis as you may get. Not all pressing needs are of crisis proportions,

---

[1] In the Appendix there is a song written by Mrs. William Banks in response to a request that I made while lecturing at Capital Bible Seminary. I noted how Titus 3:14 almost rhymed and could readily be put to music and that I hoped someone would do so since it is an important text that needs to be stressed. The tune is contemporary and could be taught to young people as well as adults.

of course, but everyone in a crisis has pressing needs. The wise counselor will be one who turns to the members of the body for help. He realizes that alone he cannot provide all of the help to meet every crisis. He must mobilize the entire body not only to pray—as important as that may be—but also to "engage in good deeds."

Long before a crisis arises, the wise pastor has been organizing his people for it. When the crisis comes, he does not need to scurry about finding out who can do what, if persuaded. He *knows* where to turn for what from whom.

And, in closing this section, let me remind you, that the counselor himself, by his knowledge of the Scriptures, by his conviction that God's Word has the answers, and by his firm personal structure, becomes a needed steady influence upon the person in crisis. He must be a man with God's viewpoint—i.e., a man of strength and hope.

Speaking of hope, and of the biblical viewpoint that brings it, leads us to the last point in this lecture: opportunity for growth. The poem once more; this time in its entirety:

The counselee's *state*

   may be sorry or great

Depending on what he has *done*.

If his *motives* are true

   when he seeks help from you

Your battle's already half won.

What his *resources* are

   will determine by far

If he'll lose or gain victory.

And through crisis he'll *grow*

if plainly you show

Opportunity through this [here] In-ven-tor-y.

That is the key. The crisis is not to defeat him; he is to defeat it. The counselee must be given a vision of overcoming evil with good, of turning tragedy into triumph. He must see that it is God's purpose to use crosses to lead to resurrections. When sin abounds—and we must be entirely realistic about the *abounding* nature of sin— nevertheless, the counselor must point out, grace even more abounds. There is a solution to every problem! But that is not all. It is a solution that is designed to lead one *beyond* the place where he was before the problem emerged. Though man was created lower than the angels, and by sin descended into a still lower position, Christ's redemption did not merely put man back again into his original condition; He has raised him far above the angels. It is *more* than redemption! In Christ, humanity has been raised far above every principality and power of the universe to the right hand of God! That is a super-redemptive salvation.

The counselor, therefore in every crisis must seek out the opportunity for growth, the road to triumph, and the way to demonstrate that grace more abounds. This super-redemptive viewpoint, above all else, should provide the needed hope.

A crisis is a sanctification context. It provides the opportunity to examine the old ways and put off those that are displeasing to God, while discovering and seeking to pursue the new ones set forth by God.

In a true crisis old ways come loose; old patterns crumble. A crisis is a time when something new must happen ("I must go on alone without John since his death," "I must now face the future as a single unwed parent with a child," "The house was wiped out in a flood; what do we do now?"). It is because of the absolute necessity of newness that the opportunity for growth is afforded. "If there must be change," the counselor may observe, "then let's be sure that it is God's change that occurs." The crisis should be seen as a divine catalyst for good. Your inventory of the counselee should aim at discovering whether he has such a biblical viewpoint. If he does not, you must make every effort to help him to acquire it. That notion of crisis as divinely catalytic cuts straight across the pathways of confusion and despair. It is a challenge flung in the face of the crisis; in it is a hope larger, fuller and more solid than tragedy. That hope will not fail, for it is founded on the faithfulness of the heavenly Father. It grows tall from the soil of the super-redemptive message of the whole Bible. Job learned it at length: "The Lord blessed the latter days of Job more than his beginning," we read (Job 42:12). Joseph experienced it, and Jesus accomplished it!

So, in full face of the fury, a believer's heart can be calm, his pathway can be clear and his life can *sprout* with *good green growth*. That is how to help another to view a crisis.

Let me close, then, not with a final recitation of the poem—as you expected—but with a summary. First aid for crisis counselors requires an analysis of the situation. That analysis demands a grasp of the facts: gathering data, reinterpreting data, assessing data, sorting-out data and programming data. It also requires an inventory of the person in crisis. Again, five elements stand out:

> The counselee's state
>
> The counselee's response
>
> The counselee's motives
>
> The counselee's resources, and
>
> The counselee's growth.

If you can remain alert to these matters when helping persons in crisis, doubtless, your ministry will be a great blessing to many.

CHAPTER IV.

DIRECTION

Today is my last opportunity to speak to you. While every aspect of crisis counseling is important, what I have to say *today* is *most* critical. If the rest has not been done properly, it will be difficult to do *this* well. But if *all* of the rest is done, and even if it is done *well*, unless this last element is achieved, everything else will have been done in vain. Yet right here is where so many counselors fail—either they do not know how to give direction to a person in crisis or they wonder whether they should.

It is necessary to analyze the crisis situation, discovering the true dimensions of the problem, learning how to recognize its parts and how to arrange them in logical segments of manageable size, and limiting it through understanding the place of Jesus Christ in the crisis. Gathering, reinterpreting, assessing, sorting and programming the facts are vital, preliminary steps, all of which have as *their* goal *doing* something about them. So analysis of the crisis is not an end in itself; analysis is done to provide the right sort of material, arranged according to biblical priorities, *for action.*

The same is true of the work of taking an inventory.

A personal inventory of the counselee is taken to enable both the counselor and the counselee to understand his strengths and weaknesses, his fears and faith, his knowledge and ignorance, *in order to* help prepare him, and encourage him, and guide him in taking the actions that he must in order to meet the crisis God's way. That is why his state, his responses to the crisis thus far, his motives, his reliance upon resources, and his viewpoint toward the crisis as an opportunity for growth are all of significance to the counselor. He wants to know about these factors just as he wants to know about the situation, because he recognizes that *this* counselee with all of his peculiarities, must meet *this* crisis situation with all of its particular configurations.

Some may think that the rigidity of the structure that I have suggested for discovering facts about the situation and the person will tend to make a counselor advise every counselee in a stereotyped manner according to a canned and refrigerated, cut-and-dried pattern. But that sort of thing is precisely what I am trying to avoid. It is because I am concerned about the *uniqueness* of every counseling case, that I have spent time trying to make you fully concerned about the many sides of each. You will notice that G-R-A-S-P involves five factors of analysis and the poem entitled "Inventory" also contains five elements. Try as I may, I could reduce neither to a lesser number. The reason for a list of no less than ten items to check out in every crisis is to be sure that no essential ingredient may be by-passed. The rigid structure pertains only to rigidity in gathering *all* of the variables that lead to the final combination that one must face in helping someone in a crisis. It is a rigid stance *against* stereotyping.

The place to look for the sort of rigidity that leads to stereotyping is in *this* lecture not in the previous ones—because this is the one that has to do with directions for decision and action. If here, I were to come up with five or more elements, watch out; then you could be sure that the data gathered in analysis and through inventory are not being given their proper weight. Decisions and actions would be shaped instead, by a prefabricated plan, rather than by the Scriptures applied directly to the data at hand.

But I do not have a five item check list for direction in counseling; I have but three, and the third item is not always pertinent. The data in each case must determine whether or not this item is of significance.

My mnemonic today, then, is quite simple. We are concerned with issues. Remember, a crisis always raises one or more issues that demand a response. A crisis is a situation requiring change. Therefore *action* is the key to resolving a crisis—and, of course, the decision *not* to act, is itself an action of the most profound importance. Since *action* is at the heart of directing counselees how to handle issues, my three letter word today is A-C-T, ACT.

These three letters stand for direction that is
Authoritative

Concrete

Tentative.

Analysis, Inventory and Direction; that is what the counselor must be prepared to bring to a crisis. Ability, knowledge, wisdom and courage in pursuing each of these activities is of utmost importance.

But before I speak of direction, let me discuss for a moment why direction is important. There are two basic reasons. First, when a crisis arises, it comes as a storm that foams up issues which demand decision and action. That demand puts the person in the crisis under pressure. That pressure comes from without but also triggers pressure from within. A person in a crisis—especially one who has asked for the help of a counselor—is *always* a person who is under heavy emotional pressure. His emotions are aroused for action. That is good and should give hope of effecting change quickly, but when emotion *prevails,* the logical side cannot always be depended upon to operate as efficiently as one might wish. Therefore, the presence of another, who is trusted and trustworthy, can be an important asset, since he stands at a greater emotional distance from the issue, and can make a less clouded assessment of it. Direction, then, is of importance even if it takes only the form of giving a second biblical opinion on the crisis.

There is, however, a second reason why direction is important. It is because, as I said before, action cannot be avoided. The crisis itself demands action; that, we saw, is inherent in the nature of a crisis. But now, I want to point out, that it is true that the *person* in crisis also demands action. It is the nature of a problem of crisis proportions to so excite the person involved that he becomes mobilized for action. If a person were not so intensely involved, he would not be in crisis. Nor, it should be observed, is it wrong (in itself) to allow one's self to be emotionally activated by a crisis. God made us that way. Stoicism, with its doctrine of the dispassionate disposition, is not Christian. Jesus wept (John 11:35); He cried down woes on the Scribes (Matthew 23); He turned on the Pharisees with anger (Mark 3:5); and when He drove out the money changers, he cried "Zeal for My Father's house has *eaten me up!* All of that is evidence of strong emotion (much of it—incidentally—exhibited in crisis situations). So, I want to repeat, it is not wrong to become emotionally aroused over a crisis. That emotion leads to the mobilization of all of the bodily faculties. This mobilization and energizing of the body and mind occurs in order to prepare one to meet a difficult situation. That is good, not bad, *if* the energy is controlled by scriptural principles and focused biblically. Emotion becomes bad if, unharnassed, it takes over and gains control of the person. If there is doubt or uncertainty about the situation or about what God requires of the one who faces it, emotion is likely to take over. A "double minded man is unstable in all his ways" (James 1:8). If, instead of welcoming the bodily tension, the counselee fears it and through that fear triggers additional anxiety, which causes more tension that he fears . . . and so on, the bodily stimulation can escalate out of control and the emotion that should act as a servant can become an unwelcome and terrifying master. Lastly, if energy that is mobilized for action is not put to work constructively doing those things that are required by God in His Word, that energy will be used destructively. The body will be injured internally, sleeplessness and anxiety may occur, and foolish and unwise decisions are likely to be made.

That is why directive counseling is so vital to a person in crisis. Rogerian, non-directive counseling, reveals its utter poverty, *perhaps most clearly,* when one uses it to try to help someone in a crisis.

When in a crisis, the counselee is reaching for the panic button, a wise directive counselor is always ready to point to other more advisable moves. He does not hesitate to show him other biblical buttons that he should push instead. Indeed, it is his task to uncover these buttons.

That is why direction is so vital in a crisis. The takeover of emotion narrows one's vision to a small unrealistic and unchristian band of possible actions ("I'll sell my house and move to Florida, I'll never be able to live alone," or "I can't face this; all I can do is lie about it"). A counselor can help broaden the band again, pointing to the true options set forth in the Scriptures. But one must *know* those options if he would be a faithful counselor.

Psychology does not prepare one to know biblical answers. That is another reason why *Christian* counseling by pastors who know the Word in depth is essential.

Before I consider direction in its three dimensions, I should like to mention the importance of another element that is a part of all counseling that—in a crisis, especially—takes on particular significance. It is the importance of a personal presence. Both the word *parakaleo* and the word *noutheteo* speak of help from the outside. They picture the helper standing beside or in front of the counselee to assist, encourage and confront in whatever ways may be necessary. In some of the counseling situations to which I have referred thus far, that personal element is prominent. For instance, both in II John (written to warn against extending hospitality to false teachers) and III John (written to insist upon hospitality for true teachers in spite of a schizmatic condition in the congregation) John speaks of earnestly wishing to be *with* the readers that their joy may be full. He speaks (further) of making plans to do just that. In writing to the divided Philippian church about the need for unity, Paul twice refers to his absence in strong and moving words (1:27; 2:12). There is no question about the fact that he would like to be present personally to resolve the issues. Like John, he recognized the desirability of having a counselor on hand to help those who are facing the crisis. Even though he himself could not be present, John sent Demetrius to help Gaius, and Paul did not merely *tell* Euodia and Syntache to be reconciled, he asked the pastor of the church to see to it that this reconciliation takes place.[1] Paul counted on the power of a personal presence.

What makes the presence of an outside party in a crisis important in all of these instances, is not merely the comfort and encouragement that he might offer. That, everyone knows about already, and so it goes without saying. There is another equally critical element in these biblical accounts that stands out: it is an emphasis upon the structure that these involved outsiders bring to those who, because of fear, weakness, lack of knowledge or confusion, so desperately need. When things are out of control—or are likely to get out of

[1] Philippians 4:2,3. Cf. more detailed comments on this matter in *Shepherding God's Flock,* Vol. III, pp. 70-72.

hand—someone present, who has deep concern, who knows and loves the Word of God, and who can minister through bringing structured control to the person in crisis, is a valuable asset. Counselees often have expressed it this way:

"Thanks, not only for helping me to understand what God wants me to do, but also for insisting that I do it."

People—especially confused people in a crisis—know that they need such help.

All right. Now for A-C-T. Direction in counseling, first of all, must be *authoritative*. When a woman says "I want to divorce my husband," and you (as her counselor) know that she does not have biblical grounds for doing so, it is not enough to urge her to change her mind on principles of expediency. You do not ultimately argue that it will cause more harm than good, that the children will be adversely affected, etc.; instead you must go right to the heart of the issue and tell her: "You may not do so; it would be sin." And, you back up what you say with an exposition of the Word of God.

Authority in counseling, just like authority in preaching, is on two levels. There is the authority of the message and there is an authority of the messenger. The latter is a derived authority and stems primarily from his appointment as the message bearer. In the final analysis, it is the fact that one ministers God's Word that constitutes the fundamental element in his authority.

Since that is the case, it is essential to bring scriptural content to bear upon the crisis issues. The divorce question, mentioned above, can be settled authoritatively in no other way. The matter is not settled, however, merely by quoting a verse as if to do so has some magical power. Every verse used, unless entirely transparent to *both* parties, should be explained in terms of its contextual and grammatical import. The *telos,* or purpose, as well as the meaning of the passage, should be made crystal clear. Counselors must take the time to do so. It is only when a truth of the Bible is *understood,* and when it is *evident* that the Bible actually does teach that truth, that a believer comes under the full weight of its authority. Thus, in counseling, the truth of what the counselor says should be shown so plainly to be biblical that the counselee—even if he did not before—

knows now what the verses that the counselor used mean, *and* what meaning they have for his situation.

The authority of the individual comes from the fact that he is true to the Book, resting all that he says upon its teaching and becoming a faithful and helpful interpreter for others. When in his life, he manifests the truth that he unfolds, that does not add authority to the message, it only adds authority to the messenger. It does do two other things, however. First, it keeps down any unnecessary confusion between the message that he speaks and the message that he lives. Secondly, harmony of message in word and life *demonstrates* the practicality and *possibility* of obedience to the counselee, and it shows him how to put it into effect. This affords great hope. It is confusing to insist on faith from others while showing no faith in them. It is difficult to understand truth abstractly without a model.

A faithful counselor will always distinguish between those truths about which he is sure and those about which he yet has some question. "I think . . . " will be reserved for the latter, while he will say clearly about the former "God says" or "the Bible teaches." Since the teacher of the Word shall incur stricter judgment (James 3:1), the counselor will want to be very sure before he speaks with such finality. He does not want to be found misrepresenting God. But when he is sure, he can do no less than speak with authority.

He will be sure of his ground, as a result, and will prove a great blessing in crisis counseling, if he takes the time to study the Scriptures regularly, and labors long and hard over the difficult portions. A background in psychology, I think you can see, is not a background calculated to produce authority. For that, one must have a background in the Scriptures. Unless he has spent much time in preparation, thinking problems through in advance according to the biblical principles that apply, under the pressure of a crisis he will prove to be but a broken reed. It is in a crisis, when the tops of the trees are touching the ground, and when the shingles are coming off, that he must be a steady and sure influence. But he will be like a house built on the rock *only* if he *hears* Christ's words and *does* them.

When everything else is coming apart, the person in crisis wants to know what it is that is immovable. He wants a solid place to plant his feet firmly. The counselor who can point him to the appropriate portions of the "Word of our God" that "stands forever" (Isaiah 40:8) will bring the help that he needs most. Authority in a crisis is the most vital factor of all; without it, all that is done is but speculation and guesswork.

Since people seem to find it difficult to distinguish between things that differ, let me say just a word about the difference between authority and authoritarianism. There is a difference, you know. Authority (for the Christian) is found in words and acts that come from God. The emphasis in such authority, as I have said, is not upon the messenger but upon his message. That is to say, authority, rightly exercised, points one to God who is *the* Authority. Authoritarianism, on the contrary, points away from God and, instead, focuses upon the messenger. His manner, his position, etc. become the most vital facts. It is so bad a distortion of authority that the divine message is made to exist for the sake of the human messenger. Far from confusing the two, you must see, rather, that they differ so greatly that, in fact, they are opposites.

We shall turn now from a discussion of the need for biblical authority in decision making and action to a brief consideration of the "C" in A-C-T, concreteness. Directive counseling must be concrete.

If direction is the place in which counseling founders, we shall see that it is in these waters also that she most frequently shatters her hull and sinks. In counseling and in preaching, in general, the tendency is to be general and abstract. Why? There are probably a *number* of reasons for this, but let me suggest only two. First, much of the material that pastors read is abstract. In their preaching and in their counseling, they tend to reproduce what they consume.[2] At our counseling center, as I observe our trainees, this seems to be their No. 1 problem. It most readily can be detected in their language, which is often technical. Jargon, peculiar to theologians, never should be used in counseling, unless *absolutely* necessary—and then, only in connection with careful explanation. And, when

---

[2]That is one reason why pastors should make it a habit to read books other than theological ones.

counseling in a crisis, you can see readily how such language could get in the way. Why create new and artificial problems for the counselee by talking about soteriology when you can say salvation, or the noetic effects of sin when you can talk about the way sin has affected thinking? Worse still is when ministers try to bolster their counseling with a sprinkling of psychological jargon. Not only is this inappropriate, but usually these terms are used imprecisely and with confusing results. How often have I heard a minister speak of someone having a "guilt complex," when really all that he meant was that the individual had a sense of guilt. The first expression is fuzzy and confusing; the second sharp and clean. Words like neurosis, schizophrenia and paranoia are especially bad since the words themselves have become imprecise. The word "schizophrenia," for instance, has come to mean nothing more than bizarre behavior. Like the words "red nose," it speaks *only* of effects, not of causes. You can get a red nose by falling asleep under the sun lamp, growing a pimple on it, getting punched in it, or, I suppose, in at least a hundred other ways. The same is true of bizarre behavior—it may come from significant sleep loss, the ingestion of LSD, a desire to deceive, malfunction of bodily chemistry, or who knows what? Moreover, the use of such terms points in the wrong direction. They are associated with psychiatry and therefore point to supposed psychiatric solutions, whereas terms like sin point to Jesus Christ.

But secondly, abstract concepts, language and discussion may grow out of fear. To keep a discussion either in the pulpit or in a counseling session in the realm of the abstract of course is the *safest* thing to do. You have run no risk of contradiction or argument when you tell him that he must "become more loving" toward his wife. The word love (when so used) is an abstraction, about which you and he can talk forever, and yet see no change. He can protest till the cows come home that he is "trying to be more loving," and that his wife is "an insensitive person" who just doesn't appreciate his attempts, and there is no way for you or for her to prove him wrong or right. But, if the words *love* and *insensitive* are concretized; i.e., spelled out in terms of what, specifically, they mean in this marriage, *then* there can be a monitoring of the progress of both the husband and wife. If his attempt at showing love, for instance, is first spelled out as doing one new small thing for his wife each day for a week—just to please her—and if being sensitive to his efforts is delineated as being aware of and expressing appreciation for each attempt by taking note of it and saying "thank you," then the progress or lack of it can be pinned down.

It is upon this aspect of concreteness that I wish you would focus your attention for a few more minutes. People do not change in the abstract; they change only in doing concrete things. An inconsiderate person cannot work on becoming considerate. Inconsideration and consideration are mere abstractions; they are simply words that should head columns of acts that a person does or doesn't do. A husband can't work on being considerate, but he can put his socks in the hamper each day instead of throwing them on the floor and expecting his wife to pick them up. She can screw the top back on the toothpaste tube instead of leaving it off when she has finished with it. Life consists of thousands of small things, like these, that—in and of themselves—are not very important. But when changes are made even in such small annoying patterns as these, especially if they have persisted over a considerable period of time, others can *see* that love, or concern, or considerateness is being expressed. Big changes in relationships can result from small changes in practice.

It is right here that a crisis counselor must excel. Since a crisis, by definition, is a situation requiring a change, the Christian counselor must know how to use the Scriptures in a thoroughly concrete manner. He must learn how to apply biblical truth specifically to given situations in a way that makes it plain to everyone what God requires. He must not speak in platitudes; he must work at the level where the rubber meets the road.

For example, if a husband has been caught in adultery and says that he wants to repent and rebuild his marriage, it is not enough to talk about those matters in the abstract. The counselor will want to make sure that both parties understand the nature of repentance, that forgiveness is sought and granted not only from God, but also from his wife. He will be deeply concerned that she understands forgiveness as a *promise* to remember his sin against her no more. In accordance, he will show how she must not bring the matter up again to him, to others, or to herself. It is the last point that is so difficult: how to keep from dwelling on it and, as a result, feeling sorry for herself and angry toward him. The counselor will help her to work on this *concretely;* perhaps he will suggest that she keep a tight schedule, allowing little or no time for wool gathering, that she develop a Philippians 4 *think list* of profitable mind-engaging subjects to carry about for use at times when she is tempted to sit and soliloquize. Instead, she can whip out her list, turn to the next item ("Planning menus for our family campout") and go to work on it.[3] For his part, the husband's repentance will be accepted concretely: "If, as you say, Bill, you want to rebuild your marriage on an entirely new basis, let's get to work on that right away. First, this week, you and Phyllis make a list of at least 50-100 concrete ways in which the marriage should change.[4] Next week we shall begin to work on these, one by one." When people came to John the Baptist and asked "What shall we do?," he told the tax collectors to stop stealing, the soldiers to put an end to the abuse of their power, etc. So too, modern counselors must be concrete; repentance should be followed by the specific "fruit (or change) that is appropriate to that repentance." The Christian counselor, in such situations, not only must *know how* but also must *show how* to make the changes that repentance requires.

One of the chief reasons people go to counselors is to learn the *how to* . For years they have heard the *what to* from pulpits ("study, don't merely read your Bibles," etc., etc., etc.) in a well-meant but abstract fashion. Now they want to know how to do it. Any counselor who does not wish to or does not know how to give instruction in the how to, will fail. Mark that down as a fact. The how to is simply the application of scriptural truth to specific situations. But that is the hardest, most painstaking part of counseling. Because it is so difficult, many counselors shy away from it. Yet, for this reason—because of its difficulty—it is precisely here that counselees need help most desperately. Abstracting the principles that apply to a counselee's situation is helpful. But then abandoning the counselee at the very point where those principles can begin to change life, is both cruel and counterproductive to all the good that otherwise might have been accomplished. Yet, so often this is exactly what is done. As a result, all of the previous work

---

[3]The first item on the think list which I always give the counselee as a starter is: "Items for my think list."

[4]50-100 items will assure you of a list that is concrete. People cannot think of that many options. It will also make it clear that you expect hard work.

that may have been accomplished is lost, and all of the hopes that have arisen, evaporate.

I do not wish to suggest that the counselor must make every application of every principle to every item on the counselee's list; that would be too much for him, and ultimately it would not help the counselee. But he must help him sufficiently enough to do at least three things: (1) change the situation markedly so that he begins to get a taste of what biblical living can be like, (2) turn things around enough to get him heading at last in the right direction and (3) demonstrate fully enough how to apply the Scriptures to concrete problems so that the counselee himself now knows how to do so and is, indeed, both *willing and able* to do so himself. The remaining work, then, and only then, can be safely left for the counselee to accomplish on his own.

Now, for the T in A-C-T, Tentative. Direction, in and during the crisis period, often must be tentative. What is done will be preparatory, partial or provisional. More often than not, what is done will constitute but a beginning. A calmer, more relaxed sort of counseling may then take up where crisis counseling leaves off. Since one of the chief goals of crisis counseling is to extract the emergency factor, thereby removing a good bit of pressure from the situation and deflating it from its crisis proportions, the *focus* of crisis counseling will be narrower than that of ordinary pastoral counseling. This more limited concern is reflected in what I have called tentativeness in providing direction.

Three things may be said about the tentative approach in giving direction:

1. Some directions must be *preliminary*. If, for instance, in taking the counselee's inventory, you discover that his *state* is not conducive to counseling or decision-making, you must take preliminary measures to meet the situation. If he has taken an O.D. (overdose), hospitalization probably will be required. If he is drunk, first, he must be sobered up. If he is perceptually unstable from sleep loss, a sleep binge of two days may be the most important direction that can be given. In the case of a husband and wife who are on the verge of separation, you may need to spend all of your first session persuading her to unpack her bags. But because you did not have

time to do more, you will want to set up some early walk-on-eggs measures to help them to get through those next two days until you can see them again. Before all of the data can be *grasped* or the full *inventory* of both parties can be taken, and more concrete direction can be given, you want to try to avoid any more complications, so you may give a preliminary direction like this:

"Between now and when I see you next, I want you to do three things. First, ask God to help you to hold your tongues. Secondly, whenever anything goes wrong, instead of trying to settle it yourselves—we haven't had a chance to work on how to settle differences God's way yet—on this pad of paper write down what went wrong and bring it with you the next time. Thirdly, read this book—especially noting the chapter entitled "Communication Comes First," and we shall begin to get into these matters in more detail next time."

Obviously, those directions are not optimal, but sometimes—when all of your time has been spent on getting a preliminary agreement not to leave, or on seeking agreement to let you help before taking some radical step, that is all the direction that you can give. But keep in mind, *some* direction is necessary—even if it *is* preliminary. Persons, highly motivated for action, must be given something to do. Otherwise they will do something—usually the wrong thing—anyway.

2. Some directions must be *postponed*. Whenever it is possible to put off certain decisions or actions, it is desirable to do so. Hasty decisions about large matters, always ought to be postponed until the crisis is past. The widow who has just lost her husband is in no condition now to decide to sell the business, or to move to Florida, etc. She must be counseled to postpone any such decision until later, when she can amass the facts, more calmly assess them and can make the decision in full possession of all of her faculties. You must help her to sort out the crisis issues (i.e., what must be done *now),* from other issues. Thus, she must be taught the value of having a full grasp of the situation, and an awareness of her own state before moving ahead.

3. The counselor may promise to help his counselee to face the non-crisis issues at length, and (if he has learned how to sort out, assess and program the facts of the crisis situation) he can lay out a plan for handling them in a reasonable order, *after* the more immediate and more pressing demands of the situation have been met. All of which is to say that:

Some directions must be *preparatory*. Since a counselee who is motivated and mobilized to meet a crisis will want to expend his energy by *doing something,* I have noted that the counselor must put him to work in some way. Usually, the most productive way in which to do this is to find legitimate preparatory work for him to do. The idea is not to find busy work for him to do—although that often would be preferable to some of the actions that counselees propose—but rather *legitimate* work; i.e., work that (while preparatory, to be sure,) nevertheless is work that will lead to a biblical disposition of the issues at hand. Preparatory work is action at least one step removed from final action. It involves activity that does not immediately commit one, can be changed if necessary and (when handled properly by the counselor who proposed it) has good, not evil consequences.

As far as possible, all short term work should relate to long term objectives; that is the rationale for calling it preparatory. Lists and schedules often provide the best sort of preparatory work. By them, more data can be gathered, data can be classified and plans can be sketched. Writing out one's ideas helps him to clarify them and helps the counselor to see more exactly what he is thinking. The preparation of lists is preparatory to the actions implied or proposed in them. The counselor can discuss the lists with the counselee at subsequent meetings and they can be modified prior to action. Here, for instance, are some examples of lists that might be made:

1. List all of the problems that you see on the horizon.

2. List everything that will be affected by the change, and how.

3. List all of the decisions that you think you will have to make in the next three months. Divide these into two columns: (1) those I must make right away; (2) those I can postpone for a time.

4. List the exact process of events that took place in leading to this crisis.

5. List the names of all who are affected by this crisis and state how.

6. List your responsibilities in this crisis: what they are, to whom you are responsible and what God wants you to do to discharge them.

Preparatory action brings satisfaction and relief because it takes the pressure off, begins to sort out aspects of the problem and is a way of getting a toehold on the crisis. As he prepares, and as you help him to do so, the counselee will begin to discover God's way out of the crisis. I did not list Bible study or prayer in the six examples above, because I assume all along that these will play a significant part in the counselee's preparation. Mostly, he will need direct help in this before, during, and after the preparatory work.

Well, there it is. For four days we have discussed—in a very spotty and preliminary fashion—an approach to crisis counseling. If you are dissatisfied, so am I. In four days we could only take a brief look at this critical subject. But I hope the dissatisfaction is not a dissatisfaction of disgust, but the sort of dissatisfaction that makes you determined to know more. I trust you will want to fill out the mere suggestions, illustrate and concretize my abstractions, and modify and adapt wherever your situation makes that necessary. But I hope that you will not want to leave and forget the whole business.

Of course, that's not really possible anyway. You may forget crisis counseling for a time. Indeed, you may even get along well in your pastorate without a thought of it—until one day at 2 a.m. when a drunken member of your congregation phones and on the other end of the line you hear these words:

"Pastor, I've got a gun at my head and if you don't tell me what to do, I'm gonna' pull the trigger."

What will you say? God help you if you don't know and God help that member.

EXPLANATION

In order to enable the reader to make immediate application of the biblical principles of Crisis Counseling that I have set forth in this book, I have added the ten sample cases in the following section. Each case involves a different sort of crisis that a pastor may be called upon to face.

By reading[1], discussing, practicing, role playing and evaluating each it is my hope that students (individually or in groups[2]) will learn how to *apply* crisis theory in a practical way. Those using or teaching these cases may wish to keep the following suggestions about role play in mind:

1. During group preparation of a role play for presentation it is most beneficial for each person in the group to take a turn playing the role of counselor.

2. It is perfectly all right to add any details to a case so long as it retains (1) the central problems indicated, (2) its crisis nature.

3. Role plays of counseling sessions should be condensed into fifteen minute periods (or less) to allow time for discussion and evaluation. Players should focus upon highlights and *necessary* details rather than taking time to relate all of the steps in the counseling process.

4. The fifteen minute segment should be followed by at least a fifteen minute analysis, evaluation and critique by the teacher and/or the class, stressing apparent strengths and weaknesses and adding suggestions for improvement.

---

[1]As a background for general counseling principles (and for reference), consult (especially) my earlier books: *Competent to Counsel, The Christian Counselor's Manual, The Use of the Scriptures in Counseling* and *Shepherding God's Flock,* Vol. II.
[2]In class, at ministerial meetings, etc.

5. Remember that condensing inevitably leads to a more compact and therefore abrupt and slightly unnatural approximation of the real life counseling situation. Make allowances for this in evaluation.

The questions following each case are suggestive and are aimed principally at helping the reader to orient his thinking in a preparatory way about his task in each crisis situation. Space has been provided for notations following each question. Directions for role playing also accompany each case.

CONTENTS

CRISIS CASE #1
THE DEFOMED CHILD

Picking up the phone you hear a voice urgently pleading "Pastor, you'd better come over here to the hospital right away. We need you. The baby has just been born. Alice is OK physically, but the baby isn't—he—he has some terrible deformities. They say he'll never be right. The doctor told Alice about twenty minutes ago and she became hysterical. Nobody here can seem to quiet her. Please come; maybe you can help."

Cliff and his wife Alice are members of your church. This is their first child. Both have seemed to be very stable people.

Using the information in the preceding lectures determine the answers to the following questions:

1. What do you know already, before going to the hospital?

2. On your way to the hospital, you try to think through the major objectives that you will try to reach. What are they?

3. From the list of objectives, formulate a plan of action by which you may structure your visit at the hospital. Set forth this plan by steps.

Role Play: From these conclusions, enact the confrontation at the hospital.

CRISIS CASE #2
"HER BAGS ARE PACKED"

Pastor, I'm so glad you're here!" Martin blurts out as he rushes through the front door of your study. "Martha is outside in the car and she refuses to come in . . . but she says that she'll talk to you You will talk to her, won't you?"

"Martin, please get hold of yourself," you reply. "Try to tell me what's happened, you are not making much sense."

"Well, pastor, she says she's leaving me. Her bags are packed and in the car trunk. I only convinced her to stop by here at the last minute. She was heading for the train station. She says that she'll listen to you, but that what you say had better be good, because unless it is, she's going and I'll never see her again. Pastor, please help. Please don't let me down. I love her. I don't want her to leave. Please talk to her—everything now depends on you!"

Questions:

1. What will you say to Martin immediately?

2. What will you try to get Martha to do?

3. How will you attempt to achieve this?

Role Play: Have the narrator relate the details as given above. Role play the counselor's response to Martin and his subsequent encounter with Martha.

CRISIS CASE #3
"I'M NOTHING BUT A MILLSTONE"

". . . So that's why I called you and asked you to come," says Bart as he concludes a tale of utter defeat, failure and sin. "There is no use to try to go on. Everything I do is a failure; my wife and my children would be better off without me. I'm nothing but a millstone around their neck. I can't keep a job, I'm drunk half the time, and when I'm sober I'm so worried about the bills that have piled up and what I am doing to the family, that I'm not worth anything even then. Unless you can show me that there is some way out of this mess, I've decided to end it all. This bottle of pills will do the trick quickly and painlessly."

1. How will you respond to Bart?

2. What will your immediate objectives be?

3. What will you try to do next?

Role Play: Act out two or three possible approaches to this situation. Try to stress the essential elements that must be included in any approach.

CRISIS CASE #4
"YOU TELL HER, PASTOR . . . "

Crushed, Mike did not know what to do. Nor did he know how to break the news. So he called you. You came. He asked you to remain and tell Brenda. As soon as she regained full consciousness you told her. Her words that follow are the climax of her response.

"But Pastor, I don't want to die! I'm only 43 years old! My husband needs me, the children are not yet raised and . . . Oh . . . Oh . . . Oh . . . What will I do?"

Brenda breaks into uncontrollable sobbing and buries her face in the pillow of the hospital bed. Not many hours before, her husband Mike had rushed her to the hospital for what seemed to be a serious, but (nonetheless) routine appendectomy. When the surgeon emerged from the operating room, he told Mike that he had found more than they had bargained for—there was cancer everywhere. He suggested also that from the looks of things Brenda might not live much longer. That was when Mike called you.

Questions

1. What is happening here?

2. Was this the time and place to tell Brenda?

3. What can you do to help her and Mike, now/later?

Role Play: Take it from the top, starting with Mike's phone call and moving beyond the point reached in the description above. Show how a Christian counselor might handle this situation. If you wish to change anything in the sequence of events as they are described, please do so.

CRISIS CASE #5
"A DIRTY LITTLE SLUT"

"But you did, you did!" screamed her mother; "you've lied and deceived us . . . and now see what it has led to!"

"You're mother's right" said her father angrily, "you are nothing but a dirty little slut! Think of it, pastor; she told us five months ago that she would never see that punk again, and now we not only find out that she's been sneaking out to see him, but to top it all off, as a result she's pregnant. What are we going to do?"

You reply "I know that both of you are angry, hurt and deeply disappointed, but . . . "

1. What will you say next?

2. How would you best be able to help the members of this family?

Role Play: Follow the format above and proceed from there.

CRISIS CASE #6
"I'LL KILL HER!"

"How can he do this to me? I've given him the best years of my life! I mothered his children, raised them all through thick and thin, and now—when the last one has just gone off to college—now when I thought that the two of us really could start to enjoy each other again with a new freedom, he tells me this! Think of it! He says I'm boring and dull and that he plans to run off with another woman. I'll kill her if he does; I'll kill that house-breaking hussy! I'll kill him too! Oh, pastor, what will I do? I love him. I don't want to lose him. I can't go on without him. Why did God let this happen? Can you do something to stop him?"

Marge has just finished telling you her story in a state of uncontrollably mixed emotions. She sits there in your study waiting for an answer. You are shocked. You had no inkling of a problem in this home. You can hardly believe your ears. Curt, her husband, is the Church School superintendent and Marge, a faithful leader of Pioneer Girls. "Could this really be happening to them?" you wonder.

1. Given your state and hers, what can you best do at the moment?

2. Later on?

Role Play: You may want to describe more than one counseling session in this role play.

CRISIS CASE #7
"WON'T TALK, EAT, MOVE"

She's been that way for hours, pastor. We don't know what's wrong, and we don't know what to do about it. She just sits there and stares; won't talk, won't eat, won't move. As I said before, all we know is that when she got that phone call, she cried out "O my God, no!" and sat down. There was no one on the phone when we got around to hanging up the receiver. Can you help us?"

1. Can you? If so, how?

2. If not, why not?

Role Play: Show clearly what you will do and say in this situation.

CRISIS CASE #8
SELL AND MOVE?

"He was buried only last week, but already I'm so lonesome and I miss him so much that I . . . " Millie, the 73 year old widow of an elder of your church whose funeral you conducted breaks up in tears. After a time she continues: "It's the hollow ring of the house. I forget for a moment and call to him and then I remember that there will be no answer. I sit at our table . . . alone. I sleep in our bed . . . alone. There is too much about this place that reminds me of him. Already I can see that I'd probably be better to get out of here. I've had a couple of real estate people call and ask about selling. I was wondering if I'd like it in Florida. What do you think, pastor?"

1. Well, she's asked for advice; What will you tell her and how will you back it up scripturally?

2. How can you best protect and guide Millie at this time?

Role Play: Millie has tossed the ball to you. What will you do with it?

CRISIS CASE #9
A PROPOSITION?

Passing by the men's room in the far corner of the all-but-empty church basement after the evening service you are brought to a halt by the sound of two voices that are all too audible:

"No, I won't do it again. I'm tired of it. I'm trying to quit. It's sin and I know that the Lord doesn't want me to go on."

"But Harry, I've told you before . . . it's not sin when two persons are in love with each other as we are. Please, just once more. Just *this* time . . . . "

1. Can this be what it sounds like? And can that be Harry, your organist, and Jerry, one of your deacons? Well, it sure seems so. Then, what do you do next?

2. later?

Role Play: The next move is yours, pastor. What will you do? Show us.

CRISIS CASE #10
ONLY KIDDING

"Pastor, I appreciate the fact that you were willing to come over right way when it was so late." So speaks Nell as she opens the conversation. Her husband Stanley, a long time member of the congregation is uncomfortably slumped down into the corner of the sofa, stone silent. She continues: "I wouldn't have dreamed of calling you under any circumstances unless it was serious. But this . . . this is too much!"

"Oh Nell, I told you—you're making too much out of it. Getting the pastor out of bed and all of that, why—"

"Too much out of it! How can you say that Stanley? Pastor, do you know what he proposed to me no more than an hour ago? He asked me if I'd be willing to participate in a swinging party this weekend. He wants to swap me off to another man so he can have sex with his wife!"

"I was only kidding. I told you that . . . !"

"Kidding? People don't kid about those things. Besides, I know you—I know you weren't kidding. You had that gleam in your eye— the same one you get whenever you see a pretty face and a sexy figure."

"Have it your way then . . . . "

And so it goes. Now, Pastor, they turn to you. What will you do?

Role Play: Be sure that you try to develop the crisis nature of the situation adequately and how you would seek to relieve it.

THE USE OF
THE SCRIPTURES
IN COUNSELING

TABLE OF CONTENTS

PREFACE

I send forth this volume in the hope that it will help many—both as a stimulus and as a guide in the work of biblical counseling. Varied forces are at work today to pry Christians loose from a biblical base. Some claim that the Bible cannot be used as a textbook for counseling, and that any attempt to do so violates its purpose and plan. Others maintain that we have not become biblical enough. Although this volume does not answer such critics directly (see my book *Your Place in the Counseling Revolution* for a fuller discussion of this matter), nothing could serve as a more powerful refutation than to set forth successfully a positive biblical perspective and methodology as I have tried to do here. I shall allow the reader to judge for himself whether, indeed, I have succeeded. This book, together with its practical outworkings in *The Christian Counselor's Manual*, while (obviously) quite imperfect, I think that you will agree, nevertheless plainly shows that biblical counseling not only can be, but is a reality. May this volume contribute to reaching an understanding of those guidelines that are needed to help pastors and other Christian counselors keep from wandering off the narrow way that (unfortunately) so many have found too strait for their liking.

Jay E. Adams
Westminster Seminary
Philadelphia, Pa.
1975

175

INTRODUCTION

The controlling design of this book is to be as concrete, informative, and practical as possible. Yet there is at the outset a certain amount of foundational work that must be done in order to support the more concrete structures that I hope to build. So, let us break the ground and pour the footing.

CHAPTER I
Christian Counseling Is Scriptural[1]

You Must Use the Scriptures in Counseling

I do not think that I need to labor this point at Dallas Seminary. I am sure that the reason why I was invited to deliver these lectures in the first place was because of our common conviction about this vital imperative.[2] Therefore, since I think that I can safely assume that we are in basic agreement about this, since I have argued the issue elsewhere in print[3] and since I am certain that your interest lies more in questions growing out of problems connected with the ways and means of using the Scriptures in counseling, I shall quickly move beyond this point. But before I do, perhaps a word or two would be in order.

You Must Have Conviction, Courage and a Steady Determination to Use the Scriptures in Counseling

First, you may think that it will be easy to graduate from this school, take up your work in a conservative pastorate, and as a part of your effort there, begin to do biblical counseling. Please believe me when I say that it will not be that simple. The pressures exerted against a ministry of biblical counseling are great, as you will discover all too soon. For one thing, when you begin to counsel biblically some counselees will rebel. They will protest that you are

---

[1]The first eight chapters of this book were given as the W. H. Griffith Thomas Memorial Lectures at Dallas Theological Seminary, November 6-9, 1973. Subsequently, they were published in the four issues of *Bibliotheca Sacra* during the year 1973. They have been revised and additional chapters have been included for use in this volume.
[2]I have retained much of the original lecture flavor in these chapters.
[3]Jay Adams, *The Christian Counselor's Manual,* pp. 92-97.

being unduly hard on them, and will demand an easier way out. After all, scriptural counsel is often *hard*. Sin creates no *easy* problems; they are all so difficult that it took nothing less than the death of Christ to meet them. Untangling men from the webs of sin can be quite a painful process. The hard (but needed) directions that you will give to others from God's Word about repentance, confession of sin, reconciliation with one's brother, and so on, will not sit right with those who want to remove the miseries caused by sin without dealing with the sin itself. Though men want it, you must tell them that there is no such instant holiness.

Second, because sinners (and never forget that *Christians* are sinners, too) always want to do things the easy way,[4] they often will insist on bypassing the hard work of determing from the Scriptures what God's solutions to their problems may be. Instead, they will run to faith healers, exorcists, and those who claim to receive extra-biblical guidance or revelation for quick answers; they will plead experience as the interpreter of the Scriptures[5] or will try to use the Bible as a talisman from which to extract magical answers. For instance, more than once parents will appear for counseling dragging their rebellious teenager, whom they have failed to discipline for the past seventeen years, and say (in effect), "OK, do it to him." They expect the counselor to put two feathers in his hair, do a short rain dance, wave the Bible over the boy's head seven times and pronounce him "cured." Such people are not happy when they learn that they may have to spend from six to eight weeks establishing Christian communication and developing biblical relationships with their son. They wanted a medicine man, not a Christian counselor. To resist these tendencies and instead hold out for careful exegesis and application will not always be easy.

Third, you will find too that even in the midst of the present disillusionments with it, many Americans still worship science—and science falsely so-called. How else could B. F. Skinner, who pontificates that man is merely an animal, and that the world's problems can be solved by scientific retraining, command such a

---

[4]That is one major reason why people get into trouble in the first place and find it necessary to seek counseling.
[5]A very prevalent problem in our irrational day.

large hearing today? Members of your congregation, elders, deacons, and fellow ministers (not to speak of Christians who are psychiatrists and psychologists) may turn on the pressure and try to dissuade you from any resolute determination to make your counseling wholly scriptural. They may insist that you cannot use the Bible as a textbook for counseling, try to shame you into thinking that seminary has inadequately trained you for the work, tempt you to buy all sorts of shiny psychological wares to use as adjuncts to the Bible, and generally demand that you abandon what they may imply or openly state to be an arrogant, insular, and hopelessly inadequate basis for counseling. They may even warn and threaten, as they caricature the biblical method: "Think of the harm that you may do by simply handing out Bible verses like prescriptions and pills."

All these—and a dozen more—pressures will be exerted upon you to give up any idea of a scripturally founded and functioning system of counseling. Combined with personal doubts that may arise during times of discouragement, these pressures can be greater than you now may think.

What then can be done to meet and to resist effectively all such pressures? There is but one answer: during periods of pressure look to the Scriptures for their help in doing this too. The counselor's Counselor is the Holy Spirit, speaking by His Word. All of which leads us to an examination of the important question:

What Does Scriptural Counseling Involve?

Your encouragement and assurance will come from an understanding of this matter. The answer to the question is that counseling that is truly scriptural is (1) motivated by the Scriptures, (2) founded presuppositionally upon the Scriptures, (3) structured by the goals and objectives of the Scriptures, and (4) developed systematically in terms of the practices and principles modeled and enjoined in the Scriptures. To put it simply, scriptural counseling is counseling that is *wholly* scriptural. The Christian counselor uses the Scriptures as the sole guide for both counselor and counselee. He rejects eclecticism. He refuses to mix man's ideas with God's. Like every faithful preacher of the Word, he acknowledges the Scriptures to be the only source of divine authority and, therefore, judges all other matters by the teaching of the Scriptures.

181

In short, such counseling takes the Scriptures seriously when they say that they are able to make the man of God[6] "adequate," and equip him for "every good work."[7] In the passage from which those words come, Paul piled words and phrases upon one another to convey the idea of *complete adequacy*: the Scriptures not only make the Christian minister "adequate" for his work, but, as Paul put it, "entirely equip him for it." Not only do they thoroughly anticipate and show him how to meet all possible pastoral counseling situations, but by doing so they make him adequate (Paul insisted) "for *every*"—not just for some but—"*every* good work" that his office requires of him. Because the minister, *par excellence,* must counsel as part of his life calling,[8] he knows, therefore, that God's written Word will adequately equip him for this phase of ministerial work. While all sorts of other resources may be useful illustratively and in other secondary ways, the basic principles for the practice of counseling are *all* given in the Bible. Counseling that relies upon these principles is scriptural. This leads us to the main matter before us:

The Use of the Scriptures in Counseling
The Scriptures are the Counselor's Textbook for Counseling

Like his Lord—who was the wonderful Counselor predicted by Isaiah—the counselor will find that all that he needs for the work of counseling is in the Bible. Jesus Christ needed no other text to become the world's only perfect Counselor. He was that because He used the Scriptures more fully than anyone else either before or since. His counsel was perfect because it was *wholly* scriptural in the absolute sense of those words. The minister who engages in scriptural counseling, like Him, believes that because the Holy Spirit inspired the Book for that purpose, the Bible *must* be used in counseling.

---

[6]In the pastorals this designation, picked up from the Old Testament, is used for the Christian minister. Cf. I Timothy 6:1. See also Deut. 33:1; Josh. 14:6; I Sam 9:6; I Kings 17:18,24; II Kings 1:10,12; 4:7; 5:8.

[7]II Timothy 3:17.

[8]For the argumentation behind this assertion see Jay E. Adams, *Competent to Counsel,* pp. 42ff. and *The Christian Counselor's Manual,* pp. 93-95.

Arguments that one does not use the Bible as a textbook for architecture or for mechanical drawing beg the question. If God has assigned the task of nouthetic confrontation to ministers as part of their life calling[9] and He has given the Scriptures to them to equip them fully for this life calling, then it follows that the Scriptures, while treating other matters as well, adequately furnish all that ministers need to counsel. Remember, the Scriptures do not purport to give shipbuilders or architects or electrical engineers detailed information for pursuing their arts, but they *do* claim to equip ministers adequately for theirs. Indeed, where else may one turn to obtain the precise data needed to meet the two major issues in counseling: namely, the problem of how to love God and the problem of how to love one's neighbor? After all, we spend little time discussing counselee problems about things; it is in relationships with God and with other persons that counseling problems develop. The Scriptures, in *focusing* upon these two questions, provide "all things" pertaining to and necessary for "life and godliness." With Martin Lloyd-Jones, the Christian counselor affirms,". . .every conceivable view of life and of men is invariably dealt with somewhere or another in the Scriptures."[10] When it comes to counseling, then, eclecticism is not an option. The issue resolves itself quite simply into this: if a principle is new to or different from those that are advocated in the Scriptures, it is wrong; if it is not, it is unnecessary.

It is at this point that so many of the self-styled professionals balk. They want the Bible in part, but not *solely,* as the basis for their counseling. Yet, just because of the fundamental nature of the question, it is right here that one makes the most vital decision about counseling; it is here that he decides whether his counseling will be wholly scriptural (and, therefore, Christian), or whether it will be something else.

[9]See argumentation for this in Adams, *Competent to Counsel,* pp. 42ff.; *The Christian Counselor's Manual,* pp. 93-95.

[10]Martin Lloyd-Jones, *Truth Unchanged, Unchanging* (New York, 1955), p. 16.

*The Scriptures Tell the Counselor All That He Needs
to Know About God, His Neighbor, Himself
and the Relationships Between These*

They speak of man's nature, as a creature who bears God's image and likeness, his basic problem (sin) and God's solution in Christ. They tell him what counseling should be, provide the content (i.e., the counsel) for it, detail the qualifications required of those who do it, and govern and regulate the methodology that may be used in it. What more is needed? Apart from the Bible, who else has such information?

You Must See Scriptural Counseling Alone as Adequate to Meet Man's Problems

All right, we have generalized enough. *How* does this all come out in the wash? *What* does scriptural counseling mean in concrete contexts? Let us conclude this article with some examples of scriptural counseling that will serve to point up more vividly what I have been saying.

Start with the most difficult counseling problem of all: death. To be more specific, let us ask who best counsels a grief-stricken widow following the death of her husband? Who is adequate for this task? Is the psychiatrist? The clinical psychologist? You know that he is not; and so does he. Quite seriously, what does he have to offer? On the other hand, are you competent? Armed with God's scriptural promises you *know* that you are adequate. You know that among God's children you *can* (as Paul put it) "comfort one another" with God's words (I Thessalonians 4:18); you know that God has said that the scriptural data in I Thessalonians 4 will act as an anchor for the believer to keep his grief from drifting into despair, and that they will moderate that grief by balancing it with hope, so that in the end, through scriptural counsel the widow is enabled to sorrow in a way different from others "who have no hope" (Thessalonians 4:13).[11]

And to the surviving one who does not know Christ, in that hour the

---

[11]Cf. Jay Adams, *Shepherding God's Flock*, Vol. 1 (Presbyterian & Reformed Pub. Co.: Nutley, 1974), Appendix A, pp. 135-156 for a fuller discussion of grief as a counseling opportunity.

only word that can make any real difference is the redemptive word of the gospel, by which, in God's providence, the Christian counselor may be used to bring eternal life to her out of the occasion of death. If the Christian counselor can handle the most serious counseling problem adequately, there should be reason to suppose that he can handle others that pose less difficulty too.

"Not fair," I can almost *hear* someone say. "You've stacked the deck in your favor; everyone knows that death (at least until recently) has been the peculiar province of pastors." While I do not think that it is at all unfair to begin with life's most difficult counseling problem, since it so clearly points up the contrast between psychiatric inadequacy and scriptural provision, and since it so pointedly shows who it is that really is engaged in "depth counseling," and who on the other hand has but thin soup to offer, I am, nevertheless, quite willing to leave the matter right here and take up a different one.

What about a marriage that has been strained to its breaking point? Two people, let us say two *Christians,* fighting and arguing sit before a non-Christian counselor. As they spit out acrimonious words of bitterness and discouragement and declare that there is "nothing left" to their marriage, that they "loathe rather than love" one another, what does the unbelieving counselor have to offer? In this day of unparalleled marital failure, on what thin thread can he hang hope? From what source can he promise change? By what authority can he insist upon reconciliation (indeed, does he even believe reconciliation to be possible, or desirable)? Is he adequate?

The scriptural counselor, in contrast, is able to meet the situation adequately. He says (in effect) with the full authority of God: "Since the information that you have given me indicates that you have no scriptural warrant for dissolving this marriage, there is but one course open to you: repentance and reconciliation followed by the building of an entirely new relationship that is pleasing to God." In contrast to the non-Christian, because he does not speak out of his own authority, the scriptural counselor speaks with confidence, knowing the goal and how to reach it. "Happily," he continues, "the Scriptures contain all of the information that you need to make these changes a reality, and—what is more—the Holy Spirit, who provided these instructions, promises also to give the strength to follow them, to all Christians who sincerely wish to do so and who step out in obedience by faith."

After detailing some of the many hopeful biblical specifics about such change (I shall not do so here as I have already done this elsewhere[12]), confidently he can encourage and persuade them: "If you mean business with God, even though your marriage presently is in a desperate condition, within a few weeks you can have instead a marriage that sings! Indeed, there is no reason why the first steps toward God's dramatic change cannot be taken *this week,* beginning *today.* What do you say?"

I ask you, *who* is adequate for such things? The answer: Christian counselors who use the Scriptures *authoritatively* to give *hope* through God's *promises* and *concrete instruction*—and no one else.

It is precisely because the will of God is made known authoritatively in these divinely inspired writings that the Christian may counsel with confidence. He does not need to guess about homosexuality or drunkenness, for instance, nor does he need to wait for the latest (changeable) scientific pronouncements to discover whether these human deviations stem from sickness or from learned behavior. God has spoken and clearly declared both to be *sins.* Therein lies hope. God has not promised to cure every illness, He has said nothing about changing genetic structures, but in Christ He has provided freedom from every *sin.* Together with a long string of similar difficulties, God has shown that those who trust Christ not only can be forgiven and cleansed, but also can fully overcome both of these sins. He says to converted Corinthians, using the past tense, "Such *were* some of you; but you were washed, but you were sanctified" (I Corinthians 6:11).

Absolute authority, Christ's commandments and precise pronouncements, are all but universally decried as restrictive and evil by those who eject the Scriptures from counseling. They make no distinction between authority and authoritarianism. Unwittingly

---

[12]Adams, *Competent to Counsel,* pp. 231ff.; *The Christian Counselor's Manual,* pp. 161-216.

thereby they jettison the basis for all hope, both for themselves and for their counselees.

When God authoritatively directs His children to forsake any sin or to follow any path of righteousness, the Christian may take hope. For apart from authoritative directions all is in flux, nothing is certain—there is no foundation for hope. Although his first reaction may be dismay when he recognizes how far his present life patterns have veered from God's way, upon repentance and further reflection the counselee should realize that whenever the heavenly Father requires anything of His children, He always provides instruction and power to meet those requirements. That means, for example, that when He says that we must "walk no longer as the Gentiles walk" (Ephesians 4:17) in Christ God will *enable* us to walk differently. Every directive of God—no matter how far short of it that we may come at the moment—serves to provide a solid foundation for the Christian's hope. Both counselor and counselee, therefore, may take heart in scriptural counseling for the very reason that it is authoritative.

"Still," you protest, "marriage counseling, like counseling the grief stricken, is not quite the same thing as dealing with those who are depressed, or those who exhibit bizarre behavior. What of the use of the Scriptures in those cases?"[13] Fair enough; let us consider another example. Fred's behavior, over a period of several years, at times became so bizarre that he was jailed, sent to two mental institutions, received a series of shock treatments, was placed on heavy medications and was subjected to intensive psychotherapy and various psychiatric treatments; all to no avail. When he came for scriptural counseling, it was as a last resort. But after six sessions his problem was solved. He has been leading a successful life as a productive Christian for over two years.

What made the difference? Biblical convictions. Since no evidence of organic damage or malfunction had been discovered during extensive medical tests, the Christian counselor rightly assumed that the roots of the problem were likely to be imbedded in the soil of sin. With that conviction he set to work.

---

[13]Cf. Jay Adams, "A Christian View of Schizophrenia" in Peter Magaro (ed.), *The Construction of Madness* (Pergamon Press, Inc., Elmsford: 1975).

His goal was not to treat symptoms (as had been done previously by those who administered shock treatments and by those who prescribed medication), nor was he intent upon discovering who had maltreated Fred in the past (as were others who had spent long hours dredging up all manner of parental and societal abuses in hopes of freeing the poor "victim" of a "tyrannical superego"). Nor did the biblical counselor focus upon feelings (as a third group of counselors had when they spent months attempting, by reflecting his emotional responses, to draw solutions out of his own storehouse of resources). What did he do? Simply this: he set out in search of the sin or sins that he supposed were at the bottom of the difficulty. A few weeks later, through proper questioning, he discovered that Fred had been sinning against his body, the temple of the Holy Spirit, by failing to get adequate sleep. Every effect of LSD or other hallucinogenic drugs may be caused by significant sleep loss (an important fact for seminary students and faculty to remember during exam periods, incidentally). Fred's bizarre behavior always followed periods of sleep loss. Fred was convicted of his sin against God and, following forgiveness, was placed on a carefully monitored sleep regimen, his daily schedule was revised according to biblical life priorities, and the problem was erased.

How did the counselor know to do this? Well, he went in search of sin because he believed the Bible. The Bible knows only two categories of causes for bizarre behavior: (1) organic causes, (2) non-organic causes. Organic factors may be hereditary or later acquired through accident, toxic destruction of brain cells, etc. Some—but not all—organic problems may be due to the sin of the individual (e.g., drug abuse may impair normal bodily functioning). On the other hand, all non-organic problems are represented in the Scriptures as stemming from the counselee's sin. There is no third, neutral category or subcategory that allows for non-organic difficulties for which the counselee may not be held personally responsible. On the basis of these biblical presuppositions, the Christian counselor began his search.

It is important to note that the Freudians and Rogerians who treated Fred also did so *on the basis of their presuppositions*. The former presupposed that Fred's problem stemmed from past malsocialization; the latter, from failure to actualize his full potential. If Fred had been treated by a Skinnerian behaviorist, he too would have dealt with him on the basis of his conviction that man is only an animal and that a new set of environmental contingencies (or learning conditions) must be substituted for the previous ones which had brought about the undesirable behavior.

Every counselor, then, comes into counseling with presuppositions. These presuppositions pertain to all of the fundamental questions of life—its purpose (or lack of it), its problems, their solutions, the nature of man and the relationships which he sustains to others and to his world. Most important, every one of those presuppositions, wittingly or unwittingly, either includes or excludes God the Father, the Son, and the Holy Spirit. If, then, counseling begins with such presuppositions, how vital to begin with the right ones! And these are found only in the Scriptures.

Each counselor finds what he is searching for. The Freudian looks for others who "did it to him," and since parents, educators and even preachers and Sunday school teachers are sinners, he has little trouble finding many persons who have wronged the counselee. The Rogerian looks for insights from within the counselee that may be drawn out from a fully prepackaged supply of potential resources upon which the counselee has failed to rely. Since no sinful counselee lives up to his full potential, Rogerians may elicit some such insights. The Skinnerian looks for environmental changes that must be made in order to reshape his behavior. He will find much in the environment that needs to be altered. But, notice, not one of them looks for sin. Indeed, if he discovers it by accident, he renames it. Instead, the sin becomes an "emotional problem" or "immaturity" or "insecurity" or a "neurosis" or "mental illness" or something else that better fits the system built upon his unbiblical presuppositions.

Reinterpreting sin redirects one from real solutions involving regeneration, forgiveness, sanctification, etc., to some lesser inadequate remedy that never can satisfy the radical needs of condemned and corrupted man which took nothing less than the death of the Son of God to meet. Only scriptural counseling, grounded upon scriptural presuppositions, can do that.

189

Because of these facts, you must "be steadfast, immovable, always abounding in the work of the Lord, knowing that your labor is not in vain in the Lord" (I Corinthians 15:58). When you counsel, it should be with hope, with expectation that since it is scriptural your efforts will not be in vain. If your counseling labors are done "in the Lord," that is, in obedience to His Word and in reliance upon His power, then they will issue in the Lord's results, in the Lord's time and in the Lord's way.

No other counselor has such assurance. At best, he knows that he has opted for some system (or eclectic amalgam from various systems) over against others. For a number of reasons this proves most dissatisfying. If he is a Freudian, he knows that more than half of the psychiatric world itself has abandoned his position and that vigorous attacks built upon strong arguments have been mounted against his views. Only the most arrogant psychiatrist today could be wholly "sold" on psychoanalysis if he has stood in full face of the prevailing winds. Moreover, look at the plethora of psychoanalytic cults, offshoots, and isms from which he must choose. Which sort of psychoanalysis will you have: classical Freudianism, neo-Freudianism, dynamic Freudianism, or what? Each of these differs from the next, not as conservative churches or denominations who agree on the fundamentals, but as widely as Orthodox Presbyterians and the Church of Rome. When one begins to branch out beyond the avowedly psychoanalytic schools to the existentialists, the Rogerians, the Behaviorists, the Transactional Analysts, the many sorts of group therapists, the Crisis Interventionists, the Rational Therapists, the Reality Therapists, the Radical Therapists, the Primal Screamers, the followers of Laing and so on and on and on, he begins to see that confusion reigns.

And unlike the Christian counselor, the rest have no standard, no way to know and no way to be sure who is right. What a difference it makes to have the authoritative Word of God!

The unbelieving counselor, seated in his plush, expensive furniture, surrounded by hundreds of books on psychology and psychiatry, with every word may seem to exude an outward confidence and certainty that one might have thought originated on

Mount Olympus. Yet, unless he is incredibly naive, unless the volumes on his shelves are there for impression alone, he knows that every statement, that every judgment, that every decision that he makes in counseling is challenged and countered by scores of authors from an equal number of viewpoints. Psychiatric jargon or prestige, which may be heavily plastered over inner insecurities, ought never to be equated with psychiatric knowledge or wisdom.[14]

The truth of the matter is that the Christian counselor who determines by the grace of God to know and use the Scriptures in his counseling is the only one who can ever have a solid basis for what he says and does. While there may be any number of issues about which he has not yet come to a fully biblical understanding, nevertheless, because he has the Scriptures, on all of the fundamental questions of life he not only knows but is fully assured of the truth and of the will of God.

Let no one, therefore, tell you that the scriptural counselor is inadequate and that he must take a back seat while learning from his pagan counterpart. The opposite is true, and it is about time that Christian counselors began to make the fact known.

In closing, I cannot help but think of the Psalmist when he wrote: "I have more insight than all my teachers, for your testimonies are my meditation" (Psalm 119:99). To those of you who believe this, let your prayer, together with him, be:

> Sustain me according to your Word that I may live; and do not let me be put to shame because of my hope (Psalm 119:116).

---

[14]For interesting comments on this subject, see David S. Viscott, *The Making of a Psychiatrist* (Greenwich, 1972), pp. 24,25,84.

CHAPTER II

Understanding Problems Biblically

The use of the Scriptures in counseling involves the interaction of no less than five essential factors. These are:

1. A biblical understanding of the counselee's problem, stemming from . . .

2. A clear understanding of the Holy Spirit's *telos* in scriptural passages appropriate to both the problem and the solution, and . . .

3. A meeting of man's problem and God's full solution in counseling, according to . . .

4. The formulation of a biblical plan of action, leading toward . . .

5. Commitment to scriptural action by the counselee . . .

all prayerfully accomplished by the enabling power (grace) of the Holy Spirit. It will be necessary to examine each of these five factors in some detail.

The Counselor Must Reach a Biblical Understanding of the Counselee's Problem

As you can see from that statement, biblical counselors cannot be satisfied simply to trust the word of the counselee, the report of some referring agency, the conclusions of standardized tests, or even their own first impressions about the counselee's problem. Rather, they must engage in a twofold process of research: (1) They must search out, discover and interpret according to biblical norms all of the significant data concerning the problem that may be provided by the counselee, parents, spouse, or others who may be involved. Data, we have shown elsewhere, are not limited to verbal material obtained

192

during counseling sessions.[1] Written information, in the form of lists prepared by counselees, records kept on Discovering Problem Pattern forms, failures and difficulties encountered in accomplishing initial homework assignments, as well as many sorts of non-verbal or halo behavior, are examples of other important sources for obtaining data.

Today's mail brings a letter from a Christian physician overseas who is working in tandem with a graduate of our counseling program whom we shall call John. He writes:

> The problem of generalizing was mine last week with a bank manager patient whom I could not persuade to go back to work . . . I thought it was that he had made the bank his idol, and the image was beginning to crack . . . however John got through to the problem straight away when he found that in fact the man had been storing up resentment over a senior man's laziness to such a degree (while blandly going on maintaining a stiff upper lip English smile) that he could not face going into the bank anymore.

Notice several facts in that account. First, note how he says, "John got through to the problem. . .when he *found*. . . ." While I do not know the details of the case, from the brief record at least three things seem to be apparent: (a) John probed for the significant data. Prior to counseling, the bank manager had been disguising the true problem which John had to "find"; (b) the physician, even though (rightly) thinking in biblical categories ("I thought that he had made the bank his idol. . ."), was wrong in his original assumption because he did not gather the significant data necessary to make a correct evaluation of the problem (probably he did not have adequate time to do so and, therefore, referred the counselee to John); (c) these data, when discovered, were analyzed and defined biblically. Judged by scriptural norms, John and his colleague rightly discussed the problem in biblical terms. They concluded: "the man had been storing up resentment." One can see that, behind that evaluation,

[1] Jay E. Adams, *The Christian Counselor's Manual,* pp. 257-59, 308, 310, 313-16.

these biblical counselors were vitally aware of such passages as Ephesians 4:26b: "Do not let the sun go down on your anger." They did not label the problem as a neurosis or blunt the truth by excusing the counselee's behavior as a justifiable "defense mechanism." Nor in this case did they speak even of "repression" (a word that carries heavy Freudian freight). They labelled the sin biblically for what it was—resentment.

Other labels at first might be considered kindlier; but in fact they are not. John and his friend are doing the kindest thing possible in calling sin "sin." There is no hope in speaking of neuroses, defense mechanisms or repressions; God has not promised to do anything about such problems. But every Christian knows that Jesus came to deal with sin. Labeling sin "sin" then is kindly because it gives hope; it points to the true problem and to God's solution.

Other labels not only remove hope and confuse the situation, but point in wrong directions. Psychiatric labels point toward psychiatric solutions. Thus they redirect both counselor and counselee away from the Scriptures. No one recommends repentance as the solution for neurosis! When the true problem, therefore, is sin, all such misdirection is cruel because it points away from the only true solution to the counselee's problem and, of even greater moment, is the fact that this redirection itself is sin. Ultimately it constitutes rebellion against God by the rejection of His Word, His Son and His Spirit as irrelevant or inadequate.[2]

---

[2]This is a very common failing among Christians who are psychiatrists or psychologists. Take, for example, the words of David A. Blaiklock in his book *Release From Tension* (Grand Rapids, 1969), in which he advocates altering the biblical picture for the benefit of the counselee: "Thus it behooves Christians who have little tendency to worry to make a worrying Christian's lot harder by loading him with guilt produced by their condemnation of the 'sin of worry,' without leading him gently to the true answer" (p. 49). Blaiklock thinks that he has a truer answer than the biblical answer which is that worry is a violation of God's commandment (Matt. 6:31,34; Phil. 4:6) and therefore is sin. Blaiklock thinks not. What does he think is truer about worry? He says that it is in part hereditary (p. 49), but of more importance is—"the effect of the vital first five years" (p. 50). That is truer, kinder? Sin, as every believer knows, can be removed in Christ. But what hope is there for the "hereditary" worrier who is also stuck with past programming? Blaiklock, because he thinks he can be kinder than the Scriptures, cruelly takes away the worrying believer's hope. Fortunately it can be restored, for in every directive of God to His children there is hope; directives speak of possibility. He never directs them without providing the means for fulfilling His directives. Cf. Jay Adams, *What To Do About Worry* (Nutley, 1971).

It is important, then, for Christian counselors to discover all of the relevant data concerning the counselee's problem(s) and to interpret the meaning of these data biblically. If there is an organic base, or if there are organic aspects to the problem, he will want to know this so that he may be able to enlist medical help in accordance with biblical principles.[3] If the difficulty is a non-organic problem in living, he will want to call sin "sin" and handle it accordingly. Nothing is of more importance to the entire counseling process than the foundation; if that is out of line, all else is likely to be off kilter too.

(2) The other side of the research process in which the counselor must engage before, during, and after every counseling session involves the discovery of the biblical norms by which symptoms, behavior, and other data may be evaluated and understood. In order to label problems biblically, he will need to know, for instance, that the Scriptures describe drunkenness as sin. He will not approach the problem under any illusion that the counselee is suffering from "the disease of alcoholism" (whatever that may be).

Because such research requires the kind of knowledge of the Scriptures that Paul describes as "the word of Christ dwelling richly within" (Colossians 3:16),[4] the best background for a Christian counselor is not training in psychology or psychiatry, but a good theological seminary education. He will need to know how to exegete the Scriptures, faithfully studying them regularly in order to steep himself in God's promises, warnings, prohibitions, injunctions, and methods. The good counselor will be helpful because he brings a "rich" supply of biblical truth into the counseling situation. From this supply he can retrieve much material previously studied, understood, and stored up for just such occasions.

Not every sort of exegesis, however, can so supply the counselor; Paul is speaking of exegesis with a practical slant. (It is Christ's word ministered to others "with all wisdom" that he has in mind.) But how does one acquire this sort of exegetical capability? The only adequate way for a counselor to learn to exegete the Scriptures in a

[3]Cf. Jay E. Adams, pp. 105ff., and *The Christian Counselor's Manual*, pp. 437-43.
[4]For further discussion of counselor qualifications, cf. Adams, *Competent to Counsel*, pp. 59ff., and *The Christian Counselor's Manual*, pp. 13-15.

practical (rather than in a merely theoretical) manner is to begin to exegete the Scriptures *personally*. That is to say, mere storage of facts is not in view of Paul's words "richly dwelling within," but rather facts transformed into life. Good counselors are concerned about becoming wise in their own personal living and, as a result, they also become wise in the ministry of the Word to others.

In the sort of study contemplated, then, the counselor does not study *first* for information to use in preaching or in counseling. Instead, he studies always with an eye on his own life. As he does so, the understanding of a verb form may bring conviction of sin, the import of a personal pronoun may occasion a burst of song or thanksgiving. Such study is not abstract; it requires personally involved exegesis. In this study the counselor's own life in relationship to God and his neighbor is always under review. He studies *beneath* rather than *above* the Scriptures. And. . .it is just *because* he has experienced the truth of God exposing his own sin, piercing through every joint to the marrow, judging the desires and thoughts of his heart, encouraging by its promises, comforting, healing, motivating—that he is able to minister that same Word to others in wisdom.

Since the counselee's non-organic problems are hamartiagenic ("sin-engendered"), the counselor himself is familiar with them. They are not different in kind from his own. Therefore, the solutions that he has found *personally* he is able to use *practically*. By this I do not mean that he must experience every situation in exactly the same way that the counselee has. He does not need to sin every sin—to commit adultery in order to know how to help an adulterer. The temptations spun out of his own adulterous heart, as well as the possibility of generalizing from biblical help that he has received in other sin experiences, are quite adequate to enable him to minister the Word sympathetically. With Paul, he is able to "comfort those who are afflicted" with the "same comfort" that he received "when afflicted" (although afflicted, perhaps, in quite a different way). This, Paul says, he can do for those who are "in *any* affliction" (cf. II Corinthians 1:3-7).

So we see first of all that in his use of the Scriptures in counseling the Christian counselor must depend upon the Bible from the outset to obtain a biblical understanding of the counselee's problem(s).

This understanding may be reached only by researching the problem according to biblical methods, out of biblical motives, using biblical categories for definition and labeling. And it can never be purely academic, for counseling from start to finish deals with matters in which every counselor himself is intimately involved.

We must turn now to the second factor that is always present whenever the Scriptures are used properly in counseling.

CHAPTER III

Understanding the Scriptures Telically

A Clear Understanding of the Holy Spirit's *Telos* in Scriptural Passages Appropiate to Both the Problem and the Solution

Note well, the *telos* (or purpose) of a passage should be central to everything that is done in counseling; that means that it is the vital factor even in the selection of the passage *as appropriate* to the problem at hand.

The *telic* side of exegesis has been either ignored, underplayed, or unknown by many pastors. Sadly this fact is all too apparent to those who have studied this question in the history of preaching. If any one fact is evident, it is this: preachers, good Christian men who meant well, nevertheless have persisted in using the Scriptures for their own purposes rather than for the purposes for which they were given. Often because blissfully unaware of the Holy Spirit's intention in placing a passage where it occurs, they have generated the most incredible interpretations and dogmas and have given some of the most horrendous advice, all in the name of God. Fortunately, on the other hand, in God's providence much truth has been preached from passages that say nothing about it! And all that may be said about the vital place that *telic* exegesis must play in preaching pertains with equal force to the use of the Scriptures in Christian counseling.

I have spoken already about the importance of authority in counseling.[1] Authority arises from knowing that what the counselor says truly comes from God. That cannot be known unless the counselor shows the counselee that the directive, warning, or

---

[1] But see also Jay Adams, *Shepherding God's Flock,* Vol. II, pp. 14,105ff.

promise about which he is speaking comes from the Scriptures. The authority will be lacking unless (a) the counselor knows the *telos* of the passage, (b) uses it for the same purpose as that for which the Holy Spirit gave it, and (c) demonstrates to the counselee that this is in truth its purpose and meaning. Because the matter under discussion is of such vital importance, I shall linger for a while over each of those necessary elements in establishing scriptural authority for one's counsel. With Paul, the counselor must be able to say in good conscience, "For I do not, like so many, peddle an adulterated message of God" (II Corinthians 2:17).

(a) The counselor must know the *telos* of every passage that he uses in counseling. It is not enough to understand the grammatical-historical, biblical-theological or systematic, and rhetorical aspects of a passage. These are essential, and I should be the last one to say anything to undermine such work, for each of these elements plays a vital part in biblical exegesis. Indeed, without their assistance often it is impossible either to discover the *telos* or to be sure even when one has done so. Yet it is possible to have all of these matters in mind in exegesis and still *misuse* a portion of Scripture in preaching or counseling. Thus, the story of the Seeking Father and the Pouting Elder Brother instead becomes the Parable of the Prodigal Son; the two commandments to love God and neighbor are psychologized by those who want to add to them a third commandment, "love yourself," which they then make basic to the other two, in spite of the fact that this is a thought repugnant to the entire Bible, and the clear statement of Christ that he is speaking of *two* commandments only: "On these *two* commandments hang all the law and the prophets."

(b) The counselor must know the *purpose* of the passage; that is, he must know what God intended to do to the reader (warn, encourage, motivate, etc.) with those words. Then, he must make God's purpose his own in the application of the passage to human needs. But to do this he must develop an exegetical conscience by which he determines never to use a passage for any purpose other than that purpose, or those purposes for which God gave it (often, of course, there are sub *tele* involved in a larger telic unit). This determination will make him faithful not only as an interpreter, but also in his *use* of the Scriptures.

It was at this point that some Puritan preachers and commentators set Protestantism back several generations. They abandoned the superior method used by Calvin which focused upon telic matters in the text. Instead, it became their practice to discuss lengthy questions from the whole corpus of systematic theology as these had any bearing upon a word or phrase, no matter how remote that connection might be. Contextually there was no warrant for this practice; and, indeed, it often obscured important contextual connections and distracted one from the main purpose and proper use of the passage. No wonder many of their commentaries were interminable. And to these doctrinal discussions some of them often appended a series of "improvements" or "uses" of the text. Under such rubrics every sort of tenuous and sometimes moralizing relationship of the passage to life was explored. The passage was wrung dry.

God's words must be used to achieve God's purposes. Obviously, therefore, flip-and-point methods of using the Scriptures are taboo, since they ignore telic considerations. Along with such techniques we must reject Bible prescription methods in which the counselor in effect tears out a page of Scripture and hands it to the counselee without explanation as the remedy for his problem.[2] For all of the understanding of it that he has, it might have been scrawled in a Latin that can be translated only by a pharmacist! All of which leads to the third point.

(c) The Scriptures must be "opened" (i.e., "explained," cf. Luke 24:32) if counselors would have the hearts of their counselees to

---

[2]Not that God in His wise providence cannot use His Word even when given in this form. Ordinarily what is meant by handing out Scripture verses like prescriptions is that the Bible is used in a magical manner, much more like a talisman than a divine Revelation. The Bible passage (like a prescription) is supposed to effect results whether understood by the recipient or not. All such usage is itself unbiblical and must be rejected. But Jim, a physician friend of mine, objects to the rejection of the image of the prescription. "Instead of stressing the aspects just mentioned," he observes, "why not focus upon the positive (highly instructive) aspects of the comparison, like the need for careful diagnosis, the need for a thorough knowledge of medicines and their effects, etc., all of which have to do with *care* by the doctor, or in your case by the counselor?" He has a point! If we take Jim's word to heart, we shall note the essential differences between counseling and the writing of medical prescriptions, and end up with *both* the ideas of care on the part of the counselor and understanding and commitment by the counselee.

burn within them like those of the disciples who walked the Emmaus road with Christ. When *He* is disclosed to them as the subject of "all" of the Scriptures, moralizing will disappear, irrelevant material will evaporate and the *telos* of the passage will find its proper place in Christ.

But how does one discover the *telos* of any passage? (1) By studying with the *telic* goal in mind (one rarely finds what he does not seek), and in that search (2) by looking for *telic* cues. Often these cues are overt; but some are more evident than others. Some *telic* statements have to do with the *whole* of the Scriptures, as for example when Paul wrote that the Scriptures have two purposes: "to make one wise unto salvation" and to "teach, convict, correct, and train in righteousness" (II Timothy 3:15-16). Thus any given passage primarily will have either an evangelistic or edificational goal. In Luke 24:27, Christ referred to Himself as the subject of "all of the Scriptures," which is perhaps the most basic and comprehensive *telos* of all. Christ Himself is the Savior and Head of His church who has made salvation and Christian growth a reality. The Christian counselor, therefore, must see Christ in every passage that he uses and introduce the counselee to Him there. This means that he may never use the Scriptures moralistically or humanistically. But, while never forgetting this redemptive base, he also must select passages because of their particular *telic* emphases, beginning broadly by dividing Bible books and counseling portions, according to their major emphases, into the two main purposes mentioned above: evangelism and edification.

John's gospel and first epistle provide the most obvious sorts of *telic* notes: the first was "written. . . that you may *believe,*" and the second "written to you who believe. . . that you may *know.*" Is there any wonder then that verses like John 1:12; 3:16; 3:36; 5:24; 14:1-6 and many others have been used so frequently by the Spirit of God to bring men to belief? After all, the Gospel of John, we are clearly told, was written for this very purpose. Likewise one should turn to the first epistle when counseling with a believer who lacks assurance of salvation. This is particularly necessary when counseling those who today similarly are plagued with a new kind of legalistic Gnosticism that teaches that only a small group of persons has a right to assurance. Characteristically, such preachers use I John not to bring assurance but to destroy what they believe to be false assurance. God's purpose in the book is positive, theirs negative.[3]

Portions of biblical books are devoted to different purposes. When the writer of Hebrews says, "Therefore leaving the elementary teaching about Christ, let us press on..." (6:1), he is giving the reader a *telic* cue to a shift in emphasis (all, of course, within the scope of the broader *telos* or tele for which the book of Hebrews was written). Ephesians 1-3 cannot be separated from Ephesians 4-6, since the two sections are hinged together by that crucial "therefore" in Ephesians 4:1 which shows that the doctrine taught in the first half has vital implications for the practical Christian living enjoined in the second half. Yet, it is important for the counselor to know that the latter portion of Ephesians shows *how* Christians, as members of Christ's redeemed body (the theme of the former), can learn to function together in love and unity.

Phrases like "Brethren, I would not have you to be ignorant concerning..." (I Thessalonians 4:13); "Wherefore, comfort one another with these words" (I Thessalonians 4:18); "I have written... to encourage you and to testify that this is the true grace of God" (I Peter 5:12); "I wish, therefore, always to remind you of these matters..." (II Peter 1:12,13); "I am writing you to arouse your pure minds by way of remembrance" (II Peter 3:1); "I found it necessary to write you appealing that you vigorously defend the faith once for all delivered to the saints" (Jude 3); "prescribe and teach these things" (I Timothy 4:11); "remind them of these things and solemnly charge them in the presence of God..." (II Timothy 2:14) are just a few of the many *telic* cues by which the counselor can be guided infallibly in determining the Holy Spirit's intentions in any given passage of the Scriptures.

Even when *telic* cues do not appear overtly, the *telic* quest still must be carried on. And this quest may be pursued successfully, for although the *tele* may not always be as apparent as in the New Testament examples mentioned above, they may be found by looking for *telic* thrusts and emphases. Thus, for example, there are few overt *telic* cues in Philippians, but the student who seeks to discover the main *tele* behind the writing of that book will have little

---

[3]A frequently observed problem of preachers is that of using a passage that has a positive *telos* negatively.

trouble uncovering such purposes as (a) Paul's desire to thank the Philippians for their gift, (b) his concern to explain the working of God's providence in his imprisonment, (c) his interest in healing the division in the Philippian church, and (d) his wish to calm their fears about Epaphroditus.

"The *telic* note is important, I can see, for establishing authority in counseling and thus assuring both the counselor and counselee that the analysis of his problem and the solutions offered are well founded, but how does this work in actual practice?" you may ask. This important question leads naturally into a discussion of the third factor.

CHAPTER IV

Bringing These Two Understandings Together

There Must Be a Meeting of Man's Problem and God's Full Solution in Counseling

Let us begin by comparing the approaches of two counselors at work. They both face the same problem: young parents have come seeking help in the discipline of seven-year-old Johnny, their first and only child. Johnny, like all other seven-year-olds, is a sinner who, in this case, has been allowed to develop a disturbingly rebellious sinful life style through parental permissiveness occasioned by their fear, poor instruction, and general laziness.

One minister, steeped in the modified Rogerianistic-behaviorism advocated in some recent books by Christian authors who have baptized such strange views into the faith unconverted,[1] finds himself in difficult straits since he considers spanking a "last resort." He points to Proverbs 23:7 and reads "As a man thinketh in his heart, so is he." From that proof text he develops the thesis for the parents that they must carefully instruct their child about the reasons for the family rules so that through proper understanding of these, at length correct behavior may be achieved. It does not take a prophet to predict the consequences of such an approach.

In contrast, a thoroughly biblical counselor will handle the problem quite differently. To begin with, he will think of the *problem* biblically—that is, rebellious behavior is *sin*. Because he sees the problem in those terms rather than as a problem in understanding, he will move toward a different sort of solution. Having rejected the compromise with behaviorism that leads to the

---

[1]Cf., e.g., Bruce Narramore, *Help I'm A Parent* (Grand Rapids, 1972), in which spanking is considered "a last resort" to be used only "when all other methods have failed" (pp. 107-8).

notion that spanking is a last resort, instead he will urge these parents to use it consistently as a vital biblical disciplinary method. He will turn for instruction to Proverbs 22:15, "Foolishness is bound up in the heart of a child, but the rod of discipline will drive it far from him."[2] But he also will instruct them that punishment is not enough; together with the punishment the child must be confronted nouthetically about his sin and his need for a Savior who can change him, and whose redemptive help he needs to overcome his sin. In order to emphasize this balanced two-pronged scriptural approach, he will discuss Proverbs 29:15, "The rod *and* reproof give wisdom, but an undisciplined child causes his mother shame," and Ephesians 6:4: "Fathers, . . bring up your children in the discipline *and* nouthetic confrontation of the Lord."[3]

Because of his eclectic approach, the first counselor has been influenced to use the Scriptures superficially. He comes to the Scriptures prejudiced by his psychological rather than biblical background. Careful grammatical-historical, contextual, systematic and *telic* use of the Scriptures by the second pastor leads him to avoid such errors. He moves in the right direction because his basic commitment is to the Bible rather than to psychological or psychiatric theory. First, because he is biblically based, he rejects Rogerian and Behavioristic inroads. Secondly, because he is careful about his exegesis, he cannot settle for a superficial use of Proverbs 23:7: "As a man thinketh in his heart, so is he." Unlike many of the proverbs, that verse has a context. It is part of a warning against taking the words of one's host seriously when he urges you to eat more food. The exegete does not wrench it from that setting. Rather, properly translating and using the verse *for the purpose for which it was given,* he understands it to say, as the Berkeley version more accurately translates it:

[2]He might calm any fears that they may have over using spanking in punishment by discussing Prov. 23:13-14, a passage intended to give reassurance and from which he also will want to explain that such obedience as the rod brings is essential to creating conditions in which to teach children the way of salvation (v. 14).

[3]He will not fail to stress biblical rewards either, noting (as Paul observes in Eph. 6:1 when quoting the children's commandment) that the commandment to "honor" one's "father and mother" is "the first commandment with a *promise*" (reward).

Eat not the bread of him whose eye is selfish, neither desire his delicacies, *for as one who inwardly figures the cost so is he;* "eat and drink," he says to you, but his heart is not with you.

He does not fall into the trap of developing a false philosophical, psychological, or counseling principle that says, "changed behavior flows only from changed understanding" from this verse. Rather, as he reflects upon the biblical passages that *do* speak of changing behavior through discipline, he discovers that *both* the rod and reproof (which further investigation shows involves what the New Testament calls nouthetic admonition) "give wisdom" (Prov. 29:15). His psychological theory, then, develops *from* the scriptural data; it is not superimposed upon the Scriptures. Because it does, it will not cramp him but rather will allow room enough for different sorts of changes to be effected through different sorts of discipline.

Because the former counselor's thinking is not fully biblical from start to finish, his view of discipline is narrowed and restricted. The latter, willing to submit to the Word of God, is free to reject all other theories that contradict and to open himself fully to the breadth of biblical truth. The former cannot see how a change in living also can lead to a change of thinking. He cannot understand how the rod can drive out foolishness and give wisdom, for he is chained to the psychological notions (weakly supported by a biblical passage that has nothing to do with the subject) that rules always must be explained in order to be effective and that changes in behavior always must be preceded by changes in thought. The real problem you see, arises when one interprets the Scriptures in the light of modern thought, according to his own superficial exegesis or in some other way that allows the Scriptures only to trickle through a man-made funnel. The full message of the Bible, thus, is withheld and scriptural authority is weakened.

Let us consider another example. In his book, *The Bible in Pastoral Care,* Wayne Oates suggests using the Bible as a kind of Rorschach test or (as he actually calls the recommended practice) the pastor's "thematic apperception test." Quoting the liberal Oskar Pfister[4] with approval when he wrote, "Tell me what you find in the

---

[4]Pfister was a psychoanalyst and good friend of Freud as well as a liberal pastor.
[5]Wayne E. Oates, *The Bible in Pastoral Care* (Philadelphia, 1953), pp. 22-23.

Bible, and I will tell you what you are," Oates says that the Bible must be seen as 'a means of insight into the deeper problems of people."[5] By this he does not mean that the Bible's *content* reveals these insights, but that the *use* that one makes of the Bible will give the counselor insight. Bad as that may be, I quote it not to show how far astray that counselors may go in using the Bible in ways in which it was never intended to be used, but rather as background for the particular misuse of the Scriptures that Oates demonstrates when trying to support his "apperception" thesis, namely, the practice of *projecting one's own ideas into the text*. The apperception idea is an indorsement of the practice of projection, and Oates' misuse of the Scriptures in attempting to find biblical support itself quite adequately illustrates and demonstrates the practice! He turns to James 1:22-24.

> Be doers of the word, and not hearers only, deceiving yourselves. For if any one is a hearer of the word and not a doer, he is like a man who observes his natural face in a mirror; for he observes himself and goes away and at once forgets what he was like.

Then he comments:

> The implication is that the Bible is a mirror into which a person projects his own concept of himself, and which in turn reflects it back with accuracy.[6]

I shall not take your time to comment on this "projective exegesis" by which Oates attempts to find scriptural support for the unbiblical and exceedingly dangerous practice of a projective use of the Bible. If the quotation itself is not sufficient warning against the practice, any argumentation would be unconvincing. Clearly Oates has a theory to support; so he comes to the Bible and grinds his axe upon it. *Telic* considerations, contextual exegesis and biblical theological understandings all give way to a projective psychologizing of the text.

One of the most commonly found examples of the projection of psychological concepts external to the Scriptures into the Bible is

[6]Ibid.

207

the practice (to which I alluded earlier) of "discovering" in the Bible that Christ really summed up the whole law in three rather than two commandments. The sober fact is that He did not. When Christ spoke of two commandments: love for God and love for one's neighbor (Matt. 22:34-40), He intended to say exactly that and nothing else. Yet psychologizing Christians have added a third even more basic commandment: love yourself. Some go so far as to claim that unless a person first learns to love himself properly, he will never learn to love his neighbor.

The argument sounds somewhat plausible at first, for how can one know how to love another unless he knows how to love himself? If he thinks (wrongly) that a practice is desirable, he may urge it upon his neighbor to his injury. And, after all, isn't that what Jesus meant by the words "as yourself"?

But a moment's reflection shows that all such argumentation misses the point—the Scriptures, not one's personal experience, must tell us what constitutes love to another. One cannot go wrong in loving another when he does what the Bible says.

When Christ urged Christians to love their neighbors as themselves, He did not intend to say that this would entail doing for another precisely what one does for himself. Instead (as in Christ's "first" commandment) the stress in the "second" is upon the intensity and devotedness of the love rather than upon the identity or similarity of action. Remember, Jesus pointed out that the second is *like* the first. The words, "as yourself" in the second parallel the phrase in the first commandment to love God "with all you heart . . . ."The emphasis is not upon the content of the love (that is found in the commandments themselves), but upon its fervency and genuineness: "Love God as *enthusiastically* as you love yourself." Beyond this, the fact that Christ distinguishes only "two commandments" (v. 40) itself is decisive.

Psychologizing the passage leads to pernicious errors. (1) God's Word is misrepresented. (2) One's own life rather than God's Word becomes the standard for behavior. (3) Endless speculation over matters like proper and improper "self love" and "self concept" is generated. It is very dangerous to make a big point over that about which Christ made no point at all (indeed, He explicitly excluded it by the word "two").

Elsewhere I have considered this matter more fully.[7] Here, let me simply say one more word. Counselors who focus on improving self-concepts and who try to teach counselees how to love themselves will find themselves spinning their wheels. Much time and energy can be wasted trying to strengthen egos. Not one word in the Scriptures encourages such activities. They are as futile as the pursuit of happiness. For a good self-concept never arises from seeking it directly. It is the by-product of loving God and one's neighbor. The Christian who concentrates on those two commandments will have little problem with the "third," for Jesus said, "He who has found his life shall lose it, and he who has lost his life for my sake shall find it" (Matt. 10:39).

Let me summarize what I have said. First, the counselee's problem must be understood and evaluated scripturally. Secondly, the Holy Spirit's *telos* in every passage used in counseling must be sought and, when found, must govern its use; and thirdly, there must be a meeting of man's problem and God's full solution. These goals can be achieved only by counselors who allow neither a distortion, dilution, nor admixture of the biblical data to enter the counseling situation, whether introduced by the counselee or by their own misuse of the Scriptures. Nothing less than this is the biblical norm against which we must measure our counseling and toward which we must ask God's Spirit to enable us to make progress continually.

[7]Adams, *The Christian Counselor's Manual,* pp. 142-44.

CHAPTER V
Forming Biblical Plans of Action

"I'm OK; You're OK"—the words may be modern, but the idea behind them is not new. They represent exactly the false, humanistic viewpoint of the rich young ruler when he called Christ "Good Master." When Tom Harris urges us to become OK by means of Transactional Analysis, he is asking us to do so without the aid of the Christ of the Scriptures. After all, he tells us, "truth is not . . . bound in a black book."[1]

Because the rich young ruler thought he was OK and that Christ was OK (in the same way), Jesus challenged his use of the word: "Why do you call me good? There is no one who is good except God" (Luke 18:19). Whenever it appears, that concept of goodness must be challenged. First, the rich young ruler could not be allowed to continue to think of Christ as good in the same sense in which he considered himself good. Unless he was willing to admit that Jesus was God, he would have to revise his language to fit the facts. All others are sinners. On the other hand, he needed to see just that—*he* was a sinner. Outwardly he had conformed to the Law, but inwardly he had broken it all as Christ so clearly demonstrated by exposing his idolatrous worship of riches.

Transactional Analysis and all other unscriptural systems that seek to change men likewise fail on both of these counts: (1) they underestimate man's problem, and consequently (2) they underestimate what it takes to solve that problem. Freudians view the counselee as a victim of poor socialization and, therefore, think that since the problem was brought about by man, man can solve it. The expert analyst/therapist can undo (at least) some of what man has done. The Rogerians think man is good at the core and his problem

---

[1]Thomas A. Harris, *I'm OK—You're OK* (New York, 1967), p. 230.

is a failure to actualize untapped resources. Hence, they attempt to draw out from him the answers that they believe he has the capability of producing. The solution lies in realizing his potential. He, rather than others, is his problem, but by the same token, he is also his own adequate solution. Behaviorists, who think that all human problems stem from poor learning caused by faulty conditioning, naturally see the solution in relearning through reconditioning. The manipulation of environmental contingencies is what is needed. Transactional Analysis sees crossed transactions (or relationships) as the problem. This situation may be remedied by learning to make paired transactions on the adult level. In all of these systems, and indeed in every non-biblical counseling system, man is the measure of all things.

But into the midst of this humanistic confusion God interposes His divine revelation—the Bible. From this Book we learn that we are all *not* OK. Indeed, our condition is not repairable. Our problem is sin. We have rebelled against our holy Creator, breaking His laws and incurring His wrath. As sinners, we cannot manufacture holiness with dirty hands. A righteous God has declared that He will punish us for our sin. We have no way in ourselves—through other sinful human beings, or by the manipulation of the environment— of appeasing Him. If, like Job, we try to speak to Him on the same transactional level, He Himself crosses out our transaction as He declares, "Who is this that darkens counsel by words without knowledge?" (Job 38:2).[2] But when, instead, we recognize our sin, become "as a child," and trust in complete dependence upon the sinless Son of God, who died for our sins and rose bodily from the dead, we receive forgiveness and learn the joy of the Cross transaction by which we say "Abba" to our loving heavenly Father. Our problem is not an immaturity that can be solved by becoming more adult; like the rich young ruler, we think we have come of age when our greatest need is to become like a little child.

We have discussed three of the five factors in scriptural counseling. Let us now consider the fourth factor in scriptural counseling.

---

[2]T. A. fundamentally constitutes an attack upon all authority structures, which means that it is (at bottom) an attack upon God Himself who is the Ultimate Authority.

The Counselor Must Help the Counselee
to Formulate a Biblical Plan of Action

You can see that this is exactly what is missing in each of the schemes just mentioned. The adherents to these schemes do not depend upon the Bible for help. Nor can they. Their systems do not allow for God's Word. Freudians think that the Bible is part of the problem rather than the source of solutions. Rogerians see no need for any outside help; to them the Bible is irrelevant. Behaviorists consider Scripture but myth that must be removed as a harmful or (at best) useless contingency, and the Transactional Analysis people find in the Bible a major reason for the crossed parent/child transactional problems that they wish to combat.

Scriptural counseling does not mix well with other ingredients. Those who propound other theories know this and often say so (Freud, for instance, called religion a neurosis.); when will Christians become aware of the incompatibility and likewise say so? It is time for us to stand up and echo God's declaration: "My thoughts are not your thoughts. Neither are your ways my ways" (Isaiah 55:8). Apart from the Scriptures, no man's plans can be adequate. When God commands, "Let the wicked forsake his way, and the unrighteous man his thoughts; and let him return to the Lord" (v. 7), He is speaking of the *only* road to forgiveness. He continues, "let him return to the Lord" (v. 7), He is speaking of the *only* road to forgiveness. He continues, "Let him return to the Lord . . . for He will abundantly pardon" (v. 7). It is clear that Isaiah was foreshadowing the words of Jesus when He said, "I am *the* way . . . no one comes to the Father but by me" (John 14:6). How could it be otherwise? How could we think that humanistic analyses of man's problems could lead to Christian theistic solutions? When will we come to see that there are not twenty ways or four ways, but only two—God's way and all others?

Listen to Isaiah again: "For as the heavens are higher than the earth, so are my ways higher than your ways, and my thoughts than your thoughts" (Isaiah 55:9). And once more, Isaiah connects the ability to return to God with a power that comes from His own Word. That word, like the rain and snow that do not return to heaven before they water the earth and bring forth fruit, will not return void. It too will bear fruit, accomplishing the purpose for which it is sent. Remember that this fifty-fifth chapter of Isaiah opens with an invitation to all those who are in need: "Ho everyone who thirsts, come. . . ." You might have supposed that the prophet was speaking to psychoanalytic patients who had been paying fifty dollars for a half hour's treatment when he asks: How much longer will God's people "spend money for what is not bread, and wages for what does not satisfy?" (Isaiah 55:1,2). All psychological and psychiatric systems that reject the Bible must themselves be rejected for that very reason. Since the message of God's Word is what is needed, therefore, and since no one else will turn to the Scriptures to find it, it is incumbent upon the Christian counselor to help the counselee to formulate a biblical plan of action.

What is a biblical plan of action and how may it be formulated? A biblical plan of action (1) grows out of and at every point is consistent with biblical presuppositions and principles, (2) aims at biblical goals, (3) depends upon biblical methods, and (4) is pursued and accomplished from biblical motives. It is a plan in which the yeasty principles and practices of the Scriptures have been kneaded into the dough of the situation so that they permeate all.

(1) When I say that a biblical plan of action grows out of and at every point is consistent with biblical presuppositions and principles, I hope to distinguish between two things: those biblical directives, warnings, promises, and so forth, that apply specifically to the counselee's problem, and those that apply in a more general way. While the Scriptures deal with *every* situation that the Christian minister faces in the course of his legitimate work, while they contain all of the data that are necessary for life and godliness, this information comes neither in the form of an encyclopedia, nor as a ready reference manual. Rather, God, in His wisdom, gave it to us in many different forms—narrative, poetry, letters, songs, prophecies, apocalyptic, drama, gospel, wisdom literature, and proverbs—from which the presuppositions and principles must be derived. Not infrequently, of course, these principles are stated directly and at times even propositionally.

Often, the very situation faced by the counselor was handled in the biblical record. This is to be expected since sinners and their

213

problems have not changed all that much. Thus, when Paul wrote, "Fathers do not provoke your children to anger but bring them up in the discipline and nouthetic confrontation of the Lord" (Eph. 6:4), he was giving directions that can be applied explicitly to every Christian parent in every era. The way that God disciplines is the norm by which all Christian discipline must be guided. That is why the passage sounds so contemporary. Looking on a woman to lust after her is adultery of the heart in any country, century, or culture. The application to contemporary cases is direct. That is why when a Christian wife wants to divorce her non-Christian husband even though he desires to continue the marriage, a Christian counselor can say without qualification, "That would be sin; you cannot do it." In support of his assertion he may cite I Corinthians 7:13 and apply it directly.

However, there is another class of problems to which the Scriptures apply less directly. When a pastor must decide whether to reject a call to another church, when a young woman has to determine whether she will accept a proposal for marriage, and in hundreds of decisions (both large and small), the biblical principles must be brought to bear upon the question in such a way that they box in the number of possible answers. Such application of the Scriptures requires time, knowledge, and wisdom.[3]

One of the reasons why Christian counselors find themselves faced continually by counselees with a myriad of such questions is because many conservative pastors have failed to teach their members *how to use the Bible practically* to deal with such matters. They have taught (successfully) the factual study of the Bible— members from infancy, it seems, can recite verses and retrieve even esoteric biblical data for the next Bible quiz. Yet they do not know how to consult the Bible helpfully in times of need or decision. I am certainly not against factual learning. But if learning never progresses beyond this to its practical (or *telic*) applications, it is not merely rendered useless, but positively harmful. Learning for its own sake leads to a kind of gnosticism in which the Bible becomes impractical for anything other than for argumentation. The Bible's use is limited to learning history and doctrine, or perhaps (at best) it

---

[3]Cf. Archibald Alexander Hodge, *The Confession of Faith* (Reprint of 1869 ed.; London, 1964), p. 39.

may be used for moralizing. But as a Book to which one can turn for satisfying redemptive solutions to life's problems—the Bible remains closed. When seminaries begin to teach pastors how to teach members of their congregations how to use the Bible for such purposes, the church will come to newness of life. Pastors who teach this way will save themselves and their members many heartaches and hours of unnecessary counseling.

At any rate, to begin with, *counselors* must learn how to use the Bible practically, and in the process they will find it necessary to teach counselees how to do so too.

A biblical plan of action that grows out of and at every point is consistent with biblical presuppositions, then, may do so either directly or indirectly. When Tom says, "I can't overcome my temper; I guess that Barb will just have to accept me as I am," the counselor may reply with confidence: "If you are truly a Christian, Tom, there is every hope that you can change, for the fruit of the Spirit is self-control. Barb should not accept you as you are since God doesn't." But when the counselor lays out a plan for Tom and Barb, *based on* the biblical principles taught in Ephesians 4:25-32, he may not speak at every point with quite the same authority. Instead, after a full discussion of the passage he may close like this: " . . . So, you see, there is hope. And the principles for putting off temper tantrums are clear—(1) daily communication rather than allowing the sun to go down on your anger; (2) words that build up and help another rather than tear him down; (3) forgiveness rather than slander, gossip, or malice. Now, let me suggest one way in which you can begin to put these principles into practice. If every day or so you meet to hold a conference . . . ," and so on. The counselor must distinguish clearly between the biblical *principles* and the suggested *plan* for putting those principles into action. The principles, if properly understood, are unalterable; the plan of implementation is negotiable. Principles must be applied; like dough and yeast, they must be worked into the actual problem situation. Yet, because situations differ, there may be many ways of doing so. It may be that regular use of a conference table will prove to be a vital part of the solution for Tom and Barb. On the other hand, different implementation of the same principles may be necessary for the counselor's very next case. The accomplished pianist learns basic principles and skills; after that he can play any piece, adapting his acquired abilities to the particular dimensions of each new tune.

But one thing is clear; in almost *every instance* of counseling success the one factor that seemed to make the difference was the implementation of biblical principles by means of a *concrete* plan of action. Without concrete application, the plan—no matter how biblical and wise (abstractly considered)—will fail. The biblical principles must be kneaded into the dough of the counselee's life.

Presumably it appears that while preachers and counselors are strong on the *what to,* they are weak on the *how to.* How often have we all preached abstractly: for example, "Don't read your Bible; study it." Enthusiastic members leave the service committed to remedying the defect. Monday they start in at Genesis 1:1, this time determined to study. By Thursday they have given up the task (since they didn't know *how to* do anything different from before). Sermons like that need to be accompanied by an announcement like this: " . . . and if you don't know how to study the Bible, be at church before the Sunday evening service when we shall begin a twelve-week course on the practical study of the Scriptures."

Counselors too need to keep in mind the fact that it is not enough to urge confused, undisciplined, disorganized, discouraged or hopeless people to stop unbiblical practices.[4] "How?" is the insistent question that they must be prepared to answer with a biblically grounded plan of implementation. But they must not wait for the counselee to articulate the question. Assuming that most counselees will be deficient not only about what-type material but also about the how-type, they will initiate the discussion themselves. Counselors, for example, will want to stock up on recommended devotional booklets to hand to couples who need to learn how to begin to read and pray together. They also may wish to devote some time to explaining some of the pitfalls to avoid and to making positive suggestions about time, method and regularity.

(2) But, secondly, a biblical plan of action aims at biblical goals.

---

[4]Counseling and preaching are complementary. Some advise, "Don't preach when you counsel." Why not? If one's preaching is good, it will have many characteristics in common with good counseling. The advice properly applies only to poor preaching.

Christian counselors may not accept just *any* goal. That is one reason why the usual behavioristic approach to goal-setting cannot be adopted by Christian counselors. Behavioristic counselors, by and large, will take on counselees with the intention of helping them to meet any goals that counselees wish to set for themselves.[5] If a counselee wishes to learn how to make friends, keep a job, or become a good father, the Christian counselor knows that these goals must be discussed and shaped *from a scriptural viewpoint.* Consequently he will interpose questions like these: Should the counselee expect to keep a job, given his irresponsible behavior? Does he want to work for the glory of God? Can he be counseled adequately apart from an understanding and acceptance of the fundamental work ethic in Colossians 3:22-26, summed up in the words, "It is the Lord Christ whom you serve"? Such matters must be of uppermost concern to a Christian counselor. The *goals* of the counselee, then, must be discussed, evaluated, and often altered in the light of the Scriptures.

Moreover, goals cannot be abstracted from life styles and life commitments. Christian counselors (unlike behaviorists) must counsel the whole man. If, for example, a homosexual wishes to learn how to make a decision about his occupation, a behaviorist may work on that goal, feeling no compulsion to handle the problem of homosexuality. But Christian counselors cannot divorce the homosexual problem, or, for that matter, the more general problem of the counselee's relationship to Jesus Christ from the question of occupational choice. Phobias will be dealt with from a biblical stance—the fear of man will be related to biblical wisdom which begins with the fear of God. Problems may be isolated for analysis and worked on individually, but never out of context.

To continue, the Christian counselor, therefore, must use the Scriptures to evaluate and, thus, ultimately to determine every goal. Goals like integration, security, adaptation, and so forth, cannot be adopted uncritically. For instance, William Glasser, author of the well-known volume *Reality Therapy,* has written: "A normal being is one who functions effectively, has some degree of happiness, and achieves something worthwhile to himself within the rules of the

[5]Cf. John D. Krumboltz, ed., *Revolution in Counseling* (Boston, 1966), pp. 9ff.

society in which he lives."[6] This definition of normality, the goal of Glasser's counseling, is faulty in several ways. But it must be rejected fundamentally, because it is humanistic, man-centered. Man is the goal setter and the evaluator. Each individual sets goals and evaluates according to his own subjective standards and the standards of others around him. Glasser, then, wants to please the counselee and at the same time to please society. No absolute objective standard is consulted. Consequently, the counselee is caught in the relativistic subjectivism of individual preferences, desires, and distortions of reality. Glasser thinks this is right so long as the individual can get away with being that way—or as he puts it: remains "within the rules of the society." That latter standard, the norms of the society, is no better than the former. For what cultural norms boil down to is this—Glasser wants to make the counselee to function smoothly within his society, whatever the rules of that society may be. If the counselee lives in a headhunting society, presumably Reality Therapy will help him to function effectively as a headhunter.

The Christian counselor should recognize that he can adopt neither the subjective standard of sinful individual desires nor the corporate standards of sinful societies as the goals or norms of counseling. He should realize that to make sinful man the standard is to set sinful goals for the counselee. He knows that God frequently requires Christians to set themselves *against* their own sinful desires and *against* the sinful norms of society. The faithful fathers of Hebrews 11 looked beyond themselves and away from society to the true and living God and to His heavenly city. They functioned according to another set of standards—a heavenly one. Where did they get it? From God's Word. They believed His promises and lived by faith in accordance with His directives even though that frequently flung them headlong into conflict with those around them. So, it is clear that one's counseling is scriptural only when he sets scriptural goals and works toward them.

Ultimately all scriptural goals may be summed up in one goal: to glorify God. In doing so, with Paul, Christian counselors will seek to "present every man complete in Christ" (Colossians 1:28). This may

<hr>

[6]William Glasser, *Mental Health or Mental Illness?* (New York, 1970), p. 1.

be accomplished by holding up before each counselee no less a goal than God's standard, namely "the fulness of Christ" (Ephesians 4:13b). God is satisfied with nothing less than the goal of becoming like Him. But the only way that one can know what Christ is like is through the Scriptures.

(3) Next, a biblical plan of action depends upon biblical methods. Here is where many Christians founder. They can agree upon the need for biblical goals and objectives, "but," say they, "why can't we use any method that achieves the goal? If Rogerian, Freudian, or Skinnerian methods are helpful in making a counselee more like Christ, then we shall use them."

In these post-Watergate days, it would seem superfluous to stress the fact that good ends do not justify questionable means. As a matter of fact, only means biblically justifiable can bring about biblical ends. Humanistic means cannot be employed in achieving Christian maturity. Freud knew nothing of means that would lead to Christlikeness. Rogerian methodology does not bring holiness. Skinnerian manipulation does not produce the fruit of the Spirit. Precisely because it is *His* fruit, the Holy Spirit's methods of fruit growing must be sought, found and used. And these can be found only in the Spirit's Book, the Bible.

I do not wish to labor this vital point, as I have dealt with it elsewhere in depth.[7] Instead, let me point out that it can only be with grave concern, therefore, that today we see the wholesale uncritical adoption of pagan methodologies by genuine Christians, who doubtless mean well and who hope thereby to reach the same goals as we. Yet, they are currently busily introducing (to the great injury of Christ's church) the methods of Encounter and Group Therapy, of Transactional Analysis, of Gestalt Therapy and of Behaviorism, just as they formerly uncritically brought Freudianism and Rogerianism into the church. We must resist this tendency to believe that means are unimportant. The ark of God must be borne on poles; it cannot be transported by oxcart.

(4) Finally, let me simply mention the fact that a biblical plan of

---

[7]Jay E. Adams, *The Christian Counselor's Manual,* pp. 5-8. Cf. also Jay E. Adams, *What About Nouthetic Counseling?* pp.73-75.

219

action, though biblical in every other respect, may fail because it was sought and carried out from non-biblical motives. Biblical counselors will always be concerned about the motives of their counselees.

The area of motive is planted thickly with thorny questions. I shall mention but one. While, on the one hand, counselors must inquire about and discuss motives, on the other hand they are incapable of judging motives, for it is God alone who judges the "heart and the reins." Man looks only on the outward appearance. Having done their best to explain the proper biblical motivation behind the proposed plan of action, and having stressed the need for sincerity and warned against proceeding from lesser motivation, the counselor must prayerfully leave the outcome to God.[8]

Let us take an example. Pat, a professing Christian, comes highly motivated to win back her husband, who has just left home and declares that he will never return. She begs, "I'll do anything to get Larry back! Just tell me what to do, please." The alert counselor will be wary of her *motives,* as well as her *objectives.* And if her words may be taken literally, when she says "I'll do anything . . . ," then he knows also that her strong desire would lead her to adopt biblical or non-biblical *methods* for achieving her end. He will soon bring the discussion around to goals and motives. He will say something like this: "Pat, as a Christian your goal must be to please God, regardless of the consequences. You must be willing to lose Larry if in the providence of God that should be the outcome. You cannot do what the Bible says simply as a technique or gimmick to get him back. It is true that if anything will bring Larry home again, it will be Christian behavior on your part, but you cannot make the changes that you must make primarily for that reason. You must be clear in your own mind that what God requires of you at this time must be done— *whether Larry returns or not.* You must do it out of genuine repentance and out of faith and love for God; because *He* says that this is what you must do. If Larry returns, then your secondary hope will be realized; but even if he doesn't, when your primary hope has been to please God, you will not be disappointed. Not only will you be what God wants you to be, but in His mercy you will realize His

---

[8]Not implying, of course, that ultimately motivation may not become known through life styles, and may even lead to church discipline: "By their fruit you will know them."

blessing to carry you through the midst of the trial. In no other way can you face the two possible outcomes with peace and assurance."

Counselees, then, should be instructed that at bottom the only scriptural motive for action is to please God. This leads very naturally to the next consideration.

CHAPTER VI
Working the Plan

Commitment to Scriptural Action by the Counselee

This is the fifth factor in the use of the Scriptures in counseling. Noble goals and motives, correct plans and procedures, while essential to any ensuing scriptural action on the part of the counselee, can never be substituted for it. He must become convicted by the Scriptures to make a commitment to take this biblical course of action.

Commitment to the biblical plan of action is, of course, altogether essential, for unless the counselee actually does what God requires, all else will have been in vain. Exposition, conviction of sin, understanding and even belief that this plan is biblical and would succeed—all will have been useless if he does not in fact follow it. "Why wouldn't he do so if he saw all of that?" you may wonder. Well, listen to four common responses with which every counselor is familiar:

"I can't."

"I won't."

"It would be too embarrassing."

"I'm afraid."

When a counselee has confessed his sin of gossip to God and sought forgiveness, he may be faced with the need to seek forgiveness from the persons about whom he spread the gossip. Any one of the four above replies may be forthcoming. The counselor must be prepared to meet each, scripturally of course.

"I can't" may be interpreted in at least two ways: (1) it would be too hard; (2) I don't know how to do it. The latter response may be handled in a number of ways. For instance, by using a scriptural model ("Here is how Paul faced trouble. Let's look at Philippians 1"); the concreteness needed can be emphasized by the selection of a concrete passage. Or the counselor may take the principle and apply it directly in a concrete fashion: "Since you must not let the sun go down on your anger, it will be necessary for you to see Brad right away."

If by "can't" he means, "It would be too hard" or "I simply don't have what it takes," the counselor can give strong assurance from the Scriptures that God never calls upon His children to do that which they cannot do by His strength. Using the line of argument from I Corinthians 10:13 suggested in my pamphlet, *Christ and Your Problems,* he can both give hope and press the counselee's responsibility upon him. Sometimes "I can't" at first seems to mean "It would be too hard," but in reality turns out to mean "I don't know how." That, naturally, can be a good reason for thinking the task is too hard. The counselor should be alert to all of the possibilities.

But suppose the response is "I won't." Here again at least two possibilities exist. Often, recalcitrant counselees, because of the perverseness of sinful human nature, balk just before they give in. Automobile salesmen call this the kicking-the-tires routine. Counselors will encounter it frequently enough to become aware of it. Firm continued insistence upon the biblical principle, leaving the counselee with the responsibility to do as God requires after prayer for help, often will be rewarded. Once the Word of God has been presented clearly and conviction is present, resistance soon may break down. The counselee will report that between the sessions he did what he had intended not to do—and frequently—on the very next day.

"I won't," however, may be indicative of a more serious problem. Actual rebellious resistance may lie behind the reply. In such cases, after a reasonable amount of time to determine whether, in fact, the problem is rebellion or some other, if the counselor is convinced upon sufficient grounds that there is an unwillingness to accept the authority of Jesus Christ in the Scriptures, he must warn the counselee (and be prepared to back up the warning if necessary) that such rebellion against Christ can lead only to church discipline. If adequate warning is met with a stiff-necked response, the actual process of discipline must be instituted, hopefully leading at length to repentance and the fruits appropriate to repentance, but if not, revealing what can only be interpreted by the church as such serious rejection of the authority of Christ as to force the elders of the congregation to expel him for this and to look on him "as a heathen and a publican."

The response, "It would be too embarrassing," must be met with gentle firmness. "Of course, it will be embarrassing; I did not say that it would be easy or pleasant," the counselor may reply. He may continue, "Sin always leads to embarrassment—now or later. How much better to deal with it now; remove the offending thorn and be over and done with it. Then you will not have to go on with the threat of embarrassment and the guilt of your sin continually before you." To reinforce this biblical principle, the counselor may refer to Psalm 32, which David wrote in order to encourage Christians to deal with sin quickly. In it he explained his own misery occasioned by delay. Concluding the Psalm he warns not to be stubborn like the horse or mule that must be dragged to confession.

"I'm afraid," may call for much the same approach, but, if the fear is severe or complicated, may also demand a challenge to Christian courage that goes beyond. A reminder that Christians have not been given "a spirit of timidity, but of power and love and discipline" (II Timothy 1:7) will need to be given: "The Holy Spirit will give you power to overcome your fear through love and discipline." John says, "Mature love casts out fear" (I John 4:18). "You must show your love for God by doing what He requires in spite of your fears. Prayerfully discipline yourself to do this task by submitting closely to the Word of God, and you will be able to overcome the most fearful problem, no matter what it may be. Once you have torn yourself away from your feeling of fear to obey God, you will discover that the fear will lessen or disappear altogether, since a large part of fear is the fear of experiencing the feeling of fear itself."[1]

---

[1] Indeed, when one out of love for God and/or neighbor does what the Scriptures require *regardless of the consequences* ("If I panic, I panic. It will be rough, but I'll survive."), for the first time he begins to free himself of fear. Fearing fear brings fear. It is like a self-fulfilling prophecy. Not trying to stop the fear experience stops it.

When a counselee commits himself to a biblical plan of action, it may be well for the counselor to check out carefully precisely what the counselee intends to do and how. If, for instance, he is to seek forgiveness from another, it might be well to ask the counselee to tell him in a dry run just about what he will say and how. If he will do so in a letter, then the counselee might be encouraged to bring in a rough draft for evaluation before writing and mailing the final copy. Suggestions for saying it differently or changing a phrase or two in the letter may make a great difference.

The counselor will be aware of possible pitfalls and warn against these. The counselee may plan to say, "Joe, I came to apologize for my nasty response toward you when you pulled that dirty financial deal on me." The counselor will point out that this will not do, for the counselee is mixing accusations with apology. He will help him to see that first he must remove the log from his own eye, and that only after that matter is dealt with and forgiveness has been received can the other question be raised separately at a subsequent point. Moreover, the counselor will note that emotionally-laden words like "dirty deal" serve only to incite wrath rather than bring about reconciliation.

And finally, when commitments to hard tasks are made, it is wise frequently (especially when the counselee is reluctant or afraid) to ask him to suggest and agree upon an early date when he plans to do it. Abraham "arose early" to sacrifice his son Isaac. This was probably the most unpleasant task to which he had ever been called. So . . . he got right to it, as soon as possible. The longer a difficult assignment is delayed, the more likely we are to worry about it, making the task seem all the more formidable and finding that we are less able to comply.

In conclusion, then, the counselee must be helped to formulate and to carry out a biblical plan of action. But even when he does, he may not then say to God, "I'm OK; You're OK," for, as we shall see in the next chapter, all of the credit, all of the glory, all of the honor must go to neither the counselee nor the counselor, but to the Spirit of the living God, who by His Word and power has *at every point* been the One who enabled the counseling to reach a successful end.

CHAPTER VII
The Spirit and the Scriptures

We have seen how the Scriptures must permeate Christian counseling from start to finish. The counselee's problem can be understood christianly only as it is evaluated biblically. The solution to his problem, likewise, must be found in the Scriptures. How the latter is applied to the former, how a concrete plan of action may be formulated and carried out—all of these steps in counseling are dependent upon the Scriptures.

When a Christian comes to his pastor for help, therefore, he should expect him to offer help, like the Levite, from the Scriptures. God Himself said: "For the lips of a priest should keep knowledge, and men should seek the law from his mouth, because he is the messenger of the Lord of hosts" (Malachi 2:7; cf. also Nehemiah 8:7-9). There should be no question, then, for either the counselee or the counselor over whether the counsel that the Lord's messenger gives should be scriptural counsel. To be obedient to God, the New Testament minister can do no less than his Old Testament predecessor.

But there is another angle from which this matter may be approached. The reason why Christian counseling depends so heavily upon the Scriptures at every point is because the Scriptures are the peculiar product of the Counselor Himself. When I say that the Counselor Himself is the Author of the Scriptures, I refer, of course, not to the human counselor, but to the Holy Spirit, who is called by John "the paraclete" (counselor) and by Isaiah "the Spirit of Counsel" (Isaiah 11:2). He is the Spirit by whom God breathed out His Words in written form in the Scriptures, the One who patiently spent long years bearing along men of God that by His holy superintendence they might write inerrant counsel. It should be no surprise, then, to find that He works through the Bible when

226

carrying out His paracletic functions. This, as a matter of fact, is precisely what Paul asserted in Romans 15:4 when he explained: "For whatever was written in earlier times was written for our instruction, that through perseverance and the *paraclesis* of the Scriptures we might have hope." Just a few verses later (v. 13) he added: "Now may the God of hope fill you with all joy and peace in believing, that you may abound in hope by the power of the Spirit." Hope, Paul at first says, comes from the Scriptures, but then he claims that hope comes from the Holy Spirit. There is no contradiction. Paul has no difficulty in sometimes identifying the source of this paracletic work as the Spirit and at other times as the Scriptures since it is *by means of the Scriptures* that the Spirit counsels.

The interchange of such terminology in speaking of books and authors is well known even among ourselves. We may say with equal ease and without occasioning the slightest misunderstanding, "The source of the quotation is C. S. Lewis" or "The source is *The Lion, the Witch and the Wardrobe*." Thus, in a similar sense, but with further qualification respecting the human agency that was involved in the writing of the Bible, an Old Testament quotation may be introduced with the words "The Holy Spirit, by the mouth of our father David, said . . . ." (Acts 4:25; cf. also Acts 1:16; Hebrews 3:7).

So, to begin with, we must be aware of the fact that the counsel of the Holy Spirit is closely connected with the Scriptures. Indeed, that counsel is identical with, and found only in, the pages of the Bible. That is why Paul can speak of the *paraclesis* (or counsel) of the Scriptures.

Recognition of this identification is fundamental to all Christian counseling. The fact should influence both the counselor and the counselee to a significant degree. The attitude of the counselor must be confidence and relief: "I do not have to *counsel alone;* when I counsel biblically, I use divine truth and the Holy Spirit has promised to work through my counseling." On the other side of the desk, the counselee also may rejoice in the fact that he does not have to *change alone;* indeed he knows that he cannot. When he walks in God's will, it is because he walks "in (or by) the Spirit"; when he begins to love, show self-control, enjoy peace, and so forth, he acknowledges that he did not produce these blessings himself. With

Paul he calls them the "fruit (i.e., the product) of the Spirit." Both must come to see what, in Ezekiel's prophecy, points to the central fact: "I will put my Spirit within you and cause you to *walk in my statutes*" (Ezekiel 36:27). Thus He promises to enable Christians to *learn* and to *live* according to God's revealed will.

As a matter of fact, it is the Holy Spirit who accomplishes each of these things for both the counselor and the counselee:

1. He illuminates the believer's mind so that he can interpret the Scriptures, giving ability to understand and wisdom to know how to live according to the will of God. This He does as *the Spirit of truth* (John 14:17; 15:26; 16:13) *and of wisdom* (Isa. 11:2; I Cor. 2:13).

2. He gives power both to will and to do that will of God whenever believers step out by faith in obedience to scriptural injunctions (Ezek. 36:27). This He does as *the Spirit of holiness* (Rom. 1:4).

The Spirit, then, gives power to *know* and power to *do*. This twofold work of the Spirit is vital, for the counselor must *know* the truth of God in order to counsel and, as we have seen, he must have courage to *say and do* as God wishes in spite of opposition or strong temptations to veer from the scriptural course. Likewise, the counselee needs to *learn* of his condition and what God requires him to do about it; he then needs strength and patience to *effect* the needed changes. The Spirit, through His Word, provides all that is required to meet these needs. In scriptural counseling the Spirit works—as He wills—on both sides of the counseling desk; He comes at the problem from each end; He works in the counselor and in the counselee.

Let us now reconsider one or two of the five factors mentioned previously to see how the Holy Spirit brings each of these into play in counseling by means of the Scriptures. Those factors were:

1. A biblical understanding of the counselee's problem, stemming from . . .
2. A clear recognition of the Holy Spirit's purpose in scriptural passages appropriate to both the problem and the solution, and . . .
3. A meeting of man's problem and God's full solution in counseling, according to . . .
4. The formulation of a biblical plan of action, leading toward . . .
5. Commitment to scriptural action by the counselee.

Consider, for example, the first factor: *A biblical understanding of the counselee's problem*. It is the work of the Holy Spirit to bring conviction of sin (John 16:8); it is also the function of the Scriptures to do so (Ja. 2:9: "convicted by the law as a transgressor"). Again, there is no contradiction: the Holy Spirit does His convicting work *by means of* the Scriptures. In his second letter to young Timothy, Paul directs him to "preach the Word" (II Tim. 4:2). In explanation he continues: "reprove, rebuke, exhort." The word "reprove" actually is the term that elsewhere is translated "convict." In Titus 1:9, Paul wrote " . . . holding fast the faithful word which is in accordance with the teaching, that he may be able . . . to convict"; and in Titus 2:15, he urged, "These things speak and exhort and convict with all authority." Plainly, in these passages concerning "conviction," it is not Timothy or Titus who "convicts"; it is the Holy Spirit. But it is equally evident that He uses the human preacher or counselor as His agent and the Scriptures as the means for bringing about conviction.

There can be no true understanding of a problem in living, then, unless the Holy Spirit enables the counselee to see himself in that Word as in a mirror and, thereby, convicts him of his sin. Every such problem is plainly described (not projected) there. The Holy Spirit enables the counselee to see sin as sin—as rebellion against God by the transgression of His law. But since behavior can be identified as sin only when evaluated by God's standard, counselors must employ the Scriptures if they would seek to bring counselees to an understanding of the true nature of their problems, and if they would have them to be motivated to do as God says. As Paul put it, "I would not have come to know sin except through the law" (Roman 7:7). Therefore, all modern attempts to understand man's problem fail, for while sin brings about alienation or estrangement, it cannot be *equated* with alienation or estrangement. While sin leads to poor patterns of learning and maladaptation, it cannot be *equated* with failure to learn or adapt. While sin disorients one toward life, that is not its essential feature. Problems in living can be understood properly only when the basic dimension of sin as rebellion against God through lawlessness is seen in them; and there is absolutely no reason to expect this to happen unless the Holy Spirit enables one to understand his problem in the light of the Scriptures. Whenever the Spirit gives such understanding, it leads to conviction.

Thus, it is accurate to say that when a Christian counselee has a biblical understanding of his problem, he is not merely able to tag it or to label it scripturally; rather, for him to understand the problem biblically is for him to become convicted over the fact that fundamentally his problem is with God. Such conviction comes only from the Holy Spirit working by His Word.

But we have seen that the Holy Spirit not only helps the counselee, He also helps the counselor. In bringing counsel to His church, the Holy Spirit has chosen to work through those in whom the Word of Christ "dwells richly" (Col. 3:16), or as Paul noted elsewhere: by those who are filled with all knowledge and able to confront one another nouthetically" (Rom. 15:14). Such knowledge and wisdom come, as I Corinthians 2 makes clear, from the Holy Spirit. So from each side of the counseling context, both the counselor's scriptural knowledge and wisdom, through which the Holy Spirit prepares him to give biblical counsel, and the counselee's biblical understanding of the problem leading to conviction of sin and repentance, are the result of the work of the Holy Spirit using the Scriptures. Neither counselor nor counselee can take credit for anything productive that comes from counseling; it is always the "fruit of the Spirit."

Thus, the Holy Spirit always must be acknowledged to be the Spirit of counsel, the Spirit of truth, the Spirit of wisdom, and the Spirit of holiness. The use of the genitive in each of these descriptions of the Spirit shows Him to be the *source* of these blessings. All knowledge of God and of what His children may do to please Him is the result of the Spirit's bringing knowledge and understanding with conviction through His Word.

CHAPTER VIII
The Spiritual Struggle in Counseling

But it is not enough to know God's Word, to be convicted of sin and to repent. How does scriptural counseling prevent sinful behavior and attitudes for the future? The greatest problem with which Christians struggle is in obeying the directive: "The things you have learned and received and heard and seen in me, practice these things; and the God of peace shall be with you" (Phil. 4:9). It is one thing to hear the truth, to know the truth, to see it in practice—and even to be convicted about one's failures and what God wants done to meet them—it is quite another to "walk" in the truth." How does the Spirit "cause" one to "walk" in God's "statutes" (Ezek. 36:27) To put it another way, how can the struggle against the "desire of the flesh" mentioned in Galatians 5:16 be waged successfully? This is the fundamental problem of counseling—to effect change that sticks. A brief consideration of the passage in Galatians may help.

First, notice the "flesh sets its desire *against* the Spirit and the Spirit against the flesh" (v. 17). The two, Paul continues, are "in opposition to one another." And, note, it is because of this fleshly opposition that "you may not do the things that you please" (v. 17). The "things that you please," here, refers to those things that Christians, *as Christians* wish to do to please God.

At least three questions that are pertinent to counseling leap from the text:

(1) What is the "flesh" mentioned in these verses?
(2) Generally, how may one overcome the desire of the flesh?
(3) Specifically, how is this accomplished in the counseling context?

The First Question

What is "flesh?" Much study has been given to the question of Paul's use of the term "flesh." Beyond the ordinary uses of this word

231

in the writings of Paul and other authors, it is well known that there is a peculiar Pauline usage that occurs primarily (though not exclusively; cf. Rom. 13:14; Eph. 2:3) in these verses in Galatians and in Romans, chapters 7-8. In each of these passages, flesh is set in antithesis to something else. A study of the term in such antithetical usage yields the following information. On the one hand, "flesh" is set in contrast to the *Spirit,* to the new *mind* given by Christ and to the *inner man.* On the other hand, "flesh" is identified with the *old man,* the *body of sin,* the *mortal body,* the *members of the body,* the *body of this death,* the *deeds of the body,* the *former manner of life, sin that indwells, sin in the members,* and *evil that is present in me.*

One thing seems evident; in the struggle the opposing forces are clearly identified. Let us consider the enemies. Against the flesh are arrayed the Spirit (i.e., the Holy Spirit) and the Christian, who in Christ has a new *mind* and who in his *inner man,* (i.e., in his deepest desires) wishes to please God and to overthrow the flesh. The struggle is carried on within the believer. But the deeds of the flesh are also something for which the believer is responsible. These are the fulfillment of the desire of the flesh. The "desire of the flesh," or the "evil that is present in me," or the "sin in my members," however, can be counteracted rather than carried into effect (Gal. 5:16) so that "the desire of the flesh" need not issue in "the deeds of the flesh."

Did Paul believe in a Greek dualism in which the fleshly body was set over against the soul, the former being evil and the latter holy? Is that what we are confronted with here? Absolutely not. Christianity came into a Greek world with a message that scandalized the Greeks precisely because Christian preachers taught that the body was not essentially evil but good and that, indeed, it would be fully redeemed at the resurrection. The incarnation of Christ forever puts the lie to all Greek or Gnostic notions that there is a body/soul, evil/good cleavage. Christian anthropology always has resisted any such dualistic ideas.

But because some theologians (rightly) feared dualistic notions in which the body might be declared to be evil *per se,* they (wrongly) shied away from the obvious import of Paul's words when he spoke of sin in the flesh. "Flesh" in such passages, they contended, must refer to something other than the fleshly body. Hence, by some the word was conveniently equated with "self"; by others it was said to be used in a purely "ethical" sense. Whichever way one went, he always was careful to strip away from the term any direct corporeal reference.

One can only laud the desire to defeat dualism that led to these interpretations, but the desire grew out of fear and, alas, led to another problem—how could the "flesh" be dealt with when it was merely an ethical concept or when it represented a self which was not identical to the "inner man" or the "mind" of the believer? The battle too often became an abstract concept that was out of reach rather than the crucial life factor with which every believer must grapple.

Of great significance in this discussion is the fact that, in spite of everything, *flesh* does have as its primary referent the corporeal. That fundamental feature cannot be removed so facilely. Look, for instance, at its synonyms and associations: the *body* of sin, the mortal *body,* the *members* of the *body,* the deeds of the *body,* the *body* of this death, sin in the *members* (of the *body*), and so forth. Surely, in such company as it keeps, "flesh," even here, *must* be understood to refer to the corporeal unless there are stronger reasons, than to date have been forthcoming, to divest it of such content. Note also that flesh is contrasted with the *inner man.* While the term *outer man* is not used, it clearly is implied.[1] What is the contrast to *inner man* if it is not the body?

Does that not leave us with a dualism then? No, not at all; rather it presents us with an antithesis and an antagonism. That such an antithesis is in view in Galatians 5 and in Romans 6-8 everyone agrees. There is an antithesis on the one hand, between the Spirit and the inner man that He is renewing, and on the other hand, the believer's body *as it is still wrongly habituated.*[2]

"Flesh" as Paul uses it in a negative sense, then, means just that: a body habituated to the ways of the world rather than to the ways of God. The idea of bodily habituation appears frequently in the pertinent contexts. The *flesh* is the "former manner of life" or "previous habits" also referred to as "the old man" in Ephesians 4:22. It is "the old man with his *practices*" in Colossians 3:9.[3] It is the

---

[1]And, in Rom. 2:28 the phrase "outward in the flesh" does occur.
[2]Including the brain.
[3]Note, *praxis,* a manner, practice, or way of life, is used; not merely *ergon,* a deed.

sinful ways that have been programmed and patterned into life by our sinful natures through continuous yielding of the "members" of the body to sin (Rom. 6:13,19). Before salvation, the Christian was a willing slave who offered the members of his body as instruments to carry out the wishes of his master, sin. Now, with the same willingness, he must learn to yield the members of his body to God.

The power of habit is great. It is not easy to please God in a body that is still in part habituated to sin. Though he may wish inwardly to cease lying, to control his tongue, to stop losing his temper, or to eliminate scores of other vices, the believer finds that the battle against the habituated desires of the body is hard. There are victories, but they do not come easily. Indeed, in his own strength he will fail to win the struggle. But that is not the dismal conclusion of the matter, for Paul both in Galatians and in Romans plainly points to the way to victory. And this fact leads us to a consideration of the next point.

The Second Question

Generally speaking, how may one overcome the desire of the flesh? Paul's answer is explicit: "Walk by the Spirit, and you will not carry out the desire of the flesh" (Gal. 5:16). Two verses later (v. 18) he speaks of this walk as Spirit "led." Moreover, in Romans 8:13-14, he affirms: "If you are living according to the flesh, you must die; but if by the Spirit you are putting to death the deeds of the body you will live. For all who are being led by the Spirit of God, these are the sons of God."

The Scriptures are unequivocal: it is the Spirit of God who, in opposition to the flesh, leads the believer into a new way of life. Christian counseling therefore requires the Spirit's leading work. We must consider this leading in some detail, however, for again leading is not what it often (superficially) has been claimed to be.

What is the leading of the Spirit, and how does it take place? The answer to that question is: it is a leading into the new ways of the new life, into the paths of righteousness; it is leading that occurs in obedience to the Scriptures. It is the same as Ezekiel's "causing to walk" in God's "statutes."

When a counselee says, "But I don't feel led . . . ," the counselor must point out to him that in so using such a phrase he is not speaking biblically, for there are only two passages in which the leading of the Spirit is mentioned (Rom. 8:1-15; Gal. 5:16-18), and in neither of these does leading have anything to do with guidance in decision making through feelings. Rather, in these passages the Christian is identified as one who is led by the Spirit into a new life pleasing to God. The stress in this leading is upon the power that He provides to produce a new *way* of life. For instance, in Romans 8 the preceding thirteen verses pertain to the Christian life, which is described as a "walk according to the Spirit" (v. 4), a "mind set on the Spirit" (v. 6), "being in the Spirit" (v. 9) and "living" according to the Spirit (v. 12). Indeed, being Spirit "led" is closely connected with "putting to death the deeds of the body by the Spirit" (v. 13). A son of God, then, is one who, by the shepherdly work of the Spirit, is led in the paths of righteousness. He is one who is being led to walk in new ways by putting to death the sinful habit practices of the old man, and who in their place, is producing the fruit of the Spirit. In short, what Paul says is that you can tell who is a believer by observing the process of sanctification at work within him. You know the Spirit is present in those in whom His work is evident.

In Galatians 5:16, Paul commands, "Walk by the Spirit and you will not carry out the desire of the flesh." It is the Spirit who effectively enables the believer to keep the desire of the flesh (that is, the sinful responses that the body is programmed, and therefore desires, or finds easy, to express) from issuing into the "deeds of the flesh." This he does by leading him into new habit patterns appropriate to the new walk of a child of God. Another way to put it is to say that the believer is led to produce the "fruit of the Spirit."

The process of sanctification is always in view when Paul writes of the Spirit leading. There is not the slightest idea of special revelation, impressions and feelings or any other subjective method of guidance under consideration. Rather, in both passages the power of the Spirit that enables the believer to overcome the desire of the flesh and to learn new patterns of life is the subject of His leading. This fact moves us to the consideration of the third question.

The Third Question

Specifically, how does the Spirit enable the believer to win battles with the flesh? The answer to this lies in a matter vital to all counseling that only can be mentioned here, but is developed fully elsewhere.[4] The child's joke:

Question: When is a door not a door?
Answer: When it is ajar.

may be devoid of humor but serves well as a model for an important biblical principle that is basic to Christian counseling. Think of the joke this way:

Question: When is a door not a door?
Answer: When it has become *something else*.

What the paradigm shows is that change in counseling is not a single, but rather a two-factored process. That means that the Spirit deals with the flesh by enabling the believer to do two things.

Let's look at an example or two. A counselee has a problem overcoming habits of lying. Since becoming a Christian, he knows that lying displeases God, and he wants to stop. Yet, in spite of good intentions and prayerful effort, he discovers that whenever heavy pressures are exerted upon him, he "automatically" lies. Sometimes the lies are out of his mouth before he even recognizes that he has uttered them. The body has been programmed by long-standing practice to lie as an escape from such stresses and—faithful to all past training—thus it responds. The flesh has won again. What can be done to deal with the flesh?

Take another example. Perhaps the counselee is a Christian who has a record of stealing. He, too, finds that the temporary cessation of his former practices is not sufficient to erase the pattern itself. How does he overcome the desire of the flesh? What of drug addicts, drunkards, homosexual sinners, and a host of others who have found that it is not easy simply to quit, even when one has good intentions? How can they be helped?

The Christian counselor remembers the model:

Question: When is a thief not a thief?
When is a liar not a liar?

---

[4]Jay Adams, *The Christian Counselor's Manual*, chaps. 14-15.

Is the answer: "When he stops stealing?" or "When he stops lying?" No! That is a faulty, unbiblical single-factored answer that is bound to lead to failure. Instead, the biblical counselor remembers Ephesians 4 and Colossians 3, in which Paul insists that the "former manner of life" and the "practices" of the old man can be changed only by putting on *as well as* putting off. When a liar tries to stop lying, he is only doing part of what God requires. A liar who stops lying is still a liar who (at the moment) happens not to be lying; a thief who stops stealing is simply a thief who is between jobs.

Well, then, when is a liar not a liar; when is a thief not a thief? Answer: "When he has become something else." Specifically, what? Paul wrote: "Therefore, laying aside falsehood, speak truth each one of you with his neighbor, for we are members of one another" (Ephesians 4:25). Well, then,

Question: When is a liar not a liar?
Answer: When he has become a truth-teller—and not before.

He also wrote: "Let him who steals steal no longer; but rather let him labor, performing with his own hands what is good, in order that he may have something to share with him who has need" (Ephesians 4:28). So, then,

Question: When is a thief not a thief?
Answer: When he has become a steady worker who shares with those in need.

And so it goes.

The Spirit leads not only *out of* but also *into*; by His power the believer can learn to resist the desire of the flesh and put to death the "deeds of the body" (Roman 8:13), and in its place to produce the fruit of the Spirit. He reprograms him for righteousness. To the extent that this fruit is present the flesh cannot prevail, for it has been preempted by new patterns. After cataloging the fruit of the Spirit, Paul asserts: "Against such things there is no law." The works of the flesh are condemned by the Law; it is against the flesh. But the Spirit's fruit is the fulfillment of the Law.

Thus, the Christian counselor aims at effecting change that is permanent; change in which new ways replace old ones. Apart from the two-factored, biblical change just described, counselees will remain caught in the kiss-and-make-up syndrome. He knows that such change alone is adequate because God says so. Moreover, he knows that apart from the Scriptures this sort of change is not possible, for it is in the Scriptures alone that he can find God's alternatives to the old sinful patterns. He will not rest, therefore, until God's new ways have been introduced into the counselee's life and have begun to replace the old ones.

These changes, note, involve *biblical alternatives.* In II Timothy 3, mentioned at the outset, you will recall that Paul listed four uses that the Scriptures play in a believer's life: they teach, they convict, they correct, and . . . they *train in righteousness.* Not only do they tell us what God requires, how we have failed and what we can do to get right with God again; they also provide all that is necessary to enable us to learn how to live a new way of life that glorifies God. We do not have to be everlastingly working on the same problem. By God's grace we can make progress; we can move on to the next.

From start to finish, counseling is the work of the Spirit of God. He provides the direction and He provides the power. The ways and means, as well as the goals, equally are presented in the Scriptures. The Spirit of God works through His Word to change men. May He thus work through you as you minister that Word in Christ's Name!

CHAPTER IX
The Application of the Scriptures
to Specific Problems

In this chapter I should like further to unpack some of the principles enunciated earlier. While I hope that, in general, I have illustrated the practical use of the Scriptures throughout fully enough to be clear, nevertheless, since there is so much poor use of Scriptures it seems advisable to demonstrate the process once again in a few more instances. Briefly, therefore, I shall take up some specific situations and try to show how the Scriptures may be used in meeting concrete problems associated with each.

In order to do so, I shall turn to several of the cases set forth in *The Christian Counselor's Casebook*[1] (q.v.) and attempt to apply the foregoing principles and practices to them. I shall not discuss these cases in full, but shall focus merely upon one aspect of them—how the counselor might have used the Scriptures at some point or points in each case.

Now, first let us turn to a case in which it should be clear that the influence of the Scriptures upon the counselor must be all-determinative. In this case, you will notice that there are several problems. However, I should like to isolate but one.

"The Pistol Is at My Head"

Your telephone rings one morning at one o'clock, and you find yourself speaking with Mary, a middle-aged married woman, the mother of two teenagers, who, together with her family, is a member of your congregation. You have noticed

---

[1]Jay Adams, *The Christian Counselor's Casebook* (Presbyterian & Reformed Pub. Co., Nutley: 1974). This study book contains 140 cases in workbook form.

that she has missed services recently, but you had no other indication of any difficulty. However, there is no doubt in your mind as you listen to her now that she has been drinking heavily, and worse yet, she is threatening to commit suicide. You talk, trying to get the story. Her response to your questions about how she expects to take her life is both swift and frightening: "The pistol is at my head as I speak." You urge Mary to talk over her problem, assuring her that the situation indeed is serious and should get immediate attention. But, she refuses to tell you anything more unless you swear never to reveal to anyone what she tells you.   (Case I - 1, pp.2,3)

Obviously, this is not a full counseling situation. Indeed, it is essential for the pastor not to try to counsel under such conditions. In role playing this case trainees often attempt to counsel over the phone. That is exactly the wrong thing to do. Mary is drunk; and the counselor must recognize that it is virtually impossible to counsel her while she is intoxicated. Secondly, she is making demands which must be overcome before it is possible to do effective counseling— she wants a commitment to absolute silence. Thirdly, the immediate crisis issue is to get her to put down the gun; nothing else. The counselor should not allow himself to be moved away from that fact. It is central.

I shall not go into all of the factors that might indicate that this is a precounseling rather than a counseling situation, nor shall I discuss other interesting aspects of the case. All that I wish to note here is that the Scriptures must control the counselor at every point. In this instance, unless the counselor has a scriptural orientation, it is likely that he will go astray. I am referring specifically to the demand for confidentiality. The Christian counselor, in contrast to others, does not accept the premise that all information must be kept confidential; from time to time he may have to warn various counselees that what they are about to reveal he may not be able to keep in confidence. For example, he may not accept privileged information in confidence (for more on this, see *The Christian Counselor's Manual*[2]). And in this situation, he again is aware of the

[2]Pp. 269, 270.

direct bearing of the Bible upon Mary's request. Passages like Proverbs 12:13 and 20:25, that condemn rash vows, should make him wary of acceding to her request and giving his word to Mary. If she has committed an illegal act that should be revealed, he must for her sake, as well as for the welfare of society be free to reveal it if sufficient encouragement over a period of time does not induce her to do so herself. I shall not discuss how the counselor may go about dealing with Mary's demand; obviously there are several things that he may do. But the crucial fact is that in meeting the demand he must think *scripturally*. Thus his approach will take either the route of avoiding the issue entirely, if possible (it is difficult to reason with a drunk), or of postponement till a later point. (He may say: "Mary, you can trust me to do what the Bible tells me to do," or "Mary, this is too important a matter to discuss on the phone; I'm coming over. I'll talk to you about it then," etc.) Thus, concern for scriptural fidelity motivates him even in a time of extreme crisis. Indeed, any lesser orientation might open him to every sort of dangerous and God-dishonoring practice. It is a heavy reliance upon the Scriptures that carries the counselor through crises successfully. It is hard to act in a crisis apart from structure and well-defined principle.

"I Want to Punch Her"

"Yes, this is probably the heart of it," Louise says to the counselor. "My heart *is* filled with bitterness toward Mildred."

"Now has your friend done something to elicit this reaction?" the counselor inquires.

"Well, she always butts her nose into our family affairs. We've been having some trouble with Jeff, our 17-year-old son. And we've been seeking guidance from the Lord. But Mildred seems to think that *she* has *all* the answers. She's always saying, you shouldn't do this, you shouldn't do that, you'd better do this, you'd better do that, and on and on. Sometimes I just feel like screaming. I almost want to punch her at times! She makes me *so* mad!"

"Yes, I can see that. I know that your reaction is a natural one. Most parents are defensive when they are criticized by outsiders. But you have to see something, Louise. Letting the bitterness build up is unhealthy for you. You should try to rid yourself of it. As you have already found out, it only results in increasing your frustration."

(Case II - 14, pp. 150,151)

This case is a good example of the sort of situation in which the counselor failed because he took less than a scriptural approach to the problem. The counselor encourages Louise to talk negatively about Mildred behind her back in direct violation of Ephesians 4:31, which forbids slanderous talk, and James 4:11 which commands: "Do not speak against *(katalaleo,* which means to speak negatively against someone behind his back) a brother, brethren." Moreover, this counselor calls sinful behavior "natural" (in a good sense), thus excusing her sin, and speaks humanistically only of the consequences of her behavior for herself (God's concerns are ignored). Also, he encourages blameshifting (he indicates that Louise's behavior is the direct result of Mildred's failures). Clearly, this pastor either does not have a biblical orientation at all or he has accommodated himself to a psychological orientation.

The biblical pastor, keeping the previously mentioned passages in mind, as a guide for his own approach, might do well to introduce Romans 12:14-21 into the counseling session as a base for helping Louise to solve her problems biblically. Without spelling out the way in which the pastor might have confronted Louise (see information in *The Christian Counselor's Manual* for this), it should be evident that this portion of the Scriptures is pertinent to the problem at hand. In that passage, Paul sorts out the responsibilities ("so far as it depends upon you" v. 18), puts an end to excuses and allows for no retaliation (vv. 18-20), prohibits blameshifting, ("do not be overcome by evil" v. 21), and again and again insists that in spite of the poor behavior of others God holds the believer responsible for returning good and evil (vv. 14, 17, 20, 21). The counselor in the *Casebook* failed because he viewed the problem in the same way that Louise did. He was not coming to the problem with the "Word of Christ dwelling richly within" (Colossians 3:16). Because his viewpoint was as unscriptural as hers, he could not help her. Louise needed to be confronted with an antithetical, godly viewpoint; the last thing that she needed was more of the same. True empathy does not necessitate agreement of viewpoint, but rather concern deep enough to disagree.

Other passages that might have been used as the session progressed are Ephesians 4:26, 29, 31, 32 and I Corinthians 13:4-7.[3] Because I have written extensively about Ephesians 4 elsewhere, I shall not say more about the passage. Rather, let me at least note how the latter passage may be applied. Louise had interpreted Mildred's words and actions in the worst possible light. Love would demand, however, that they be interpreted in the best light (Cf. I Corinthians 13:7, "believes all things, hopes all things.") The counselor, instead of calling her bitterness "natural" ought to call it sinful, and should point out to Louise that God has obligated her to put the best construction upon Mildred's advice. In that way, even annoying behavior can be looked upon in terms of the good intentions possibly underlying it, thus allowing for a better relationship to develop in spite of differences of opinion or of personality. It is interesting that those who in the name of empathy (as a matter of fact true empathy demands something quite different) simply agree with a counselee soon find that agreement means that there is no further advice that can be given since they see the problem as the counselee does. There is nothing to do to help when one thinks that the counselee is already doing all that can be expected of him. The fact is that bringing the biblical viewpoint to bear upon the situation always offers a counseling alternative to the counselee's present stance toward the problem. There is always something to advise; always another way to go. This is so because if the counselee were already doing what God says to do about the problem, and were sure of it, he would have had no need to come for counsel.

The following case again illustrates the use of the Scriptures in an antithetical, confronting fashion, but from a slightly different perspective. Notice how a direct Word from God may be used to cut across false propaganda to give hope.

---

[3]The importance of using a modern translation is evident in passages like this one. Counselees, confused already by many things, do not need further complications added by the necessity for explaining KJV vocabulary like "charity."

Check Up?

You dismissed Harry six weeks ago and set up a second check-up session after the first was cancelled due to working overtime. Harry's wife called you an hour after the time of the appointment to notify you that he couldn't make it. Harry is a new Christian who has been trying to overcome drunkenness.

Harry is now sitting before you in tears confessing that he was drunk and that his problem is not solved as he had thought. "Maybe I can't stop drinking. Once a drunk always a drunk! I stayed away from all the places and people that you told me to. I even found three new ways home from work and alternate them. I guess I just don't love God enough." Harry sobbed.

"When did you get drunk and what was involved?" you inquire.

"I don't know exactly, but it began when my wife and I had an argument. She wanted to go out and I couldn't because I wanted to avoid the drinking at the club to which she wanted to go. She left anyway and I started feeling bad."

(Case II - 21, pp. 164,165)

Clearly, many things may be said about this case. But again, I wish to stress the use of the Scriptures in one respect only. People use language for two purposes: to speak to others, and to speak to themselves. They may not convince others readily, but they are usually very persuasive when talking to themselves! All of which is to say that the counselor should be aware of the damaging effects of frequently-repeated old sayings, cliches, proverbs (i.e., extra biblical proverbs), and the like.[4] Here, the statement "Once a drunk always a drunk" is a tragically false proverb that capsulizes a conviction of pagan despair. The counselor must see that Harry has become convinced that it is true. Perhaps this catch-phrase has been repeated again by him and by others. Possibly the conviction has been strengthened by statements of A.A. that support the contention. However he has reached this conclusion, you can be

[4]For more on this point, *The Christian Counselor's Manual,* pp. 103-116; 373.

sure that it needs to be dislodged before real progress can be made. A man with the conviction (or even half-conviction) that there is no way to change once he has become a drunk will not have hope enough to endure the trials and the temptations that he must face. Here then, is the place for the counselor (who has also failed in other respects because he has not taught Harry according to Ephesians 4 and Colossians 3, and the significant verse in Ephesians 5:18, that drunkenness can only be removed by the two-factored process of putting on as well as putting off) to confront the concept packaged in the statement "Once a drunk always a drunk!" with the unequivocal word of the living God to the contrary. Turning to I Corinthians 6:11,12 he not only will read "drunkards" in the list of life dominating sins delineated, but also will continue to the end of the thought: ". . . such WERE some of you." Then he may comment: "God differs with your statement. He says that these Corinthian Christians had been able to put drunkenness behind them. Notice the past tense. By the grace of God you can do so too!" Harry needs to have his pagan notion challenged by the Scriptures.

Empathy

"My situation is so different," Laurie explained. Laurie, the wife of a young seminarian, had come (she said) because "I feel obligated to David to keep working, since I want him to be able to concentrate on school. I would never forgive myself if I quit my job, because he would have to reduce his class load in order to work, and I know that he wouldn't get as much out of school. But Pastor, I tell you, my job is impossible! I can't advance because I'm pegged as being temporary. I can't tell David or he'll tell me to quit. Less qualified men are promoted before me because, as my boss seemed happy to explain, 'a man's voice on the phone commands more respect, and therefore, is more valuable to the company.' And to top it off, I get no encouragement in the work that I am doing. I am losing my self-confidence; what shall I do?"

Laurie's story tugs at your heart; not long ago you and your wife were in nearly an identical situation. You can empathize with her and are inclined to advise her that she might change jobs at the earliest opportunity. But you are not sure; "Is there more that can be done for Laurie?" you wonder.

(Case I - 47, pp. 94,95)

In this case there are many features that might be emphasized. Let me quickly run through three. First, when Laurie says "My situation is so different" the counselor, properly identifying with her (not as he was tempted to in the *Casebook* account), might have referred to I Corinthians 10:13, quoting and explaining the verse,[5] and powerfully concluding with a reference to his own experience. In part, her despair and her evident self-pity grew from her false, unbiblical notion that no one else had ever had to grapple with the difficulties with which she was struggling. The same verse also could be used to deal with her language (see previous case) which indicates that she has convinced herself that the situation is hopeless (cf. words of exaggeration: "never, impossible" and of impossibility: "can't," etc.). Secondly, I Peter 3 in general is apropos concerning her submission to her husband. She is already involved in a deception that could lead to serious marital communication problems. She first should have talked to him about her problem, and she should not have prejudged his reaction (in the actual case, he did not respond as she supposed). More specifically, by not telling him, she has made it difficult for him to exercise his responsibility to live with her "according to knowledge" (I Peter 3:7). She must be willing to reveal all such matters that deeply influence them jointly so that he can fulfill his obligation to understand her. Lastly, somewhere in this session, Laurie needs to be confronted with the biblical work ethic found at the end of the third chapter of Colossians. A Christian does not work for her boss' acclaim, nor merely for earthly rewards. "It is the Lord Christ" whom she serves. And it is the same Christ who will acknowledge her faithfulness: "Well done, you good, faithful servant."

It is possible to go on and on discussing other cases in like manner, but these should suffice to show how the Scriptures, used in counseling, guide the counselor as well as help him to guide the counselee. Each of the cases also may be examined according to the

[5]Cf. *Christ and Your Problems.*

five essentials delineated at the beginning of Chapter II. As a further exercise, I suggest that you work your way through the *Casebook,* making a list of all of the pertinent passages of Scripture that might possibly be used in each case either as a guide to the counselor in dealing with the counselee or to the counselee in dealing with his problems. The list of passages in Chapter XI will be found to be of valuable assistance in doing this.

CHAPTER X
Miscellaneous Comments About the Use
of the Scriptures in Counseling

In this chapter I shall mention several important uses of the Scriptures in counseling. To begin with let me observe that the Scriptures should be used in homework assignments. I do not have time or space here to discuss either the place or use of homework in counseling. I have done so, however in several chapters in *The Christian Counselor's Manual* (q.v., if you are unfamiliar with the idea). However, I should like to emphasize here one aspect of homework that I have not discussed elsewhere: *how* the Scriptures may be used in homework.

It is important for the counselee himself to back up all counseling, and in particular, all of the work that he accomplishes through counseling, with prayer and the assimilation of Scripture. In every instance, the Christian counselee should be questioned about the regularity of his prayer and about his Bible study habits. Here I wish to speak about the latter. If he does not study the Scriptures daily, he should be encouraged to do so and given concrete help in doing so whenever necessary. One of the most helpful ways to promote daily Scripture study on the part of the counselee is to suggest that he begin by reading the Book of Proverbs (in a modern translation together with a good Bible commentary). In doing so, unless the first nine chapters are particularly pertinent to the problems that he is confronting in counseling, it is often wise to urge him to begin with the list of single proverbs that begins in chapter 10. In this way, he can read through slowly until he strikes a proverb that seems to embody a pithy concept that he needs to grasp and knead into the dough of his life. I usually advise him to stop whenever he has struck gold in this way. First, he should study the proverb to his satisfaction so that by help of his commentaries, Bible dictionaries and other reference works (whenever necessary), he understands the import of the proverb. He should spend at least an equal amount of time thinking about how the proverb applies to his life. He may need to turn it over again and again, looking at it from various angles. Or he may wish to write out (he will discover that forcing himself to write things out often is useful for assuring himself that he is not deceiving himself) the areas of his life to which the proverb applies and how. Each area, then, should be examined carefully to discover every implication. Whenever he follows this approach he should be quite specific (e.g., after reading Proverbs 12:25, he might make a notation in his study book:[1] "Bill is worried; I must give him an encouraging word from the Scriptures about his problem").

Next, let me point out a second use of the Scriptures. The Scriptures may be used in counseling to set and guide the course for some particular counseling task that must be performed. For example, whenever a conference table is set up in a home, we hand out the following form to the counselees. You will notice how it points to the reading of a particular portion of the Scriptures that directly pertains to the matter of Christian communication. Reading and rereading that portion at the outset of the conference reminds each party of God's requirements and thereby sets the tone of the conference and helps to cut down the counterproductive sinful attitudes, words and actions that previously were destroying good relationships between the participants.

SETTING UP A CONFERENCE TABLE

PLACE
   Agree upon an area in which daily conferences may be held without interruption. Choose a table, preferably one that is not used frequently for other purposes. Hold all conferences there. If problems arise elsewhere, whenever possible wait until you reach home to discuss them—at the conference table, of course. The first week read Ephesians 4:17-32 each night before conferring.

---

[1]Keeping a Study Book for recording results of studies preserves ideas for future use. The book can be quite simply arranged with each page devoted to a passage. The page may be divided into two columns headed: Meaning of passage and Implications of passage for my life. The second column is essential if Bible Study is to become *telic* rather than merely oriented toward storage and retrieval.

Place _____ Time _____

PURPOSE

The conference table is a place to confer, not to argue. Begin by talking about yourself—your sins and failures—and settle all such matters first by asking forgiveness. Ask also for help (cf. Matthew 7:4-5).

Speak all the truth in love. Do not allow any concern to be carried over into the next day. Not all problems can be solved at one sitting. You may find it necessary to make up an agenda and schedule out the work over a period of time according to priorities. Direct all your energies toward defeating the problem, not toward the other person. Your goal is to reach biblical solutions, so always have Bibles on the table *and use them.* It helps to record the results of your work on paper. Open and close conferences with prayer. When you need help, reread Ephesians 4:25-32.

PROCEDURES

If any conferee argues, "clams up" or does anything other than confer at the table, the other must rise and stand quietly. This prearranged signal means, "In my opinion we've stopped conferring." Whether he was right or wrong in this judgment does not matter and ought not to be discussed at the moment. The person seated should then indicate his willingness to confer, and invite the other to be seated again.

The conference-table guide also points up the need for the counselees to use the Scriptures in order to reach solutions to problems. There are many ways in which people seek to solve life's questions. They may try to follow feelings or intuition, or act upon an experience. But Christian counselors will be zealous to teach counselees instead to rely upon the Bible. Therefore, as a part of their counseling they will make an effort at every appropriate point to stress the importance of consulting God's Word by giving assignments calculated to encourage and to help the counselee to learn to use the Scriptures profitably to deal with his life problems. Often this will entail instruction as to how to use the Bible practically, including directions about how to look for the *telic* emphasis of each passage. It may involve help about how to use dictionaries, commentaries, concordances and other Bible reference materials. The counselor, in each instance, must make an evaluation of the counselee's present capability to use the Scriptures effectively and not merely assume that an assignment to search the Bible for help in reaching a particular objective will be productive. The desire may be present to do so, but the counselee's lack of knowledge about how to go about the search may keep him from fulfilling that desire. Failure may further discourage him, and may confirm suspicions that the Bible is impractical.

One of the most important ends for counselors to pursue is teaching counselees *how to* find answers to life's questions in the Scriptures. Nothing will help counselees for the future more than this. Another factor in the use of the Scriptures is the importance of distinguishing between direct commands of God and valid inferences from and applications of such commands. Some matters are directly enjoined or forbidden; in others decisions must be made by inference from biblical principles. It is not necessary to spend time developing this theme here since in *The Christian Counselor's Manual* I have already done so.[2] Yet it is essential to stress the importance of making such distinctions. Otherwise, the counselee may fail to distinguish between the authority of God and the biblically-informed judgment of others. It is therefore significant when the counselor, in giving advice or in making an assignment himself makes such distinctions. Compare the following two statements: "Joe, you must stop running around with Bob's wife, and you must stop as of today!" and "Bill, you should study your Bible; I'd suggest that you might begin with the tenth chapter of Proverbs." The second differs radically from the first.

The distinction may be summarized in the following chart:

[2]Cf. pp. 16, 17, 447, 448.

BIBLICAL COMMAND	COUNSELOR'S SUGGESTION
Outcome "Joe. . . you must stop"	Specific biblical steps for reaching the outcome. "Call her today"
General biblical principles leading to the outcome. "You must study your Bible"	Outcome "Read Proverbs 10 ff."

The counselor may be very directive about commanding a certain outcome when the biblical commands directly govern it: "Joe, you must stop running around with Bob's wife." When the case is not covered directly, one can be directive only about the principles that clearly are commanded: "You should study your Bible." It is not altogether certain biblically *how* Joe must put an end to his infidelity. Indeed, the steps that he takes to achieve this end may vary under different circumstances. If he can make a clean break with a phone call today, he should do so. If, however, Bob's wife keeps on trying to reestablish the relationship, that might call for different steps. On the other hand, studying the Scriptures regularly may be enjoined as a biblical principle, but the passages with which Bill begins can only be suggested. Circumstances again, might point to entirely different passages (e.g., if Bill is an unbeliever, he should probably not begin with Proverbs but rather with the Book of John).

In considering the various ways in which the Scriptures must be used by counselors, it is important to warn against moralistic, illustrational, prescriptional and abstract usage. A final word about each of these misusages of the Scriptures is in order.

Moralistic use of the Scriptures usually involves at least two faults. The first of these is a failure to show that the intended action must be done not merely to remove some grief or trouble from the counselee, but rather must be done primarily in order to please God. Secondly, the Scriptures are used moralistically when biblical principles or practices are enjoined in order to achieve a reformation apart from the saving work of Jesus Christ (both in justification and

252

in the process of sanctification, which is the work of the Holy Spirit alone).[3]

Illustrational use of the Scriptures consists of proof-texting ideas set forth by you or someone else. The Scriptures often are used in an exemplary manner ("for instance, take the case of Daniel . . . ") to demonstrate some point that the counselor has made, a point that originally may have been taken from Rogers, Freud, Skinner, Harris, etc. The serious error involved in the illustrational use of the Scriptures is simply this: while one *sounds* scriptural, because he uses the Scriptures to back up his comments and ideas, in fact he is doing nothing more than that—using the Scriptures illustratively to BACK UP HIS OWN IDEAS. Instead, his ideas themselves must be gleaned from the Scriptures. Rather than illustrationally, the Scriptures should be used *foundationally*.

Prescriptional use of the Scriptures has already been mentioned at an earlier point in this volume, so I shall not say anything more about it here, except to remind you that the Scriptures cannot be given out to counselees as if they were a magic potion that (understood or not) will do him good. On the contrary, they must be explained and concretely applied to the specific problems that he confronts.

Abstract use of the Scriptures is closely related to the last error mentioned above. Setting forth principles and truths alone is often insufficient. The counselee usually does not know how to apply these to his life. While it is important to etch out principles so that these may be known and applied later in various circumstances, it is essential to show in the present one just *how* the principles work out. While it is true that a principle is the most practical element of all, it is also true that unless the counselee learns *how* to make principles practical by having someone *show* him *how* to do so, probably he will not find principles practical at all. Thus, the counselor, in this as well as in other things, will find himself again and again faced with the task of showing counselees *how to* use the Bible in a personal practical way.

---

[3]For counseling pamphlets that make a strong effort to overcome this problem, see my "What Do You Do When . . . " series (Presbyterian & Reformed Pub. Co., Nutley, N.J.: 1975). There are six pamphlets now available (see back cover).

All in all, there is nothing more satisfying than the proper use of the Scriptures in counseling because by such usage one does so many things at once. He helps by bringing God's sure Word to bear upon the counselee's problem. He honors God by pointing away from human wisdom to Him. He shows the counselee what a rich wealth of information is contained in the Bible, thus encouraging him to turn more often to this Source. And, he helps to instruct the counselee in the ways and means of using the Bible in days ahead for himself. Thus, by the use of the Scriptures, he helps solve problems now and prevents problems from reoccurring in the future.

CHAPTER XI
The Counselor's Topical Worklist

On the following pages, alphabetically arranged, there is a list of topics under each of which appears a limited number of selected Scripture passages. In many ways, this is a curious list, as a quick scanning will indicate. But, to counselors, the peculiar nature of the list is readily understandable and, indeed, constitutes its sole value. It is from beginning to end a counselor's list. It is a work list, based upon many of the most commonly encountered areas of needs, sins and problems faced in the counseling context, together with references to key biblical passages that have proven particularly helpful in dealing with each of these topics.

Since the choice of the specific Scripture portions will vary from counselor to counselor, according to his understanding and even his interpretation of them, sufficient space has been provided beneath each entry for other references to be added. In this way, by making one's own additions, the list may become a valuable personalized reference source that may be used for many purposes, some of which may extend beyond counseling interests. Plainly, the list is limited but hopefully it is adequate. Too many topical or scriptural references would confuse the counselor who seeks to obtain quick help (perhaps at times even in the counseling session itself). Indeed, selectivity is what makes the list most useful. Since many persons have asked for just such a list, my expectation is that it will meet a real need.

WORK LIST

Adultery
  Ex. 20:14
  II Sam. 11:2
  Prov. 2:16-18, 5:1-23,
    6:23-35; 7:5-27; 9:13-16
  Hosea, bk. of
  Mal. 2:13-16
  Matt. 5:28; 15:19; 19:9
  I Cor. 6:9-11

Alcoholism
(See Drunkenness)

Anger
  Gen. 4:5-7
  Psalm 7:11
  Prov. 14:17,29; 15:1,18;
    19:11,19; 20:3,22;
    22:24; 24:29;
    25:15,28; 29:11,22
  Mark 3:5
  Eph. 4:26-32
  Jas. 1:19,20

Anxiety (See Worry)

Associations (bad/good)
Prov. 9:6; 13:20; 14:9;
22:24; 23:20,-
21;29:24
Rom. 16:17, 18
I Cor. 5:9-13
II Cor. 6:14-18
II Tim. 3:5

Avoidance
Gen. 3:8
Prov. 18:1
I Tim. 6:11
II Tim. 2:22

Assurance
Hebrews 4:16; 6:11
I Pet. 1:3-5
II Pet. 1:10
I Jn. 5:13,18,19

Bitterness (See Resentment)

Blame Shifting
Gen. 3:12,13
Prov. 19:3

Body
Rom. 12:1,2
I Cor. 3:16,17;6:18-20;
15
II Cor. 5:1-4

Children (See Family)

Church
Eph. 4:1-16
Heb. 10:25
Rev. 2,3

Change
Ezek. 36:25-27
Matt. 16:24
Eph. 4:17-32
Col. 3:1-14
I Thess. 1:9
II Tim. 3:17
Heb. 10:25
Jas. 1:14, 15
I Pet. 3:9

Commandment
Ex. 20
Prov. 13:13
Lk. 17:3-10
John 13:34; 15:12
I John 5:2,3

Communication
Eph. 4:25-32

Conscience
Mk. 6:19
Acts 24:16
Rom. 2:15
I Cor. 8:10,12
I Tim. 1:5,19; 3:9
II Tim. 1:3
Heb. 13:18
I Pet. 3:16,21

Confession
Prov. 28:13
Jas. 5:16
I John 1:9

Conviction
John 16:7-11
II Tim. 3:17
Jude 15

Death
Psalm 23:6
Prov. 3:21-26; 14:32
I Cor. 15:54-58
Phil. 1:21,23
Heb. 2:14,15

Desire
Gen. 3:6
Ex. 20:17
Prov. 10:3,24; 11:6;
28:25
Matt. 6:21
Lk. 12:31-34
Rom. 13:14
Gal. 5:16
Eph. 2:3
Titus 2:12;3:3
Jas. 1:13-16; 4:2,3
I John 2:16
Jude 18
I Pet. 1:14; 4:2,3

Decision Making
II Tim. 3:15-18
Heb. 11:23-27

Depression
Gen. 4:6,7
Psalm 32,38,51
Prov. 18:14
II Cor. 4:8,9

Discipline
 Prov. 3:11,12; 13:24;
   19:18; 22:6,15; 23:13;
   29:15
 I Cor. 5:1-13; 11:29-34
 II Cor. 2:1-11
 Eph. 6:1-4
 I Tim. 4:7
 Heb. 12:7-11

Doubt
 Jas. 1:6-8

Drunkenness
 Prov. 20:1; 23:29-35;
   31:4-6; 23:20
 Eph. 5:18
 I Pet. 4:4

Divorce
 Gen. 2:24
 Deut. 24:1-4
 Isa. 50:1
 Jer. 3:1
 Mal. 2:16
 Matt. 5:31,32; 19:3-8
 Mk. 10:3-5
 I Cor. 7:10-24,33-
 34,39-40

Envy
 Titus 3:3
 Jas. 3:14-16
 I Pet. 2:1

Family
Gen. 2:18,24
Ex. 20:12

Father (See Family)

Fear
Gen. 3:10
Prov. 10:24; 29:25
Matt. 10:26-31
II Tim. 1:7
Heb. 2:14,15
I Pet. 3:6,13,14
I John 4:18

Husband/Wife
Gen. 2:18,24
Eph. 5:22-33
Col. 3:18-21
I Pet. 3:1-17
I Tim. 2:11-15

Forgiveness
Prov. 17:9
Matt. 6:14,15; 18:15-17
Mk. 11:25
Lk. 17:3-10
Eph. 4:32
Col. 3:13
Jas. 5:15
I John 1:8-10

Parent/Child
Gen. 2:24
II Cor. 12:14
Eph. 6:1-4
I Tim. 3:4,5

Friendship
Prov. 27:6,10; 17:9,17
John 15:13-15

Grief
Prov. 14:13; 15:13
Eph. 4:30
I Thess. 4:13-18

Gifts
Rom. 12:3-8
I Cor. 12-14
I Pet. 4:10,11

Habit
Prov. 19:19
Isa. 1:10-17
Jer. 13:23; 22:21
Rom. 6-7
Gal. 5:16-21
I Tim.
Heb. 5:13ff.
I Pet. 2:14,19

Gossip
Prov. 10:18; 11:13;
    18:8; 20:19; 26:20-22
Jas. 4:11

Homosexuality
Gen. 19
Lev. 18:22; 20:13
Rom. 1:26-32
I Cor. 6:9-11
I Tim. 1:10

Humility
Prov. 13:34; 15:33;
   16:19; 22:4; 29:23
Gal. 6:1,2
Phil. 2:1-11
Jas. 4:6,10
I Pet. 5:6,7

Hope
Prov. 10:28; 13:12
Rom. 15:4,5
I Thess. 1:3; 4:13-18
Heb. 6:11,18,19

Jealousy (See Envy)

Laziness
Prov. 12:24,27; 13:4;
   15:19; 18:9; 26:13-16
Matt. 25:26

Lying
Ex. 20:16
Prov. 12:19,22
Eph. 4:25
Col. 3:9

Love
Prov. 10:12; 17:19
Matt. 5:44; 22:39,40
Rom. 13:10
I Cor. 13
I Pet. 1:22
I John 4:10,19; 5:2,3
II John 5,6

Life-dominating Problems
I Cor. 6:9-12; 21:8
Eph. 5:18
Rev. 21:8; 22:15

Lust (See Desire)

Mother (See Family)

Obedience
I Sam. 15:22
Lk. 17:9,10
Acts 4:19; 5:29
Eph. 6:1
Heb. 5:8; 13:17
I Pet. 1:22

Listening
Prov. 5:1,2,13; 13:18;
15:31; 18:13

Peace
Prov. 3:1,2; 16:7
John 14:27
Rom. 5:1; 12:18; 14:19
Phil. 4:6-9
Col. 3:15
Heb. 12:14

Put off/Put on (See Change)

Reconciliation
Matt. 5:23,24; 18:15-17
Lk. 17:3-10

Pride
Prov. 8:13; 11:2; 13:10;
16:18; 18:12; 21:24;
27:1; 29:23

Repentance
Lk. 3:8-14; 24:47
Acts 3:19; 5:31; 17:30;
26:20
II Cor. 7:10; 12:21

Resentment
Prov. 26:24-26
Heb. 12:15

Sexuality
Gen. 2:25
I Cor. 7:1-5

Reward/Punishment
Prov. 13:24; 22:15; 29:15
II Cor. 2:6; 10:6
Heb. 10:35; 11:26
II John 8

Shame
Gen. 2:25
Prov. 11:2; 13:18
I Cor. 4:14
I Pet. 3:16

Slander (See Gossip)

Stealing
Ex. 20:15
Prov. 20:10,22; 29:24;
30:7-9
Eph. 4:28

Worry
Prov. 12:25; 14:30; 17:22
Matt. 6:24-34
Phil. 4:6,7
I Pet. 5:6,7

Work
Gen. 2:5,15; 3:17-19
Prov. 14:23; 18:9;21:5;
22:29; 24:27; 31:10-31
I Cor. 15:58
Col. 3:22-24
I Thess. 4:11
II Thess. 3:6-15

TOPICAL INDEX

Abba, 211
Abstraction, 135ff., 253
Absurd, 62
Accomodation, 28
Action, 115, 129ff., 210, 222ff.
Adaptation, 105f.
Adequacy, 182, 184
Additive, 30
Adultery, 122, 137f.
Aid, 89 ff.
Alternatives, 85ff.
Analysis, 90ff., 94ff.
Anger, 215
Application, 7
Assessment, 108
Arminianism, 62
Attitude, 104, 115
Authoritarianism, 135ff., 187
Authority, 11, 130ff., 133ff., 186f., 198, 211

Behavior, 20ff., 118f., 189, 204, 211
Biblical-theological, 5
Bitterness, 241, 243
Bizarre behavior, 162ff., 187ff.
Blameshifting, 242
Brainwashing, 20
Business life, 4

Cancer, 155ff.
Can't, 222ff.
Categories, 109
Change, 9, 19ff., 27, 101, 126, 129, 186, 227, 237
CCEF, 11
Christocentric, 5
Church, 121
Church history, 5
Commandments, 187, 199ff., 207
Common grace, 37
Complicating problems, 109

Complexity, 98, 109
Concreteness, 7, 130, 136ff., 177, 216f., 223
Context, 205
Conviction, 27, 179
Correction, 27
Courage, 86, 179
Creativity, 3
Crisis, 79ff., 241
Curriculum, 7

Data, 192ff.
Death, 155ff., 185
Defense mechanism, 194
Deformity, 146ff.
Deism, 62
Depth counseling, 185
Desire, 235
Despair, 185
Determinism, 62
Diagnosis, 22
Direction, 7, 20, 90ff., 128ff.
Discipline, 22, 206
Divorce, 94, 133f.
Dualism, 232
Drugs, 139f., 236
Drunkenness, 113, 142, 152ff., 186, 195, 236, 240, 244

Eclecticism, 7, 10, 81, 181
Electro shock therapy, 21, 187
Emergency, 92f., 112
Emotion, 88f., 113, 131, 189, 225
Encounter, 219
Enormity, 98
Equipment, 182
Establishment, 2ff.
Eureka view, 34ff.
Evangelism, 40ff., 114ff.
Evil, 242

269

Evolution, 41, 61
Exegesis, 4, 5, 11, 195ff., 199, 205
Existentialism, 62, 64
Experience, 7

Facts, 99f., 104ff., 108ff.
Family, 4, 121
Fatalism, 61, 63
Fear, 84, 126, 131, 224
Feelings, 188
First aid, 93
Flesh, 231ff.
Forgiveness, 122, 137f., 215
Freedom, 3
Freezing, 100
Frontiers, 4

Generalizing, 193
Genetic view, 21, 186
Gifts, 5f.
Godless systems, 31, 32ff.
Gossip, 222
Great Awakening, 39
Greek and Hebrew, 53
Grief, 81, 95, 96, 122f., 185
Group Therapy, 219
Growth, 126ff.
Guilt, 116

Habit, 233, 234ff.
Hallucinations, 109, 113, 116ff.
Heredity, 194
Holy Spirit, 5, 9, 27, 36, 81, 181,
    192, 198
Homosexuality, 108, 166ff., 186,
    217ff., 236
Hope, 120f., 185, 194, 227
Hospitality, 132
How to, 138ff., 216f.
Humanism, 61
Hypnotism, 19

Id, 35
Illegality, 241
Illustrations, 253
Imaginary crises, 107
Interpersonal relations, 39
Inventory, 90ff., 111 ff.
Issues, 106f.

Jargon, 35, 135f., 191

Kiss-and-make-up, 237

Labels, 108f., 194, 197
Language, 102, 107f., 225, 244
Laziness, 84
Leading, 234, 237
Limitation, 102ff.
Lobotomy, 21
Love, 69ff., 87, 122, 183ff., 185,
    199, 208f., 224
LSD, 188
Lutheran, 2
Lying, 236f.

Magic, 180
Man of God, 26, 79, 182
Manipulation, 211
Marriage, 7, 39, 149ff., 185,
    186, 220
Medical help, 9, 114
Medical model, 35
Mental illness, 22
Methodology, 26, 219ff.
Minimizing, 108
Mnemonics, 111ff.
Moralizing, 201, 252
Motives, 117ff., 220ff.
Mutual ministry, 48

Need, 124ff.
New Morality, 7

270

SCRIPTURE INDEX

274

NAME INDEX

Abraham, 225
Banks, Mrs. William, 124
Blackwood, Andrew W., 82
Blaiklock, David, 194
Caesar, Nero, 101
Calvin, John, 37
Caplau, Gerald, 81
Collins, Gary, 36
David, 227
Demetrius, 132
Diotrephes, 91, 109
Epaphroditus, 203
Euodia, 132
Freud, Sigmund, 9, 26, 35, 36, 70,
    189, 206, 253
Fromm, Eric, 36
Gaius, 91, 109, 132
Glasser, Wm., 217f.
Granberg, L. I., 36
Grounds, Vernon, 33
Harris, Thomas A., 210
Hyder, O. Quentin, 33
Isaac, 225
Job, 86ff., 115
John, 91, 109, 132
Lewis, C. S., 227
Lindemann, Eric, 81
Luke, 70
Lloyd-Jones, Martin, 183
Menninger, Karl, 22
Miller, Keith, 44
Moses, 60, 110
Oates, Wayne, 206
Paul, 5, 70, 94, 182
Peter, 92
Pfister, Oskar, 206
Rogers, Carl, 6, 9, 35, 131, 189,
    204f., 210, 253
Satan, 88
Skinner, B. F., 9, 24, 26, 35, 180,
    189, 253
Syntache, 132
Thomas, W. H. Griffith, 179
Viscott, David, 191
Zillborg, 22